Entrepreneurship
and the Experience Economy

Daniel Hjorth and Monika Kostera (Editors)

Entrepreneurship
and the Experience Economy

Copenhagen Business School Press

**Entrepreneurship
and the Experience Economy**

© Copenhagen Business School Press, 2007
Printed in Denmark by Narayana Press, Gylling
Cover design by BUSTO | Graphic Design

First edition 2007

ISBN 978-87-630-0205-9

Distribution:

Scandinavia
DJOEF/DBK, Mimersvej 4
DK-4600 Køge, Denmark
Tel +45 3269 7788
Fax +45 3269 7789

North America
International Specialized Book Services
920 NE 58th Ave., Suite 300
Portland, OR 97213, USA
Tel +1 800 944 6190
Fax +1 503 280 8832
Email: orders@isbs.com

Rest of the World
Marston Book Services, P.O. Box 269
Abingdon, Oxfordshire, OX14 4YN, UK
Tel +44 (0) 1235 465500, fax +44 (0) 1235 4656555
E-mail Direct Customers: direct.order@marston.co.uk
E-mail Booksellers: trade.order@marston.co.uk

TABLE OF CONTENTS

List of Contributors 9
Acknowledgement 10
(Be)Fore Words 11

Part I
Introduction to Experience Economy 17

Introduction 19
The Rise of the Experience Economy 19
Translating the Idea of Experience Economy into Experience 20
The Way of Entrepreneurship 21
Kinds of Experience and Motives for Translation 22

Part II
The Unique Experience 25

Chapter 1
Blood Transfusions and Constant Critique 27
Experience Entrepreneurs 33
A Historical Comparison 44
Artistic Entrepreneurship: New Blood for an Anaemic System 48
Interviews 54

Chapter 2
Film Producer Entrepreneurship, and the Experience
Economy 55
A Close-Up from the Field of Filmmaking 55
Film Production, Aesthetics, the Experience Economy and
Entrepreneurship – Introduction... 56
Narrating Knowledge – Theoretical, Epistemological, and
Methodological Notes 59
Findings and Insights – Both Theoretical and Empirical................ 61
Entrepreneurship and the Film Producer in a Relational
Perspective.. 64
Film Producers and Their Work Practices—Listening,
Intuition, and Attunement... 67

Film Producer and Aesthetic Entrepreneurship—Concluding
Remarks 69

Part III
The Mediated Experience 73

Chapter 3
Escaping and Recreating Everyday Life 75
Introduction 75
Film Festivals as a Specific Form of Film Consumption 77
Bakhtin, the Carnival and Entrepreneurship 80
Accounts of the 1993 Sarajevo Film Festival 81
The Dramatist Analysis 84
Dramatist Analysis of Accounts of the 1993 Sarajevo Film
Festival – Number One 85
Dramatist Analysis of my Festival Account – Number Two 88
Dramatist Analysis of the Festival Director's Account – Number
Three 89
Festivals between a Managed Project and an Entrepreneurial Event 90

Chapter 4
Of Angels, Demons, and Magic Items 93
The Experience Economy 93
Myth 94
The Computer 94
The Study 95
The Demon 97
The Angel 100
The Trickster 101
The Frankenstein Monster 105
The Magic Item 106
Experiencing Economy 112

Chapter 5
The Designer as the Creator of Experiences in the
Postmodern Economy 115
The Experience Economy as a Stage for the Designer 118
Experiencing Design as Product and Process 119
The Character of (Industrial) Design in the Modern and
Postmodern Era 121
Concluding Remarks 126

Chapter 6
From Becoming Enterprising to Entrepreneurial Becoming 129

The Big Secret of Success 129
Producing the "Managerial Entrepreneur" 131
"Become Enterprising!: The Enterprising Self as a Historically Singular Mode of Experience 140
"Refusing Who We Are": Studying Entrepreneurship as Ethico-Aesthetic Practice 147

Part IV
Massexperience 153

Chapter 7
Artisans of the Spectacle 155

A Theatrical Perspective on Organizations 156
The Stage is set for the Experience Economy… 156
…and the Entrepreneur Takes the Cue 158
The Workings of the Event 160
Notions of Theatricality 161
Andréasson Public Relations go Liljevalchs 164
Event Time and Space 165
Audience and Performers 167
The Protagonist 170
Plot 171
So Stockholm – Meeting, Mixing, Mingling 173
Overcoming Transience 175
Concluding Remarks: Orchestrating Experiences 177

Chapter 8
Sports as Entertainment 181

Opening 181
Purpose 185
Sports as Entertainment 186
Sports as Mass-Communicated Entertainment 188
Immaterial Resources of Sports as Entertainment 190
A Case of Kitsch in the Experience Economy 197
A Discursively Denied Swedish Practice 204
Conclusions on Inclusions and Exclusions 206

Chapter 9
Experiencing the Dairy.. **209**
Introduction 209
Method.. 213
The Case and Anderson.. 214
Mystifying 220
In Conclusion.. 227

Chapter 10
Place Branding in an Entrepreneurship Experience
Economy.. **229**
Introduction 229
Place Branding.. 231
Place Branding as an Entrepreneurial Process in an
Experience Economy 234
Method of Investigation 238
The Story of Branding Lammhult as The Kingdom of Furniture 239
Analysis of the Story 246
Conclusions 252

Chapter 11
The Event of Disorientation as a Space for Inventing
New Practice.. **257**
Introduction 258
Experience and Event.. 259
The Aesthetic Experience: Opening and Disorientation 264
The Pleasure of an Experience Economy.................... 267
Entrepreneurship and the Creation of Events in the Context of an
Experience Economy 269

Part V
Making Sense of Experience Economy **281**

Chapter 12
Kronos and Eros **283**
Organizing and Sensemaking...................................... 283
Kronos versus Eros.. 286
Studying the Experience Economy 290

Works Cited.. **295**

LIST OF CONTRIBUTORS

Senada Bahto
Växjö University
senada.bahto@vxu.se

Frederic Bill
Växjö University
frederic.bill@vxu.se

Daniel Hjorth
Copenhagen Business School
dhj.lpf@cbs.dk

Marjana Johansson
Stockholm School of Economics
marjana.Johansson@hhs.se

Ulla Johansson
Växjö University and Göteborg University
ulla.johansson@gri.gu.se

Jerzy Kociatkiewicz
University of Essex
kociak@kociak.org

Monika Kostera
Warsaw University and Växjö University
monika.kostera@vxu.se

Katja Lindqvist
Stockholm University
kli@fek.su.se

Hans Lundberg
Växjö University
hans.lundberg@vxu.se

Lovisa Näslund
Stockholm School of Economics
lovisa.naslund@hhs.se

Marcela Ramírez-Pasillas
Växjö University
marcela.ramirez-pasillas@vxu.se

Marja Soila-Wadman
Växjö University and Royal Institute of Technology
marja.soila-wadman@vxu.se

Lisbeth Svengren Holm
Stockholm University
lisbeth.svengren@fek.su.se

Dr. Richard Weiskopf
University of Innsbruck
richard.Weiskopf@uibk.ac.at

ACKNOWLEDGEMENT

The editors special thanks go to Lena Olaison (University of Essex/ Copenhagen Business School) for her work with bringing this manuscript into its published form. This work has been invaluable to us in finalizing the process.

Daniel and Monika

(BE)FORE WORDS

In the academic context the economy used to be presented as an arena for simplistic exchange where supply directs demand or demand advises supply. Economists, lead by Edith Penrose, have only slowly realized that the economy, as much as the social world at large, is genuinely relational. Early Scandinavian researchers pointed out that industrial markets should be considered as relational constructs and Manuel Castells later advised us to imagine the economy as generally networked. These invitations to a relational viewpoint suggest that both the supplier and the customer will change as their partnership evolves. As a management concern, however, this mutual learning has only been recognized as an organizational rather than an embodied phenomenon. According to Joseph Pine and James Gilmore, the authors of the pioneering but also colonizing work *The Experience Economy*, the producers of dramatic and individualized offerings seem to stand above those experiencing, as if the suppliers' minds resided over the bodies of their customers. Customers are identified as helpless clients that are told to expose themselves so that the producers can make them experience. There is obviously a need for another perspective on the experience economy, one that invites producers as well as consumers to jointly make the economy into also an arena for aesthetic and emotional encounters. This present volume seems to meet such expectations, but its different contributions also extend our understanding far beyond received knowledge of the economy.

As a point of departure for their organizing of this book, its editors, Daniel Hjorth and Monika Kostera, succinctly present their understanding of experiences: they are always embodied and immediate; there is always a subject experiencing something, space for play and new openings is always there; and experience is always about enacting, making dreams come true. These statements may well reflect wishful thinking in a world populated by human beings who are disciplined by standards and routines embedded in gravity. There is, though, a large group of citizens and consumers who acknowledge that every market resides in an experience economy that is created in order to serve them. I have the children in mind. The toys they are given, as well as the common things that they construct as toys, become part of their play and integrated into their own, always emerging worlds. Children spontaneously absorb the experiences that adults stage as education or entertainment, which, in turn, crafts their identities. While adults as producers and consumers have a need to present themselves as providers and recipients of "experiences", children treat everyday playing, spontaneous socializing, as well as educating, imposed experiences in similar ways.

Children do not only practice the saying "make an experience" and create their world out of experiences, they also epitomize entrepreneurship as social organizing, as they work on their own identities and realize the potentialities that an emergent world offers. Children spontaneously take initiative and intuitively stage the work/play needed to make imagination turn into real social projects or artifacts. Whatever the context, whether an institutionalized formal setting or a natural or manmade catastrophe, children soon establish an arena for playing. A place of refuge is spontaneously created, sometimes amidst the structure and order imposed by the adult world, sometimes when facing the disorder produced by a catastrophe. Today the information and communication technology has expanded the children's and adolescents' possibilities to create their own worlds into which elder generations then are guided. Because of their "enculturation", grown-ups lose their ability to impulsively affirm and expand upon situated experiences. Sometimes, however, people locally enact entrepreneurship in the face of an apocalypse as in the story about the Sarajevo Film Festival being told in this book. Events such as film festival, usually staged in order to cause a rupture in everyday life, thus may appear, or be experienced, as stabilizing in a world that is in physical, mental, and social disorder.

As adults we generally welcome the label and practice of a (special) experience economy that is visited when everyday life becomes too dull. We deport spontaneous experimenting, and playing to special settings in time and space where our educated submission to socially constructed and self-imposed discipline can be relaxed. This book tells several stories about how producers on the market—from film-producers and designers of products and localities, to the organizers of sports events—stage such experiences in order to deliver their audiences from the taken-for-grantedness of everyday life. On the other hand, the very mission of designed experiences is, sometimes, in the name of nostalgia, to offer, the possibility of return to everyday life where and when it used to be. Human beings seem to have an existential need for traveling in space and time, whatever the direction.

This book is obviously written by a team of dedicated authors, committed to a reporting on different images of entrepreneurship and the experience economy. Although the approaches used, whether discursive or empirical, only marginally challenge the norms of the academic community, they are but forward by authors who themselves seem to be moved by their research. Some authors have even experienced the very events that they report. Such close-up research certainly brings life to the stories told and inspires others to continue a much-needed inquiry into the interface between the experience economy and entrepreneurship as two promising fields. I see four reasons for this urge: First, the experience economy challenges, in a fundamental way, the view that entrepreneurial activity originates in innovation in physical space alone. Human ingenuity, with all its faculties, invites itself into every setting where human activity appears, establishing its own playgrounds for entrepreneurship. Schumpeter could explain why the introduction of railway technology radically changed the competitive environment for horse-drawn coaches but he obviously could not imagine the return of the coaches as exciting means of transportation within an experience economy. Second, intense human encounters, the hallmark of the experience economy, incessantly produce coincidences, which, through entrepreneurial initiative, will soon enough turn into opportunities, subsequently materializing into ventures. Third, the emergent experience economy brings promises in terms of bilateral learning and mutual identity formation. We already know that successful entrepreneurs especially appreciate critical customers as advisors on instrumental learning. What is more, entrepreneurship is as much about identity and sense making as about market and money making. The experience economy appears as a potential "democratic" arena where producers and customers are invited to jointly remake their identities and understandings of the world. Fourth, communication and information technology not only liquidates distances in space (and therefore) in time; interactive technology, in particular, promises a more dynamic and flexible stage for entrepreneurial activity.

This book itself is a meeting point for different contributors to the understanding of the experience economy. Some of them take the fine arts as their point of departure in while others keep a strong foothold in managerial, often industrial, contexts as they inquire into the world of

13

experience. This combination is captured by the idea of the "creative industries". On one hand we are told how artists may dress as entrepreneurs and what someone with an aesthetic eye may generally have to say about entrepreneurship, while on the other we see how industrial designers, farms, and industrialized localities may combine managerial and rationalistic approaches with emotional attachment and commitment to place. The book chapters invite the reader to use her or his own eyes and mind to draw personal lessons from the readings.

Reading the different contributions to this book however also enforces my desire to see more (personal) experiences of the researcher included into entrepreneurship research generally and entrepreneurship research in the context of the experience economy in particular. Knowing that somebody interweaves a personal experience when telling stories from the experience economy, as in the chapter on sports, adds an extra dimension to the reading. From my own experience, I know the excitement associated with enacting a venture in the vicinity of the experience economy. The project that comes to mind was not just about getting closer to the unfolding of the process and thus being able to reveal its micropractices, but was also intriguing because it challenged the boundary between myself as researcher and (inter)active agent. The contributors to this book invite me to further consider how, exactly, entrepreneurship and the experience economy address experience as a genuinely relational phenomenon. For researchers this means, as I see it, not denying the importance of personal involvement as a means to insight and a recognition of the need for a "bodily turn" in the social sciences. As much as embodied, tacit knowledge provides the context that renders formal knowledge its meaning, our encounters and experiences as complete human beings of flesh and blood define what contributions we may make when we present ourselves as researchers. Considering the stakeholders in the experience economy itself, chiefly its providers and consumers, experiencing, and thus learning, should be recognized as a mutual and embodied exercise.

The majority of the authors of this book are quite closely associated with the Entrepreneurship Research Group at Växjö University. The minority consists of equally dedicated "external" contributors. The constitution of this diverse, yet collective, authorship adds to the promises about the future. Any contribution to an inquiry into the experience economy must provide a minimum of variety, or "requisite" with respect to external challenges as Ashby once stated, in order to be able to grant the views and the tools that make an ever evolving world bring adventure to everyday life. The reader will encounter images of the experience economy that do not portray it as a temporary relief in the wake of a vanishing industrial economy but as a social setting where informed customers/consumers can share entrepreneurial practices with producers.

Considering the present achievement of a group of (mainly) social science researchers, the prospects for further elaboration on the ideas presented here are favorable indeed. Inviting humanities into the making of an entrepreneurial experience economy can easily be extended beyond art and media. Inquiring into experiences that encompass existential issues calls for a multidisciplinary approach across faculty borders as much as the practice of an experience economy needs cross-sectoral measures that usually thrive in a regional context.

Bengt Johannisson
Professor of entrepreneurship, Växjö University

PART I

INTRODUCTION TO EXPERIENCE ECONOMY

INTRODUCTION

DANIEL HJORTH AND MONIKA KOSTERA

The Rise of the Experience Economy

The notion of the experience economy has recently become increasingly popular and used in various discourses, especially in consultancy and popular media. The term was coined by Joseph Pine and James H. Gilmore in their book The Experience Economy: Work is Theatre and Every Business a Stage (1999) which is primarily a book of the management consulting genre. The concept has, however, also become fashionable among researchers. The Swedish government ordered a study on the topic from the KK foundation (KK-stiftelsen)– 'Mixed Experiences'–which was published the same year with the title Blandade upplevelser. A term, previously reserved for the (performing) arts, experience economy has become associated with various creative industries. Emphasizing the need for "Western economies" to face the challenge from Asia with creativity, the creative industries have been pronounced the industry/economy of the future. If we—Sweden, historically early industrialized countries, and the West—want to keep a competitive position in the increasingly globalized economy, we have to utilize our broad knowledge base and bring creativity to the markets, where the demand for experiences is growing.

In this book, we do not aim for a systematic redefinition or recontextualization of the idea of the experience economy, but rather, it is our intention to disclose how this idea is performing in a number of practices and to discuss and reflect on those. We want to explore and inquire into the actions and practices that connect "experience" and "economy" in real life organizations. The organizations we are most interested in portraying are entrepreneurial events. We do not claim that entrepreneurial organizing is the only type of process that characterizes the experience economy. We believe, however, that entrepreneurial qualities emphasize the most vital characteristics of experience: immediacy, playfulness, subjectivity, and performativity. This book will, therefore, center on how the entrepreneurial organization, in a multiplicity of ways, connects experience and economy.

The question we started to work with can be formulated as follows: Is it meaningful to speak of an experience economy? In what contexts does this idea occur and how is it put to work 'entrepreneurially' in local practices?

Translating the Idea of Experience Economy into Experience

The way that ideas manifest in local practice can be described through the model of translation (Czarniawska and Sevón, 1996). Translation describes the process of disembedding and reembedding ideas between different practices. It is an ongoing process and there are no guarantees that it will succeed (Callon, 1986). An idea travels when it becomes disembedded from its assumptions and is then transferred in the form of an object to another setting. The idea in the process of being translated acquires almost physical, objective attributes. In order to be put into action, the idea is tendered with images of action. These can be verbal or nonverbal and they enable its materialization. The idea is subjected to a 'translatable' organizing process, either via technology or organizational practices, such as management or entrepreneurship. They speed up and unify the translation process, making it continuous and magnified—management fits it into existing orders, prioritizing the benefit of control and efficiency, whereas entrepreneurship holds on to the anomaly and its new order, demanding the creation of new organisation. This reembedding phase of the idea makes the idea understandable in a new setting.

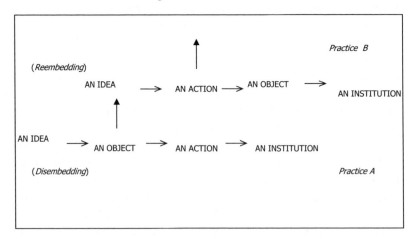

Figure 1.1 The Model of Translation of Ideas (adapted from Czarniawska and Joerges, 1996)

Applying this model of translation it is possible to trace the process of the disembedding and reembedding of the idea in different settings—that is, the process of communication between those settings. The ways in which motives and values are embedded in different settings can now be explored in more detail.

The Way of Entrepreneurship

The contributors to this volume explore how the experience economy is turned into organizational practice through the means of immediacy, subjectivity, playfulness and performativity.

By immediacy we mean the concrete situatedness of experience in time and space. Experience is not abstract, it is always contextual, socially and culturally embedded, and always embodied. By subjectivity we mean the connection of experience to the experiencing subject. There must be someone experiencing in order for an experience to take place. While experiences produce subjectivities, subject positions in turn shape experience. By playfulness we want to emphasize openness towards the emerging event: embracing whatever is in the making. Playfulness is a receptivity that moves virtualities to actualities. Finally, the performativity of experience is the quality of being enacted, its inherent actualization. It becomes real by taking place. To make sense of experience, one has to be observant of all of these qualities. This becomes, in our opinion, possible when applying qualitative, primarily narrative, approaches to/in field research.

The qualities that make possible the translation of the idea of experience economy into practice are also important characteristics of entrepreneurial events. The crossing and intersecting of entrepreneurship and experience is interesting, and persuades us to believe that an exploration of entrepreneurial experiences may generate some particularly pertinent inquiries. According to our approach, an experience economy is invented through the translation of ideas and the subsequent invention of new practices, resulting in concrete new organization. This becomes our contextual definition of entrepreneurship (fig. 2).

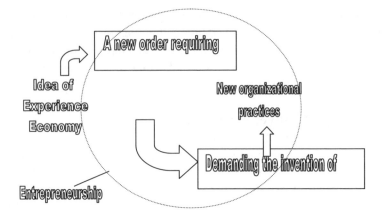

Figure 1.2 Translation of an Experience Economy into Organizational Practice

In other words, the primary aim of this book is to inquire into how (entrepreneurial) organizations make economy and experience cross in order to make up an experience economy. The cases presented by the authors cover a variety of practices, from artistic projects, sport organizations, film festivals, and the circus, to discursive uses and phenomenological references. These contributions also include a variety of reflections regarding the researcher as an experiencing subject in qualitative research. With this book we want to move beyond the buzzword and put the concept of the experience economy into some use: How can we think with this concept of experience economy when discussing entrepreneurial organizing? What does an experience economy look like close-up?

The chapters in this book demonstrate various forms that the translation actually takes place: the different motives for and manifestations of the idea of an experience economy.

Kinds of Experience and Motives for Translation

The guiding motivation for actual translation guides the presentation of the volume material. For some contributors, it is the uniqueness of the experience that matters. This is the case when artistic expressions and individual statements lead to an organized event such as the translation process of filmmaking, the creation of an art exhibition, and so forth. The producer and the consumer experience the product and/or the process subjectively and as subjective. This is the purpose and the specific character of the event.

Another common motivation is that of mediation, or the transformation of a product or event into something else, perhaps experienced as more aesthetic, more moral or generally more worthwhile. The force that drives the process is that of desire (in the Deleuzian sense), both on the side of the producer and the consumer. Examples of such events are design, technology and teaching.

Finally, some of the contributors address the notion of what we call mass-ification, whereby the experience's main trait is of being a mass event, of being collective rather than individual. The motivating force here is that of repetition (in the Deleuzian sense). This is the case with sports events and mass-produced furniture.

The contributions to this volume include: a discussion of the Sarajevo film festival; an examination of the artist as entrepreneur in the experience economy; a study of the role of design in the experience economy; an exploration of unlocking the value of peripheral traditions; a study of the film producer as entrepreneur; a consideration of sports as entertainment; an inquiry into the entrepreneurial process of creating events; a story of "necessary excess", or how entrepreneurship functions in the event industry; one essay of the social roles of computers.

PART II

THE UNIQUE EXPERIENCE

CHAPTER 1

BLOOD TRANSFUSIONS AND CONSTANT CRITIQUE
THE ARTIST AS ENTREPRENEUR IN THE EXPERIENCE ECONOMY

KATJA LINDQVIST

We went to Naples to see some art exhibitions, and to experience the former capital of southern Italy; a center for trade and politics and a baroque jewel fit between the sea and the mountains. Never was contemporary art less interesting. Paintings and installations in a quiet but freshly renovated building in the cleaned-up tourist area of town had no chance against the street-smart *ragazzi* in the Spanish quarters (quartieri spagnoli) driving on their Vespas in full speed down the alleys or against the intensive traffic and kissing along the seaside promenade. The Palace of Art, where we saw rather than experienced a contemporary art exhibition, was a closed circuit reiterating abstract notions in a strangely quiet part of this violent city. Many contemporary professionals in art attempt to break away from that disinterested, sterile space that at times frames the art experience; following artists such as the Situationists and philosophers such as Dewey.[1] Trusting the naïve force of experiment, they insert life into art, creating social situations and extending the art experience, in order to counter boring and nondeveloping art experiences. Many artists who work in this way thus comment, criticize, and challenge the contemporary art world as well as contemporary society. The context of art, the art space, is an aspect of the experience of art, and society is its extension. An aspect of contemporary artistic practice then involves philosophizing on the very conditions of art production and display, and life in a globalized, postindustrial world; and even offering alternatives to them.

---

[1] Dewey 1934.

In the 1990s the experience economy was a concept that rapidly gained supporters both among business theorists and politicians as well as sociologists. It was claimed that after the material, product force-feeding of the last century, we in late modernity long for experiences. Old services have been "discovered" and repackaged in a commercial form, often in new mediated forms.[2] Versions of the notion of an experience economy, such as the "creative industries," were also coined by governments in search of new national growth areas, and in general, creativity became a catchword for future productivity.[3] How are age-old forms of experience production and consumption, such as the arts, doing in this mediated and globalized era? Art venues and museums flourish, embraced by the tourism industry. The encounter with individual and original artworks seems as important as ever, despite the supply of mediated experiences with similar content.

Besides priests, artists are among the oldest experience suppliers of civilized society in the sense that they serve the transcendent and intellectual, as well as emotional, needs of humankind. Religion and art are forms of expression through which society and its members understand themselves and their context of living, but that also offer alternative views of things, both material and immaterial.[4] Artists deal with pure experience production, which includes creating something out of nothing, or, expressed with a marketing phrase, adding immaterial value to a material entity. The "new" economy has expanded foremost the forms and accessibility of stories and experiences of various kinds through technology. Apart from new techniques that have always interested artists, and the loss of common references (such as mythological and religious motives) in art, surprisingly little has changed with time regarding the consumption of art. Art is as a common, collective good relating to identity, the senses and cognition. It is produced to be experienced in a social context. What differentiates art produced and displayed today from that of two thousand years ago is the emphasis on the new, in contrast to the traditional. Recently many artists have left investigations of the object of art preferring, instead, to investigate the production process of art, and the social context in which art is inscribed.[5] This has resulted in art that investigates the contemporary patterns of production, distribution and consumption of art on a socie-

---

[2] Jensen 1999, Pine and Gilmore 1999, Caves 2000.
[3] Cf. DCMS 1999, AMS 2001, KK-stiftelsen 2001, 2003, Florida 2002, 2005.
[4] Cf. Huizinga 1944.
[5] A shift in interest, which itself is not new. This change is best understood as a reaction to the formal experiments in art in the 1950s and early 60s.

tal level, including investigations of capitalist society. Many artists have a critical urge, that is, an urge to ask questions about, challenge, and propose other models for the context, production, and consumption of art. In this critical tradition, many artists seek out and offer individual social spaces and social interaction that is not already choreographed, as in ordinary social interaction, or determined, as in the market. Art and artists offer a social space that is open; open for the individual to complete in ways that may differ from social norms.[6]

The development of the history of art as we know it is based on the acknowledgement of changes in style, with the greatest contemporary heroes of art being those artists who managed—preferably without the understanding of their contemporaries—to establish a new style that revolutionalized the perception of art. Breaking the rules therefore is almost the only existing current rule for art production. The "new" economy supports this artistic innovation through technological innovations. Doing things in new ways could thus be a description of contemporary artistic work.[7] In economic theory, the same description denotes entrepreneurial action. The ability to see the possibility of doing things in other ways or using resources in a different way, having one's own ideas of how to do things, as well as the strength to endure social pressures for conforming to established norms, are central to entrepreneurial thinking. By challenging established structures and modes of acting, both the entrepreneur and artist act as creative destroyers. In this sense, artists trying to change the conditions under which we encounter art bear similarities to Schumpeter's entrepreneur (*Unternehmer*) as a type of social actor. For Schumpeter two ideal modes of responding to changes in conditions for action (i.e., opportunities) exist: an adaptive, traditional one, and a creative, entrepreneurial one. The best adaptive response to changes in opportunities and conditions to act is according to Schumpeter, to accept the new conditions; but as far as possible to go on as usual. On the other hand, Schumpeter defines the creative response as action that goes outside

---

[6] For example, the diverse roles given to the producer and consumer of an art work have been challenged by many relationally interested artists. They have tried to develop art encounters that are not choreographed by one actor, but instead need the active participation of the visitor to be finished. Some examples are: public works operating in Germany and the UK; Love and Devotion, operating in Sweden; and Stalker Lab, operating in Italy.

[7] Artistic innovation and entrepreneurship can relate both to the artistic and to the enterprise side of the artists work. Innovation can be artistic, or organizational, referring to the artistic content of the art produced on the one hand, or the ways of working on the other.

the range of existing practice.[8] A creative response can never be anticipated, and in addition, shapes subsequent events and long-run outcomes of these changes in action.[9] The role or action of the entrepreneur is according to Schumpeter that of doing new things, or doing things in a new way (i.e., innovation).[10] Entrepreneurs "set up a concern embodying a new idea," whereas managing is to "head the administration of a going concern."[11]

The entrepreneurial function may be performed by a person for a limited period, after which she or he may go on to manage the successful enterprise. In this case, the person changes from an entrepreneur to a manager. There may be other persons who continuously engage in entrepreneurial action and who leave it to others to run the enterprises they have established though it is not always easy to be an entrepreneur, as it implies not doing things the proper way: [12]

The whole economic history of capitalism would be different from what it is, if new ideas had been currently and smoothly adopted, as a matter of course, by all firms to whose business they were relevant. But they were not. It is in most cases only one man or a few men who see the new possibility and are able to cope with the resistances and difficulties with which action always meets outside of the ruts of established practice.[13]

---

[8] Schumpeter 1946.

[9] This text departs from Schumpeter's functional definition of the entrepreneur, which is not entirely psychologising, and not equalling entrepreneurship with the establishment of a business. Cf. Gray 1998 and Bridge, O'Neill & Cromie 1998.

[10] According to earlier economic analyses the entrepreneur was a person inclined to risk, with an ability to manage uncertainty, making profits based on speculation and arbitrage. Cantillon 1755, Sciascia & De Vita 2004. Adam Smith in addition pointed to the entrepreneur's project orientation, taking action to realize a vision. Smith 1776. Some contemporary entrepreneurship researchers claim that entrepreneurs are those who act in a way that is "spontaneously carnival[esque]," Hjorth, Johannisson & Steyaert 2003: 99; or people who act following an "identity-related, conceptual reorientation." Svensen & Svendsen 2004: 134.

[11] Schumpeter 1946: 413. A further distinction is that inventors produce ideas, whereas entrepreneurs get these ideas into production. They get things done.

[12] Regarding the issue of determining who is an entrepreneur, Schumpeter soberly stated that we know ex post facto, what action, and who, is entrepreneurial: "Historical work alone can furnish material from which to arrive at scientifically reliable propositions about economic change and, therefore, about entrepreneurship". Schumpeter 1946/1991: 408.

[13] Schumpeter 1946: 413.

Thus entrepreneurship takes place in a social context, which is challenged by entrepreneurial action. The social space in which action takes place can be more or less predefined in terms of norms for conduct, and thus responsive to changes. The space for art in society today seems to be the only framed locus for experiments with societal space itself. Analyzing social events, philosopher Ole Fogh Kirkeby has described art as such a space for possibilities, which at the same time pointing out everyday limitations that order social action.[14] In other words, art is a social space that encourages experimentation by relieving us from many everyday social norms and legal responsibilities. This is also why art can be provocative. Art theorist Nicolas Bourriaud has also investigated the relationship between social action and art spaces. For Bourriaud the increased emphasis on human social interaction as the core of artistic works is a reaction against the increased level of planning and restriction of human encounters and social interaction in contemporary society. He sees artists creating:

> *free areas, and time spans whose rhythm contrast with those structuring everyday life, and it encourages an inter-human commerce that differs from the 'communication zones' that are imposed upon us. The present-day social context restricts the possibilities of inter-human relations all the more because it creates spaces planned to this end.*[15]

Many artists working with relational artworks may be described as social entrepreneurs, since in their artworks and artistic practice they deal with issues relating both to society at large and to the art world specifically.[16] In this sense, there is a link between entrepreneurship and artistic practice as research and development centers for society. Entrepreneurial action and artistic practice, in their attempts to reformulate frames of reference, contribute to a renegotiation of social space as well as physical space, by both displaying and using excessive energy. In doing this they not only react to but act for change.[17]

---

[14] Fogh Kirkeby 2004, 2005.

[15] Bourriaud 1998.

[16] Neither economic nor artistic development can be programmed; economic development and growth of creative activities tend to occur organically where not foreseen or planned and where there is free or nondefined space, or where reinterpretation of a given social space is allowed. As discussed by O'Connor & Wynne 1996 and Fogh Kirkeby 2005.

[17] Lefebvre 1974.

But does the artistic experimentation allowed by society apply in the art field itself as a structured field of action? The art world is not only marginal, it also seems closed. Furthermore, it is also, as in other fields of action, based on a number of outspoken or silent norms that form a code of conduct. Individual strategies for action can be defined as either more or less entrepreneurial or mainstream in relation to these codes, where mainstream is understood as a description of a strategy that closely follows received ideas of ideal artistic strategic behaviour and action. There is strong pressure on contemporary artists to continuously be entrepreneurial, i.e., to break the rules of what is perceived as art, yet at the same time pressure is also strong to conform to codes and norms of the field. How then should entrepreneurship, or innovative action, be investigated in a field that is characterized by constant innovation as well as strict rules of conduct? What does entrepreneurship mean in this field where everyone has to invent her or his own oeuvre within seemingly strictly dictated career rules?

These issues will be investigated through case studies of two artist groups and an artist based in Sweden and Denmark respectively; Johanna Billing and Konst2 based in Sweden and, the Danish group, Superflex. The common characteristics of these artists and artist groups are that they work in new ways that go beyond established career strategies in the art world, and they work expressly collaboratively.[18] In other respects, there are no stylistic similarities between the work of the various artists and groups. The contemporary artists are then compared with a Swedish artist active in the nineteenth century, to further put the contemporary norms of the art world in relief.

---

[18] The study was executed through repeated interviews in 2004-2005, and through first-hand and second-hand documents. The studied artists were initially chosen based on the author's knowledge of the contemporary art scene, on the criterion of doing something new or different. Thorough knowledge of their own phrasing of artistic ideals and ideas developed only during the study.

Experience Entrepreneurs[19]

Konst2[20]

Konst2 is an experimental art platform established by visual artists and curators Ylva Ogland and Rodrigo Mallea Lira together with Jelena Rundqvist, a curator and stylist with a background in scenography.

Konst2 started off in a venue in Skärholmen, a southern suburb of Stockholm, in 2003. In 2004, the initiators of Konst2, Ogland, Mallea Lira and Rundqvist, were appointed directors of Tensta konsthall,[21] the gallery in another suburb of Stockholm, and therefore decided that Konst2 was to be relocated to the premises of Tensta konsthall. Konst2 grew out of a discontent with the closeness and the set rules of the art world. Rundqvist, Ogland and Mallea Lira felt that the art world was very homogenous, often driven by competition and jealousy. They experienced ignorance of how the world outside the small art sphere functions, which, they felt, resulting in the unquestioning acceptance by many of current norms and hierarchies. With Konst2 they wanted to bring new people into the art world. One of their strategies for this was to locate their activities in Skärholmen.

Konst2 was explicitly established as a complement to other types of institutions and activities in the Stockholm art world, as a space for experiments in production and display of creative work. Challenging received ideas and norms of how an art institution should be run has been a central idea in the conceptualization of Konst2 as an institution. What makes Konst2 different from other institutions is that they experiment with work processes inherent in exhibition production and gallery curating, something which in turn leaves signs in the physical space of the gallery. They want to abandon the white cube art space, which in their opinion, is not real. They want history to be part of whatever takes place in their institution. In the white cube, the artists

---

[19] I wish to thank all artists and curators interviewed for this text, who told me about their work and drives and generously explained what often is taken for granted in the art world.

[20] All quotes in this section are from two interviews undertaken with Konst2 in 2004 and 2005.

[21] The first years of Tensta konsthall, established by artist Gregor Wroblewski, and with the help of curator Celia Prado, were a success story that ended in a conflict between the director and the board of trustees of the organization in 2003. The board of trustees fired the director and in early 2004 asked the establishers of Konst2 to take over the directorship of Tensta konsthall. The conflict generated a vast amount of articles and debate in media, and has been analyzed by both journalists and university students.

of Konst2 think that history is negated, resulting in the space becoming a bubble, self-sufficient and disconnected from the world outside. The only thing relating to the outside world in the white cube is that which artists bring in. The foundations of Konst2 think this is the reason why artists work so much relationally and socially at the moment.

All three founders have experience with initiating and executing projects in the art world and other creative areas in Stockholm, working in different roles mostly without funding or on a shoestring budget. They know that funding problems often exhaust participants, which creates anger and complaints. Another aspect of working on shoestring projects is the constant lack of time, which also creates frustration. Rundqvist, Mallea Lira and Ogland have also, according to themselves, always been uncompromising about believing in and daring to stand up for their ideas. They are always consciously subjective and they see their work as being about developing themselves. They and their project might be perceived by others as egotistic because of this self-conscious choice and preference. They think that it's important to have good self-confidence in order to make things happen:

> *We usually work from a gut feeling, and we also clearly state that we are a subjective institution. We depart from ourselves because we think it's a necessary condition for working with experimental art. It's about working from a feeling, and you don't always know what it's all about. That you may discover much later… The decision to go on with something is only yours to make. You can't wait to be sanctioned by anyone else before you dare to make a decision, because then you have already given the decisionmaking over to somebody else… It's about standing up for your personal direction, your own interest, and your own taste, and not taking too much impression from others. I think this is very important, for example, if you're a curator. You have to trust your own interest. And that's frightening, but also a strength.*

Working cross-disciplinarily as curators, as Konst2 does—combining art with graphic design, design, and fashion—is considered somewhat strange in the art world, according to the three founders of Konst2. Sometimes their project proposals have been met with frustration, as they have contained multiple forms of expressions, something which the art world at least temporally has been uncomfortable in accommodating. But these difficulties have been a source of energy for Konst2 to continue pursuing their vision. Konst2 also feel that they have a more subjective and direct relationship with their projects than academic curators in the art world. Many other curators, in their opinion, keep a distance from art and artists. Konst2 think it is important not to put the creative act on a pedestal; to make it into something literally untouchable. They like to work experimentally and close to the invited artists and the process itself:

[It's very important that] there is a very tight dialogue. Sometimes it is also difficult and demanding for those engaged because of the tight dialogue, which is not only theoretical but also very practical. It's the dialogue that is interesting, with the viewer and with all those involved in the processes. It's something completely different than to just leave an art piece to an exhibition that you have worked with in solitude, and then someone else is there to take care of the piece, and there is nothing between artist and curator. Then it's a completely lifeless exhibition.

They see themselves as an important addition to existing traditional institutions, since they allow for experiments that do not happen in museums or established art venues. One important effect of working experimentally is that everything takes much longer than working according to tradition or established practice. Still, for Konst2, it is worthwhile to: invent new possible ways of doing things; to try to find out for themselves how things could be done; and to be able to do this in a profound way—not just temporarily, as is the case when working in sequential projects:

We wanted to start from flexibility and investigation of how an experimental investigation could be, instead [of] from the question of how we should be. We want to allow failures and successes.

In late 2004, a year after the establishment of Konst2, Rundqvist, Ogland and Mallea Lira were offered to become directors of Tensta konsthall. Tensta konsthall is in another suburb, northwest of the city center, and in this sense can be said to fit well with the ideology of Konst2. They accepted after some hesitation and discussion.[22] Their condition was that they all work together, and only be engaged part-time. Furthermore, they did not want the leadership position for more

---

[22] The development of the crisis at Tensta konsthall was widely commented on by local and national media, and radio and newspaper reporting, postgraduate dissertations as well as a book that has been published on the topic. Ericsson 2004.

than five years. They believed that both they themselves and the institution would stagnate if they stayed on for a longer period, and because conflicts always appear when a certain management group prevails. As of 2005, the members of Konst2 all found working together with the two organisations satisfying, but each was also simultaneously engaged in individual projects and agendas beyond Tensta and Konst2. Paradoxically, some of the artists invited to do shows at Tensta konsthall were demanding a white cube context rather than dealing with traces of the previous artists and projects in their exhibition space. This, indeed has challenged the ideals and ideas of the trio running the gallery. Another challenge has been to run two parallel, independent organizations. Will running Konst2 and Tensta konsthall in parallel turn the founding troika of Konst2 into managers, or will they be able to leave the institutions as planned for new explorative initiatives? Is running two institutions at the same time a way of increasing the challenges for their own work? Will the institution of Konst2 eventually disappear, and would that be considered as a loss?

The doublemanagement arrangement has, according to the three founders/directors, given them more energy to work with both formats, which none of them want to give up. On the contrary, one feeds into the other, as the format of a set institution such as Tensta konsthall poses demands on how to present art that can be explored, elaborated, and challenged by the format of Konst2. Describing it in entrepreneurial terms, the members of Konst2 have been able to create a framework for intrapreneurship within the artworld, by being their own managers, and establishing a dual identity within a set art gallery framework. Being both entrepreneurs and their own bosses surely facilitates this strategy. Regarding the possible disappearance of Konst2, it is clear that the experimental space provided by the concept of Konst2 was not something that its founders were willing relinquish, but rather it is central to their overall creativity and work. Even though criticized in the Swedish press, the schizoid strategy of Konst2 at Tensta konsthall merits future reexamination.

Johanna Billing[23]

Swedish visual artist Johanna Billing is perhaps most known for her video works. She has enjoyed recognition since her debut in 1999 and generally works on projects that include many people. Many works, such as *Project for a revolution*, *Missing out*, and *Where she is at*, deal

---

[23] Quotations in this section are from an interview with Johanna Billing from 2004.

with formulas for performance, scripted aspirations, group dynamics, and feelings of loss. Public space and policy are also themes that recur in her works.

A focus on situations where the action undertaken is open to negotiation has become prevalent in her recent works, such as *You don't love me yet*. This work was born in 2003 out of an invitation by Galleri Index (a foundation for contemporary art) in Stockholm to cooperate in a long-term project. The piece that Billing developed centered around a song written by Roky Erickson that deals with the difficulty of maintaining intimate relationships. Her work consisted of a tour with versions of the song by Erickson sung live by young musicians in six different locations in Sweden, and elsewhere abroad. A single recording and a video were also made.[24] For Billing, apart from the topic of the artwork itself, the project was an attempt to try to connect the art and music worlds on equal terms; a way to formally investigate how an art project can be run where neither the persons involved in the artwork not the artwork's creator have full control over how it is going to evolve. This kind of insecurity and cooperation have been main ingredients in her projects, whether video productions or otherwise:

> *This music tour project was a huge project where we've been in maybe ten different places, and on almost every location there was a cooperation between an art venue and a music association, usually for the first time. And on each location the engaged parties have had to work with it apart from me, and it's been like the opposite of just sending something away with an instruction of how to install the piece. On the contrary, in this project, they have had to create something of their own as much as something that is my project. And this project has been far more site-specific than I've ever worked before.*

Billing is interested in projects where she feels that she can work closely with a process and invited persons over a period of time. She is more interested in sharing the experiences of other people, whether that is in the art world or outside of it:

> *In the beginning, I felt the art world was very closed upon itself. Artists are happy to produce art that are [sic] about art; pieces that refer to other art pieces for an initiated art public... This atti-*

---

[24] www.indexfoundation.nu

tude I find strange. I want to do something that primarily helps me communicate more with people. And I'm more interested in this than in getting good marks by the art critics. Then, of course it, would be fun if one [could] do something that both worlds find fascinating. It's boring to be against other people. They are all just people, whether inside or outside the art world. It's so terribly easy to get stuck too much in this thing that you do what you are expected to do.

According to Billing the prestigious art biennials that are commonly perceived as important for an artist career are void of real contacts. The artworks become anonymous pieces in abstract discourses staged by internationally touring curators:

It becomes so impersonal. It gets so void, so empty, that it's just some kind of representation of something. And some curators work in a very distant way in relation to artists. The individual artwork doesn't mean anything, and I feel that I don't get any contact with the public in this kind of context. And I don't even feel that my work communicates when I'm part of some of these giant, anonymous events.

KL: So it's the contact with the public or the context of the project that is important?

I think it's both. And I think that's probably where my driving force has been from the start...and then, after having taken part in some of these big exhibitions, I felt that I needed to go back to something very personal and local, and that I maybe also needed to find a new form that wasn't like the old familiar one. I prefer doing something that's constructed in a way that makes you have to work, to engage with the artwork to a hundred percent and work with it for several months, and for me it's been more rewarding to do these kind of projects. This is what I enjoy and what is worthwhile for me in the long run.

I think that my music tour project was a way for me to take it all back to where I had started. It has to be here and now, and different every time. In some way I'm doing it more difficult for myself in this way, because it's easier to do a career or to receive schol-

*arships if you are shown on a lot of biennials, and so, to say, play
with the system.*

As a part of Konst2, Billing works intimately with the creative process
of an art project, not separating the artistic creation from the organizing process of the production. Combining artistic integrity with close
cooperation with the contributors to her artworks, Billing bridges individuality and collectivism, designing collective works as individual
projects and vice versa; stepping between the role of artist and producer. This is a way of illustrating that one doesn't have to be an either
artist or producer: one can be both. Trying to break out of stated professional definitions is also a way to renegotiate received ideas about
the tasks and roles of the artist, producer, or curator. Billing, like many
other contemporary artists, challenges the received idea that artists are
those whose works are used by other professionals curating a show or
a project. As Billing, and other artists, have shown, many times the
level of originality and innovation is higher when professional identity
is not clearly defined.

Superflex[25]

Superflex is a group of Danish artists group that have worked for ten
years with social projects that aim to change and improve everyday life
for ordinary or poor people in different contexts and countries around
the world. The core members of Superflex are Rasmus Nielsen, Jakob
Fenger and Bjørnstjerne Christiansen. They met at the Copenhagen Art
Academy, where they each started to study after having left a school
for documentary photography. Art school better harbored their longing
for active interventions. They established the company while still at
the Academy.

Superflex projects include: the development and experimental implementation of a micro biogas system for domestic use in Africa and
Asia, *Supergas*; an internet TV channel and accompanying studio for
producing broadcasts, *Superchannel*; and a beer recipe made freely accessible according to an open source principle.[26]

Through these projects, Superflex has developed tools for ordinary
people to actively engage in and improve the quality of their lives. All
the tools are constructed in such a waythat they can be used by a com-

---

[25] If not otherwise stated, quotations are from an interview with Superflex conducted in 2005.
[26] Steiner & Berger 2001, Superflex 2001, 2003. E-mail invitation by E-flux for
Free Beer launch in Copenhagen 2005.

munity without needing the artists in order for the tools to live on. Superflex has opened or offered a new social space for individuals and groups to act, that may, if so desired by these individuals and groups, be continued autonomously without large investments. Their projects are emancipatory in this respect. The group describes empowerment as a main element of their projects.

The members of Superflex have always worked together. They feel they can do so much more as a group than individually. They are not interested in pursuing careers as individual artists, which seems the norm within the art school and the art world:

> *I wouldn't call it a reaction but a trend that goes on in many other areas in society as well… The production of knowledge and ideas is increasingly done in this way nowadays. You use the energy that is created naturally when working as a group. For us it just seemed more functional to work as a group from the start. Another aspect of the interest in working as a group, apart from this functional aspect, is that there is a lot of individualization taking place, in general, in society, and you could understand all the group work that has been going on during the last ten years as a reaction to that; refusal of being framed as an individualist.*

The economic model of the open source, and offering alternatives to existing power relations in business are important bases for the work and projects of Superflex, such as the Guaranà or Free Beer projects.[27] For Superflex the art world is crucial as a space where resources and flows of people come together. Superflex uses an exhibition as a point of public comment on one of their projects, and the feedback helps them develop the project further or in new directions. Superflex have chosen to display the work within the art system, even though they work as a company, because the art context offers a freedom that is not found in other sectors of society:

> *The reason we work within art is because of the possibilities it offers—a space in which to experiment, free from the bonds of convention.*[28]

---

[27] For presentations of other artistic and alternative economic strategies, cf. Maraniello et al. 2001 and Düllo & Liebl 2005.
[28] Superflex 1999: 11.

They use the art world and its economic resources for funding social projects in the world outside the art system. Superflex has worked with developing feasible alternative models of interaction, both economic and social, that try to change established power relations.[29] Superflex holds the attitude that art can do more than problematize questions in contemporary society. In fact, they put into practice alternative economic models, displaying the process and the results in the art context. Their actions have the aim of economic surplus, but in an opposite way from those of the common entrepreneur. They develop economic opportunities for other people than themselves, and they use art world money to finance projects aiming at changing economic structures outside the art world: [30]

The Biogas project emerged because Louisiana invited us for participation in a show, and we said we wanted to go to Tanzania to install a biogas system as our work for the show. Louisiana paid for transportation of the biogas system to Tanzania with money that would normally go to costs for transportation of artworks to the museum. So we flipped some economies over with that project, and that enabled it to happen. And that told us that maybe those [art] structures are not totally useless to us, that you can use the frame of an exhibition as a working area. There is some funding available sometimes, not much usually, but it is a public space that you can put people into, and then things can happen.

And the art space is also a public window, where you can show what you are doing, which is important to us. What you call the white cube seemed to be the place to be if you are interested in working like this.

KL: So the gallery space gives you freedom, more space to work. But why don't you work as a company, since you actually are one?

[The art context] gives more space, that's the main reason. Companies have to deal with the bottom line as their main objective,

---

[29] Another Danish artist with economic interests was Asger Jorn, cf. Jorn 1962. I am indebted to Rasmus Nielsen for this reference.

[30] Other artist groups have used the same method. The artist group CALC has described how they have sold items on exhibitions to fund local social/art projects in Northern Spain. Cf. CALC 2004, www.calcaxy.com.

and that can be interesting as well, but for us it is not interesting to be only a company. If we were going for that, it would be a waste of time doing all these exhibitions that take so much time and don't really bring any monetary value. But we use the identity of the company because we found that this was the most flexible identity to manoeuvre in a late capitalist environment.

Apart from the flexibility, there are also limitations with the art world, which Superflex discovered. This is a lesson learnt after various experiments with working within art spaces:

For example we've worked with exhibitions where we tried very much to create an interaction or make something that has a dynamic part in it, but art institutions are not built for that. They're not built for working with an exhibition after the opening, because after the opening staff have to start working on their next exhibition, because manpower is scarce. We have learnt not to have illusions about creating a daily active situation, since it's not possible. So now we try to be realistic about what you can do and what you can't do... The art space is a specific context and it has certain limitations, we have to accept that. Because of this we work also outside that space.

The art context is used by Superflex to reflect on and to develop the projects and models further. In other words, the art context is used as a Research and Development resource and a space for the economic undertakings of Superflex. But the production of goods is only a tool for attempting to change the existing economic and social structure of the world. Superflex is mainly interested in the development and research, and start-up phases of economic ventures. As they explain with the example of the Guaranà soft drink:

When we start a project, we basically do everything ourselves. We have to find and convince a company to help us with the first production, and we have to find a distributor, and so on. But the moment things start to roll, we can leave the project over to others more and more, and we also need to do that.

KL: Why do you need to do that?

Because we are not soft drink producers.

KL: But you are...?

We are, our interest is not to drive around in trucks and distribute soft drinks. Our interest is to make that happen. And there are other people who are much better at driving trucks than we are. That is also why we look for contributors or partners when we start up a project... We are good at dealing with contexts. I think that's what we're best at, because of our interest in the exchange between different contexts, and the value of this... I think it's more important that you are open than to be very good at something. We have never tried to be specialists, because the moment you specialize, you also fall into a category, and categories are not interesting. Making categories is a danger to the art sphere, because when you make categories, you always read something in just one special way.

To Superflex, their success in art terms—being invited to many prestigious institutions and exhibitions—has meant that they meet expectations of how they should act to capitalize on their success. But they want to continue with their investigations rather than to act predictably:

Probably the most economically successful thing [at this stage] would have been to do a retrospective. Quite a few have advised us to do that. A lot of people say to us that we should do this or that, because now we have a brand. But it never works like that. Then it's exactly starting to be driving around with a soft drink truck. But that's not interesting for us, it really doesn't make that much sense to us. Of course we want the soft drink to succeed, but it's not our business. Our business is another business. Our business is to be open to look into new situations and consider them as being new.

Because Superflex participates in another arena outside the art world, they are not confined by the rules of the art world. They can leave it to its own mechanisms and operate in society at large, where they feel they want to change power relations, and where they can really try to change the state of things.

Superflex combines economic activities in real time with artistic reflection on their ongoing work in the bracketed space and time of the art world. In this way they have time for reflection, which they would probably not have if they were running a business. On the other hand, it gives them time to develop their business. Would this combination of art and business also work the other way, as a way of enabling a fusion of art into everyday (working) life? Is this a way out of the eternal dilemma of the separation between art and life in modern society? From studies of artist-workplace cooperation projects, it seems that both cultural life and business life on a larger scale still are unripe for such a total immersion. Art is still considered something essentially separate from day-to-day business. [31] Artists like those involved with Superflex, on the other hand, are, busy bridging that perceived chasm.

A Historical Comparison

In order to give perspective to the ideas and modes of working of the artists and artist groups presented, a fourth and historical example of artistic enterprise is presented here. In many ways, Julius Kronberg, who lived and worked in the latter half of the nineteenth century in Italy and Sweden, represents a contrast to the contemporary artists already presented. At the same time, he illustrates another and historically more frequent relationship between artist, public, and commissioner. Kronberg had a close and continuous relationship with his commissioners, one with particular adjoining obligations and constrictions.

Julius Kronberg[32]

Born in 1850, Kronberg graduated from the Art Academy in Stockholm in 1870, having been supported economically by the prefect of the school. After graduation he was praised as a talented young artist, and received a scholarship for further studies. With the scholarship in his pocket, Kronberg first went to Düsseldorf, which was the leading center of influence at that time, but didn't find it rewarding. He continued to Munich and Rome to study more classical painting and styles, and there he found both influences that satisfied him and a market for his work in the continental haute bourgeois milieu.

He stayed in Rome for twelve years, building a strong reputation as a painter of mythological and literal figures, and portraits, and for knowing how to work closely with architects. Speaking Italian fluently, he also made many contacts through Swedish architects and art-

---

[31] Cf. Lindqvist 2004, Barry & Meisiek 2004.

[32] Quotations in this part are from an interview made with Heli Haapasalo, curator at the Hallwylska museet in Stockholm in 2004.

ists who passed through Rome on journeys, that were to come in handy when he returned to Stockholm after more than a decade. Kronberg worked in a style that was very much an established tradition in the nineteenth century, but by the 1880s, a new more outdoor and realistically inspired style of painting became influential in artistic circles. Its inspiration came primarily from Paris. This style of painting focused more on ordinary people (peasants, workers, residents of the countryside, women, or nightlife) than bourgeois idealistic painting. Impressionism was its main expression:

The Hallwyl palace is a kind of Gesamtkunstwerk, and Kronberg was also honored for his ability and skill in working so closely with an architect. This contact with architects, and the commissions for monumental decoration, got him into many high-society contexts, like a commission at the castle of Stockholm, which got him acquainted with the King; and a commission for the Royal Dramatic Theatre of Stockholm, and the Adolf Fredrik Church, where he was commissioned to decorate the cupola. I don't think he would have got these commissions if he hadn't personally known the architects who were involved as well. So personal contacts were clearly important.

Kronberg helped construct a *Gesamtkunstwerk*—the high bourgeois dream of self presentation—where the house represent the total fusion of art and architecture as both exterior and interior design. He was a laborer, paid by his fulfilled commissions, offering the wealthy Hallwyl family an assurance of close connections to haute bourgeois values through his nineteenth century style painting, which expressed the importance of tradition and *Bildung*—of knowing classical literature and mythology.

The space was created and designed by the architect and the artist, who was part of creating a whole, but was just as much a collaborative creation of the commissioning family, the architect, and the artist. The artist was paid well to deliver a product of guaranteed quality and to execute it according to established standards and taste. The style developed by the artist was accepted and bought, or not, by the commissioners who paid for the artworks. A skilled artist could also create demand for new products by offering new product or styles to their commissioners:[33]

> *The Hallwyl family was an extremely wealthy family, and a lot of money was spent of fixed decorations and similar [sic], because this was the way things should be done. Kronberg had rather free hands in working with the interior decoration in the Hallwyl palace, and this is maybe due to the fact that the countess, Wilhelmina von Hallwyl, was not an art connoisseuse. Instead she had to trust architect Klason and artist Kronberg, whom she commissioned to decorate the palace, to a rather high extent. It seems Kronberg could choose the motives for his paintings, and probably the countess pointed to a space and said that here they wanted something, and that Kronberg then presented sketches and ideas for her. And Kronberg and the architect whom he worked very closely with, have surely been able to persuade her of their ideas.*

Kronberg was considered by the art world to be too pompous with his historical style and arranged figures with allegorical meaning, and thus was not given many chances to show his work in public. But his connections with architects and wealthy haute bourgeois families in Sweden paid off. It was to there that we found his main niche for the coming decades of work. Kronberg worked in a style that suited the bourgeois taste during a time when the avant-garde was being born. Art was becoming perceived less as an intimate contract between commissioner and artist as part of an architectonic whole, and more as a relationship between the artist—with her or his style—and an anonymous buyer.

> *But Kronberg also wanted the countess to help him show his work publicly in exhibitions, and also works that the family had in their possession. But she didn't agree to this, and so it didn't happen. This goes to show that the countess didn't have blind faith in Kronberg, and didn't go along with all the propositions he or the architect made. But in the palace itself they got rather free hands I believe.*

---

[33] In this sense Kronberg followed an established skilled artisan strategy adopted by painters in earlier centuries. See Goldtwaite 1993.

Kronberg never succeeded in achieving some of his goals as an artist, which was, primarily a matter of the degree of his acceptance in the art world. At the end of the nineteenth century the art world became interested in a freer artist role, more oriented towards outdoor painting and natural arrangements than taste had dictated, even in the mid-nineteenth century. These artists first produced artworks that were then exhibited and sold, whereas Kronberg followed a tradition where the artist received a commission directly from the buyer. In his own time, Kronberg could be characterized as working in an older fashion. Nevertheless, there were still enough wealthy families who adhered to the kind of lifestyle that involved commissioning artists and architects for the decoration of their homes. They were paid as professionals for their work. In fact, Kronberg was one of the most economically successful artists at the turn of the century:

Even though Julius Kronberg wasn't among the celebrated artists of his time, he was one of the most economically rewarded artists, because he had all these wealthy families as customers or commissioners. At least from the Hallwyl family Kronberg was paid very substantial sums for his work. Maybe this was also because the family felt that with Kronberg they knew what he would deliver, he delivered a certain kind of motives, and the family knew how the work was undertaken, there were no unpleasant surprises in terms of motives or quality; what was delivered was genuine and reliable craftsmanship. And maybe Kronberg also was paid for loyalty, for always being accessible for different kinds of consultations or discussions on commissions.

In a way, Kronberg was an inventor as he introduced a more colorful style of painting in Stockholm during the second half of the nineteenth century, but principally he continued a tradition that was specifically academic. He found a market among families who were not interested in the art of the emerging scene that the avant-garde saw as a reinvigoration of painting. What was particular to the older relationship between commissioner and artist, was its closeness and ongoing nature, often over a number of commissions and years. The space between public/commissioner and artist was quite intimate. This type of close relationship did not prevail among most artists and customers buying from galleries and art dealers, as the dealer distanced the buyer from the artist. A somewhat similar long-term relationship still prevailed for a time between patrons such as Ernst Thiel and the newer type of artist, who was still given financial support to conduct his[34] own work. The artists eventually either sold the finished paintings on the market or to their patron, or offered them as gifts to their patrons as thanks for their support.

Artistic Entrepreneurship: New Blood for an Anaemic System

Challenges and Opportunities of Entrepreneurship in the Art Field

One of the first questions in this chapter was how entrepreneurship appears in the experience economy. Starting with the art world as a field within the experience economy, I initially defined artistic work as experience production but also a social practice, which is, today, often oriented towards reflection on social practice itself. Artistic practice was also shown to display similarities with entrepreneurial action in terms of proposing new ways of doing things and thereby challenging established norms. Following this discussion, was an investigation of artistic entrepreneurial action through a number of examples. Here I present some conclusions regarding entrepreneurship as it appears in artistic practice. First, I begin by discussing what opportunities and challenges are embraced by entrepreneurship organized to offer experiences.

The Anaemic White Cube and New Blood

For entrepreneurial artists, challenges are clearly found within the art system. These include norms, hierarchies, and gatekeeping in the art world, which cause the field to stagnate and implode. The opportunities for renewal are found outside the art system, established through experience. The artifice of the norms of the art world, or the economic order, are discovered and exposed by critical artists, and can be challenged. For entrepreneurial artists, the art world is a closed circuit in need of revitalization through fresh impulses originating outside of it. The artists presented in this chapter perceive the white cube art system as a self-referring system where everything is fixed: positions, rules for action, and strategies. By opening up toward other systems and practices, the art scenee and the abstract white cube space can be reshaped, and the distanced relationships of the global art system be developed

---

[34] Female artists in this period had difficulties advancing to such privileged positions as to receive patron support.

into a live space with shared experiences in local social environments. The artists heard in this chapter do not renounce the art world in itself, but want to add to it.

The historical comparison shows us that Kronberg was marginalized by a changing art world, where his older style of working was not accepted by the up-and-coming art community, which preferred different ways of conducting artistic and including relationships to the public. The contemporary artists discussed in this text work to create spaces of reciprocity that offer alternatives to the objectifying relationships that the international biennial art career system offers, which seem closed biennial art career system offers. These alternative relationships between artist, curator and consumer of art seems more close to the relationship Kronoberg had with his commissioners, but over the contemporary artists can never have the economic intimacy that characterised the links between many artists of the nineteenth century, such as Kronoberg, and his commissioners.[35] Johanna Billing, Konst2 and Superflex are all opposed to producing artwork in a commodified form; artworks that can be placed in any context, and that are produced and consumed without a clear relationship to the context of production. This critique of the commodification of the artwork echoes the sociologically inspired installation art of the 1960s, which was mainly critical, or Marxist, in ideology.[36] Instead, an intimacy between public, commissioner, and artist is important and stimulating to them. This is more important than acting according to the norms of the art world.[37] Kronberg, on the other hand, was a craftsman working closely with some of the most wealthy and influential persons in Sweden at the turn of the nineteenth century. Whereas our entrepreneurial contemporary artists are not dependent on their visiting public for economic support because of public support for art production and display, Kronberg was dependent on commissions. In this sense, contemporary artists can

---

[35] For a discussion of the value systems of market, government, and gift economies, cf. Klamer 2001.

[36] Marx analyzed commodities and found things were manufactured not for direct use and consumption, but for sale in the market. In a feudal or agrarian system, on the other hand, goods were primarily for immediate and local consumption and use. As referred in Bocock 1993. Cf. Fromm's analysis of Marx's notion of Man in Fromm 1961. For a historical overview of installation art, cf. Bishop 2005.

[37] Artists critique many aspects of the conditions of the contemporary art world and the effects of globalized society. A massive and excentric contemporary critique of the spectacularization of art, science and life in general is offered also in Virilio 2002. Not to forget Situationist Guy Debord's classical *La société du spectacle* from 1967.

earn income through public support for their work through projects or employment rather than by operating in a market where the working hours are determined by a commissioner. [38]

In Kronberg's time, the white cube art system was only in the process of being established. Kronberg never professionally entered this new sphere for art. He was trained and continued to work within an older tradition of large-scale painting, interior decoration, murals and commissions for decoration of public spaces. Kronberg nonetheless expressed an interest in participating in the exhibition form of displaying art, but he never got the chance. The private sphere of views and homes was his oeuvre, not the new white cube gallery sphere. In a sense, Kronberg can be seen as a role model for the type of relationship that contemporary artists long for (even though obviously some other sides of his artistry would not, such as his emphasis on craftsmanship rather than experimentation, and his loyalty to both traditional forms of expression and the taste of customers). [39] Whereas Kronberg was an artisan decorating the premises in which the Hallwyl family executed their miseenscène of haut-bourgeois life and spectacle, [40] contemporary artists want to be part of a more carnivalesque event, where ordinary people and artistic professionals jointly create an ongoing event. [41] They long, however, for the long-term and intimate relationship between artist and commissioner/public, which was customary in former centuries, and even exists today for a few artists.

Paradoxical Elements of Artistic Entrepreneurship

Entrepreneurship in the art sector is—in the examples above—about making room for doing things one's own way, despite contradicting norms. It is also about sharing this space with others. Enabling others is an important element of entrepreneurial artistic practice both inside and outside the art system. The reason for this entrepreneurial action is not found in cultural policy or current trends in grant giving, but cul-

---

[38] See discussion of the role of the funder of an artwork as cocreator of it in Santagata 1998.

[39] For a discussion of academicism and avantguardism, see Barlow 2000.

[40] Hoskins (1955) writes about the creation and cultivation of a picturesque surrounding of aristocratic life and living. Aristocratic and in later centuries haute bourgeois life had to be arranged in a picturesque way, partly literally, in order to separate and frame the life of the noble family from that of common people. The look of the place had to be paid attention to. See Zukin 1991. This urge to arrange the space according to a logic of separation and appearance seems opposite to the ambitions of both Konst2, Johanna Billing, and Superflex.

[41] See Bakhtin 1965.

tural policy phrasing and key words in grant directions may be used by artists for the artists' own ends. Other key elements of artistic entre-preneurship are collectivism, individuality, self-assurance, knowledge of limits, amateurism, process focus, challenges, and public support.

Collectivism and Individuality
Working with others gives more strength and enables more than work-ing individually. It is also more fun than working on your own. This stress on collectivism and cooperation does not negate respecting for a contributors individuality, but rather it builds on it. The strength of working as a group or in close collaboration with others is that ideas and projects can be developed, judged internally, and executed with more energy and input when there is a group engaged in hatching and realizing a common project. Hierarchies with demarcation lines be-tween positions and possibilities are not interesting. Energy flows when participants are treated as competent and important; when they are accepted for who they are and are allowed to contribute with their various experiences, knowledge, and skills. Various expressive forms are also treated equally, and are seen as complementing each other rather than being hierarchically structured or to be kept divided.[42] En-trepreneurial artists are not working solitarily, but on the contrary work in groups and networks with projects that demand organizing skills and that cherish individuality.

Self-Assurance, Knowledge of Limits, and Amateurism
All presented artists have enjoyed success in the art world even if some of them have also temporally experienced the opposite. This is an important fact to remember when considering their ideas and work. They all also express self-confidence and conviction in what they do and in their objectives. If and how these two facts are related needs to be further analyzed. All interviewed artists speak of the ne-cessity of not looking for appreciation from others when doing what one perceives as important; new ideas should not be stopped because of the limited judgment of others. These artists have also learnt the limits of the art world by working within and outside it. They have re-alistic expectations of what can and cannot be done in the art world. They go outside the art world for what cannot be pursued within it, but

---

[42] Experiments with various and combined art forms are not new, but happened on a larger scale both in the early twentieth century, and in the 1960s and 70s. In ear-lier centuries various art forms such as painting, sculpture, and architecture, were physically more intimately related in the built environment than today.

simultaneously contribute to it in ways that are fruitful both for themselves and for the art world.

Also central to all the contemporary artists presented is a love of exploration, of trying out new things that are intriguing. It is important to not only do what one is good at or what is expected, but rather to try out and learn new things. They do not consider it a failure not to know an area or how to do something. These entrepreneurial artists see themselves as professional amateurs. They work from an idea of the collective or the common, with "popular" as a cherished concept.[43]

Continuous Challenges and Process Focus

All the artists studied work with art in a way that stresses the open-ended nature of the work process and development of a project. But a focus on the process is also a point of departure for an analysis and rethinking of how things are done. Challenging received norms and routines is a way for the artists, presented in this text, to explore new possible orders, but also a way to increase the level of joy and excitement in work. They continuously challenge themselves, and find pleasure in this. Exploring is more gratifying than being rewarded by others. If this strategy in turn leads to respect and good responses from the art world, it's considered a opposite outcome.

Public Support

All the work done by these artists relies on public economic support for production and display. The art venues with which Konst2, Superflex and Johanna Billing work are all primarily publicly funded. Private money, in the form of foundation grants to young or promising artists, has given the artists opportunities to work without pressure to produce salable art pieces, but this income is usually combined with commissions from public art museums and galleries. The profit from the sales of artworks contributes very little to the income of these artists.

As shown in this study of the art field, entrepreneurship is paradoxical, cherishing and hosting conflicting values as central to the dynamics of doing something new. Entrepreneurialism relates to the organization of work rather than to innovation in artistic expression itself, even if the two cannot be clearly separated. Entrepreneurial artists operate by establishing new possible orders of things—new norms and values—and this is expressed in their forms of working, and through

---

[43] Santagata 1998.

their relationships to other partners around the artwork. The effectiveness of this strategy is shown through in the economic success of the alternative orders (as in the case of Superflex), or in social or artistic success, as measured by respect and interest from the public and other professionals in the art world.

Artistic Entrepreneurship Rephrased: Carnivalesque Space

Just as carnivals in former times were spaces where the normal rules of feudal society, with its strict regulation of status and action, were temporally inverted, art today challenges the everyday norms for action and status. It creates a space where these norms and rules may be contested or redefined.[44] In social or relational art works, these changes are tested on the actual participating audience who is active. While official feasts in medieval Europe sanctioned and reinforced existing patterns, of hierarchy, morality, and truth claims, in the carnival there was no distinction between actor and spectator, since the carnival was a popular event open to all people.[45] Bodily functions and appearance, laughter, simultaneous celebration and degradation, and ambivalence are the hallmarks of the carnivalesque; the opposite of the serious and the respectable. Here the audiences were not just passive, regarding the spectacle at a distance, but were simultaneously active, in creating it. Experience of the carnival is not something that is offered, but rather is created in the course of the event itself.

The artists presented in this chapter all give center stage to other individuals, and offer an engagement based experience as a central part of their work. When known artists hand over center stage to others it can be difficult for the art world to accept, since it is oriented towards the identification and judgment of the original work of one ceator. Art itself brings the carnivalesque into other spheres of society, but the carnivalesque, it seams, is not always easy to include in the art world on another level other than the exceptional, the popular, or the marginal. Most importantly, the experiences of the artists presented in this text illustrate that structures and norms are not fixed and unchangeable.

Challenges for artistic entrepreneurship reside not only in the artistic innovation process itself, but also in the structure of the art world, which seems to some artists closed in on itself, with rigid norms that

---

[44] A space both mental and physical, economic and relating to power, as outlined in Lefebvre 1974.

[45] Bakhtin 1965.

stifle energy and taking satisfaction in the artistic work. Artistic entrepreneurship points to the demand for alternative art encounters other than these often experienced where artworks do not communicate among themselves or with the visitor, and where personal interaction is lacking between the producer and consumer of the art experience. Entrepreneurial action in the art world today focuses on process development, which also changes the end product and the experience offered. As Fogh Kirkeby points out, an event and its experience cannot be but fractionally managed. This knowledge is the point of departure for entrepreneurial artists who invite coproducers of their art work to a simultaneous experience of production and consumption—to a carnivalesque space in which the experience is not staged, but propelled by the individuals and the collective of producers and consumers; an experience in the making.

Interviews

Johanna Billing, 2004.
Heli Haapasalo, Curator, Hallwylska museet, 2004.
Konst2 (Ylva Ogland, Rodrigo Mallea Lira, Jelena Rundqvist), 2004 and 2005.
Superflex (Jakob Fenger, Rasmus Nielsen, and Bjørnstjerne Christiansen [not interviewed]), 2005.

CHAPTER 2

FILM PRODUCER, ENTRE-PRENEURSHIP, AND THE EX-PERIENCE ECONOMY

MARJA SOILA-WADMAN

A Close-Up from the Field of Filmmaking

I can tell about a shooting phase of a film, which ended up in very good film, strong film. The shooting started with co-operation be-tween the author, who also was the scriptwriter to the film, and the director. They had been friends for years. Their families had taken holidays together, which afterwards, of course, had resulted in two theatre plays by the author.

We should start this shooting. Then it happened that the author became really damned on the director, and didn't even want to come and say hello to him. I, as a producer to the film, was obliged to jump in and finish the script together with the director. To make the script shorter was necessary, it was four hours long and we should take it down to two and a half. I was obliged to do the entire job, and run between, when these two persons were scolding each other via me.

The shooting started and it was a really trying one, there were a lot of emotions. The actor in the title role became very sick, and simultaneously, he was accused for having flied from the Swedish theatre Dramaten before some guest play... So, I had this in my ears all the time. Additionally, the director had borrowed half a million crowns in order to start a play, and for which he had rented a theatre at the same time as we were filming. The same author as for the script wrote the play. The wife of the director had the title role in the theatre play, and was also responsible for the organization of the performance.

Just as it was as worst in the shooting, and when the opening night for the theatre play was to occur, there was a press strike. In three days the newspapers weren't published, and they should have given the reviews. The whole theatre performance crashed. The director owed the bank the money and the wife phoned every second hour to the location and wanted to kill herself. She rang to our office, where the director at the same time struggled with the scriptwriter, and where the technical team told that they had had enough. So was the shooting and I tried to pat everybody and go around, and talk with the wife to the director.

This is a very typical producer task to take care of everything. If the shooting is well organized, the producer can devote oneself to tasks outside the shooting. He should not be obliged to go into the shooting. But here, there were several remarkable things, which happened. And the film is about breaking up in the age of thirty-five, forty years. The whole team was in that age. It was as if just to continue the shooting when you went home. The film became bloody good when everything had been cleared up. I imagine that also the author and the director have talked to each others since then. (Film producer Bo Jonsson, in Soila-Wadman, 2003: 76–77)

Film Production, Aesthetics, the Experience Economy and Entrepreneurship – Introduction

Film production has been viewed as the great media industry since the twentieth century. Now there are billions of people watching different kinds of movies around the world. The reason why we do it varies. It can be a question of becoming entertained by popular or artistic films, or we may want to know about different cultures, be educated, seek for information, look at our favorite film stars, see a mirror of our society and culture, and so forth. Whatever the purpose, film media has had a great influence in many societies and is an important part of the experience economy.

The importance of the aesthetic experience should be emphasized when looking at the influence of film. Welsch explains the significance of aesthetics of artwork:[46]

---

[46] Whether film can be seen as art, popular culture, entertainment, etc., has been a long discussion in film history (Söderbergh Widding, 1996), along with the discussion about what art is (Becker, 1992, Wolff, 1993). In our postindustrial world there are several borders that have been questioned. In this text I speak about art creating processes in filmmaking, with inspiration from persons in film production,

When you look at an artwork it maybe opens one's eyes so that you can see the world differently, in a new or unusual way. Art-work thus can be a tool for an intensified perception of reality. In addition to seeking enjoyment, entertainment and prosperity through art, it is also a field for cognition. In our world where flexibility is demanded this can have importance for our will to question the established ways to perception, thinking and organiz-ing. This is something, which has influence on us, both on the per-sonal plane and on the institutional plane, as well as in science and the social and the cultural fields. This in turn can open new ways of seeing life. [47]

Perhaps the aesthetic experience that film evokes in it's viewers as well as the film product itself reflect entrepreneurial potential as de-fined by Spinosa et al (1997): Entrepreneurship can be viewed as something that transforms the practices of people's everyday lives, creates the possibility to figure out one's life in a new way, and thereby participate in history making.[48] Reasoning about entrepreneur-ship can also be noticed in order to understand how the production conditions are organized when a new film is created and the crea-tive/artistic/aesthetic expression is brought about. As Bo Jonsson's story at the beginning of this chapter shows, producing a new film is risky business.[49] Certainly, the risky factors can be identified in crea-tion of the artistic/creative expression, but also when organizing the work processes and not the least in managing financial aspects of a production. A common opinion among people working in the film business is that during the production phase of a new film, it is impos-sible to know if it will be a success. All the "success factors" can be there: an interesting story, well-known actors, generous advertising, and exposure in mass media, including appreciative reviews from the critics. It is never sure, however, that enough people will want to go

---

which means that there are so many different aspects in a film, for instance, photo, sound, story, etc., that it is difficult to say where it is art, and where not.

[47] Welsch in the conference Art and Enterprise, 1996, Stockholm University, School of Business. See also Welsch 1998.

[48] See also Hjorth in this volume.

[49] Bo Jonsson has worked in film production for several decades. Currently he has a film production firm of his own. Earlier he had been CEO for Swedish Film Insti-tute and for Sandrews' feature film production. He has produced several films about "conducted tours" directed by Lasse Åberg, for example 'Sällskapsresan', 'When the Raven Flies'—a cult film on the 1970th directed by Hrafn Gunnlaugs-son, , as well as films directed by Lars Norén, Dusan Makavevj, and Jaques Tati.

and see a film, to guarantee that the money invested in the production will be repaid. Both film workers and film scientists are very conscious that the budget available and organizing the division of labor in a film team have influence on what the aesthetic product is going to look like (Hollows, 1995). The distribution of work on a film project is commonly though to be that the director is responsible for the artistic/creative part, while the producer is concerned with administration and finances (Bordwell and Thompson, 1997).

What is the Role of the Producer in Filmmaking?

The aim of this chapter is to explore some aspects of how the role of the producer is constructed in the entrepreneurial process while the filmmaking activities are being initiated, created, and organized. Like many artistic leaders, film director is often portrayed, both in media and research, as a kind of romantic hero role responsible for the artistic creation in a project (Köping and Soila-Wadman, 2005; Koivunen 2003; Wennes, 2002; Stenström, 2000). There is not much talk about the role of the producer in this process (Lanz, 2006). How many persons in the ordinary cinema audience know who the producer of a film is or what they do? After having studied some textbooks in leading film programs in the United States, Lanz argues that they portray a picture of quite neglected film producer in relation to the director as concerns the task of a creative project. Further, she stresses that the construction of the leading roles in a film team (film director and film producer) are constructed dichotomously, which maintains an ongoing competition between them. I argue that if the artistic/creative process is viewed from an entrepreneurial perspective, from the conception of the idea to the finished film, the vision and the finances realized in the tasks and the roles of the director and producer should not/must not be viewed in contrast to each other.

The information in this chapter concerning the role of the producer is mainly based on interviews with two acclaimed Swedish film producers, Bo Jonsson and Lars Jönsson,[50] who deem it of vital interest to participate in the creative process in filmmaking. Information concerning the organizing conditions on a film project is based on research for

---

[50] Lars Jönsson owns the production company Memfis Film together with his colleague Anna Anthony. They have produced several box office successes in Sweden around the turn of the millennium, for instance *Show me love* and *Lilja-4-ever*, director Lukas Moodysson; *Dalecarlians (Masjävlar)*, director Maria Blom; *Jalla!Jalla!* and *Zozo*, director Josef Fares. Several of the films have also been distributed on the international market.

my doctoral thesis (Soila-Wadman, 2003). I interviewed people in different occupational roles in film production. Additional background to the questions is given by an ethnographic study in a film project.

Narrating Knowledge – Theoretical, Epistemological, and Methodological Notes

The epistemological position in this text is based on social a constructionist approach (Berger and Luckman, 1967) and relational perspective (Dachler, Hosking and Gergen, 1995). Knowledge and meaning are negotiated by "multiloguing" (Dachler and Hosking, 1995: 6), whereby an ongoing conversation is constituted by several voices who participate in the process of constructing reality. Language coordinates action when people who are talking with each other create understanding as a shared ground for meaning making. The position of the speaking subject is problematized in this discussion following the modernist/postmodernist debate that continues to this day, wherein we find a critical perspective on the view of (hu)man as a selfconscious, autonomous, integrated, freethinking subject who constitutes himself and his world (Benhabib, 1992; Carter and Jackson, 2000; Dachler, Hosking & Gergen, ibid). This view of the subject Dachler and Hosking (1995) names as entitative or possessive individualism', and argues that it is traditional in management narratives.

For example, when talking about leadership, which has been the hot area in the management literature (Czarniawska Joerges and Wolf, 1991) leaders are considered to own certain qualities that make them suitable for their role, Dachler and Hosking continues their critical argumentation: They are supposed to be superior to their coworkers in terms of knowledge or they posess "charisma." The goals and interests of the leader are considered privileged over those of theirs who are subjected to leadership. In this model, the leader is presented as the subject and the coworkers more like objects. The central problem here is how the leader/subject is to make the coworkers/objects think, speak, or act so that they reflect the leader's perspective. As far as social relations go, the subject exploits relations in order to achieve knowledge and influence over other people and groups. Relationships are viewed as instrumental. The leader is assumed to be in control of the course of events. Discussion concerning this view of human nature can also be found in entrepreneurship research (Hosking in dialogue with Hjorth, 2004). According to an overview of entrepreneurship research conducted by Fletcher, there is also a tradition of talking about "how certain individuals display and manipulate unique personal characteristics in order to identify/exploit market opportunity" (Fletcher, 2003:125).

It is possible to describe a film producer as an individual with specific entrepreneurial personality traits and characteristics, as has been one tradition in entrepreneurship research,[51] but there have been criticisms concerning the research, which wants to explain the phenomenon with the specific traits that the entrepreneur "owns" (Shane and Venkataraman, 2000; Gartner, 2004). Certainly, there is always a human being acting in entrepreneurial processes; an experiencing, embodied subject as Johannisson (2005) points out. But entrepreneurship is also an ongoing process of interaction with other people in a specific context (see also Hjorth, Johannisson and Steayert, 2003).

In this text I explore the role of the producer by using the relational model proposed by Dachler and Hosking, but I change the word *leader* in their logic to the word *entrepreneur*. When seen from the relational perspective, discussing entrepreneurship means posing questions about the social processes within which a specific entrepreneurial model has been construed and is being continuously construed. The entrepreneur shares responsibility with others in the construction of this understanding and, in the long run its, execution. The entrepreneur is one of many voices. From a relational perspective, entrepreneurship should not be defined in accordance with arguments such as how successful or unsuccessful an entrepreneur is, or what special qualities they have. The main question is, rather, how the entrepreneur and those they interact with are responsible for the type of relations and actions that they jointly construe. The differences that exist within the understanding of oneself, the other, and the state of things should be noticed and negotiated. The entrepreneur's attention should thus move the focus to multiloguing, negotiating, networking and other social means of narrative that deal with meaning in individual and collective activities. Small talk, which is continually occurring in both the formal and informal organizational arenas is a good example, while these conversations are partly trivial, important emotions and ambitions are also expressed, and ideals, norms, and rules are created, interpreted and re-interpreted (Gustafsson, 1994; Sjöstrand and Tyrstrup, 2001).

Consequently, the interviews with my informants have been conducted as open conversations. The knowledge was narrated in interaction between the interviewees and myself in a way that gave them—

---

[51] There are parallels to leadership research where there has been interest in leadership traits (Yukl, 2002).

actors in the film business—a space to come out with their stories of everyday life (Chia, 1997; Czarniawska, 1997; Steyart and Bowen, 1997). I agree with Foss (2004) that when people tell their life stories they also make sense of their experiences, which influences their identity construction. As Dachler and Hosking (ibid.) argue, our subjectivities are created in relational, interactive processes in different contexts. Benhabib (1992) maintains that this should be seen pragmatically, which allows the subject to be considered as the author and main actor in her/his own life. The actors are a part of their particular life context and at the same time creators of it, participate in worldmaking. In this context, organizational artifacts are included, partly material but also symbolic, which create an order for aesthetic understanding of organizational life.

Since the film product is an aesthetic one, creating an understanding of organizational dynamics in an entrepreneurial project must include an aesthetic slant. This approach, in which interest has grown during the last decade, problematizes the rational analysis and emphasizes aspects like emotions, intuition, improvisation, and fantasy (Gagliardi, 1996; Guillet de Monthoux, 1993, 1998, 2000; Lindstead and Höpfl, 2000; Strati 1999). These aspects can, more or less, be found in all organizations and are important to notice according to Gagliardi (ibid.) in order to understand the moods, pathos, and sensitivity in human life. In organizations that create art they are necessary for action.

Findings and Insights – Both Theoretical and Empirical

"To Find Out the Gap on the Market"

"You don't get rich in the Swedish film business," Bo Jonsson pointed out. (Soila-Wadman 2003). Further, in a Swedish newspaper during the last years of the 20th the Swedish film producer is characterized as something like a small-scale enterpriser with unpaid invoices. The Swedish film industry cannot be compared with its huge American counterpart, but as measured by ticket sales, there have been successful Swedish repertory. Such as: *Show Me Love* aka *Fucking Åmål* (1998), *Jägarna* (Hunters, 1996), and several films directed by Lasse Åberg on 'conducted tours' (for instance *Sällskapsresan*, 1980). In spite of the risks of filmmaking, there has been a great will to make film in Sweden. Where does it come from? And how is it accomplished?

Certainly a film project, which is the organizational context where a new film is created, can be viewed as an entrepreneurial event in the sense that Hjorth puts forth in his chapter in this book: "… it changes

the style of relating to objects and people resulting in a new order..."
The process of filmmaking is centered around the aesthetic experience
connected to disorientation and creation of affects. A film project
needs its entrepreneurs—fiery spirits—to drive the risky production
process through to completion. In order for the public to come and see
a film, these entrepreneurs must have a feeling for timing in the society
in order to identify a topic for a good story. It is a question of finding
an anomaly, or a gap, where the idea can find a market, as this process
is called in the entrepreneurial literature.

According to several of my interviewees, finding a story that the
film is going to tell, and that will have enough power in it, is crucial
for the whole filmmaking process. It can be seen as the starting point
for a new film project. Judgment is needed from a producer that people
want to see the film. A director or a scriptwriter can also initiate the
idea, but they must find a producer who thinks that the idea is something worth commitment and to start further activities.

Producer Lars Jönsson told me that he wants to produce a film that
he himself wants to see. His production company Memfis Film actively looks at what is going on around us. Lars reads newspapers,
watches plenty of film, works with new, inexperienced directors and
tests new ideas. This has shown to be a fruitful strategy; quite new and
inexperienced directors have made several successful of Memfis films.
He invests much energy in the script phase and relies on his intuition
in his judgements:

> *When I was in my youth I spent lots of time in the cinema. Went to*
> *filmclubs and festivals and watched lots of great stuff from the*
> *film history. All those films are now somewhere in my backbone*
> *for inspiration and reference. Nowadays I trust my taste and intui-*
> *tion. In the beginning of your career you perhaps are not so sure*
> *about your decisions. However, my experience is that if there has*
> *been some slight feeling of uncertainty during the script phase,*
> *there often will be troubles later on in the shooting or editing*
> *phase. That is why it is better to try to work up the script so that*
> *you can trust it.* (Lars Jönsson)

To Initiate, Organize, Finance, and Manage a Film Project Needs both Planning and Improvisation

Beyond finding the idea for a new film, the activities in the start-up
phase of a film project include securing the approximately 15–20 millions crowns that a Swedish feature film costs. An agreement with a

distributor for exhibition of the film must also be reached. This is required in order to get financing from the Swedish Film Institute. A team must be created to carry out the shooting process. Finally, launching and advertising activities must be organized. To find financing and create a budget for a film in Sweden is well described by the comparison of making puzzle. There are different financiers involved in it. One of them is the Swedish state through Swedish Film Institute. The state participates in financing film production because of a cultural and political decision that film production is important for Sweden.[52]

Some producers feel it is important that the film team is committed to their vision for the project and that the team doesn't question their decisions. Several informants with different professions in film production have referred to the strict hierarchy in a film team:

The shooting process is so expensive that there is no time to begin to debate with everyone in the team when you are on location. Instead, one of the desirable skills of a producer is to be able to foresee the problems, which probably will emerge during the shooting and prepare a kind of alternative project plan for all eventualities. (Bo Jonsson in Soila-Wadman, 2003)

Several producers and directors I have interviewed have confirmed this opinion. One strategy to achieve a flexible organizing process is to set up a crew that is capable of working together. Circumstances during a shoot are often turbulent and include a lot of hard work. When creating a team this means that both professional and social skills should be taken into account when selecting crewmembers.

A Pleasure in Creative Work

Several interviewees talked about the playful processes in filmmaking, which can be both fun and serious. To start a film project is to start an adventure, too. It is impossible to predict everything that will happen when a project starts. Circumstances emerge that are impossible to control. The story in the beginning of this text is an illustration of this fact. Another example told by the producer Katinka Farago is about a house that was meant to be set on fire during shooting but that hap-

---

[52] An interesting point concerning the owner of the film is that in the Oscar's gala, as well as Guldbagge gala in Sweden, the award for the best film of the year goes to the producer.

pened to burn down a day before the shoot.[53] What to do? The plans must often be changed, which is a well-known aspect of all project research (Engwall, 1999). Of course, some enjoyment may be derived from the turbulence when it is at its worst. Everyone in film business, however, is conscious that flexibility and the talent to improvise are important, not only in front of the camera but also behind it. The concept of improvising here means being open to emerging opportunities and to finding new ways to act (Gustafsson and Lindahl 2002). It is not a question of amateurism. My interviewees told me that persons working in a film team are used to the changing conditions. They are used to finding alternative solutions and they take pleasure in these creative processes. An informant, who has been working as a producer and an assistant director, expressed it as following:

> *It is really motivating to work in the creative process. There exists an enormous creativity among filmmakers. To be near the process when it takes form and results in a film on the screen, it is an intensive experience.* (An informant in Soila-Wadman, 2003)

Entrepreneurship and the Film Producer in a Relational Perspective

It has also been discussed whether entrepreneurship could be reviewed from a widened definition beyond technology and economics, as something that has to do with history making and the creation of new styles of living (Spinosa et al., 1997).

In the following text I am going to talk about the role of producer in the relational, interactive process of filmmaking. I start with some opinions about the significance of the artistic product, which has parallels to the process of entrepreneurial organizing as an interactive event.

Film (Art) is Created in an Aesthetic Play

It is important to understand the characteristics of artistic work and how the artistic process works when trying to understand the organizing processes of that work. The idea of seeing artwork as an individual action may be exemplified by Lapierre (2001) who maintains that for an artist—designer, performer, conductor, choreographer, lighting designer, dancer, actor, etc.—the most important thing is to be true to his/her idea. In doing so, it is not a question of simply relying on one's

---

[53] Told by the film producer Katinka Farago, 1997. The film was directed by Andrej Tarkovskij.

technical skills or virtuosity, but also on one's sensibility and intelligence. Art is a means of self-fulfillment and of relating to one's time. In an art producing organization, art originates with the creators and performers, who have made art the focus of their personal and professional lives, rather than as a result of market demand.

The idea of artwork as an individual action can, however, be seen in contrast to the idea of the artwork as agent. Guillet de Monthoux (1993, 2000, 2004) claims that art is created in a circle of poets, actors, and the audience in an aesthetic play. In that play, artists are not isolated bohemians who stand above regular society but neither can technical part of an art creating team work in isolation from the aesthetic play. The creation of a work of art should not be described as something like the Mona Lisa idea of art, where a framed canvas is painted by someone famous and reminds us of something. Seeing art as an intimate dialog between a brilliant artist and his admirer is too narrow a view. This position extends the individualistic view of the artist, which has parallels to the nineteenth-century romantic notion of an artist (Becker, 1982). Art can be viewed, instead, as having an organizing ability and being dynamic human action. This idea of art implies organizing in the aesthetic field, where the artist triggers playful interpretations in a creative process. Referring to Genette, Guillet de Monthoux argues that a work of art, as exemplified in the script for a theater play or the score to an opera, is more than the written text; it also includes execution on stage and comes into being between its manifestations.

To View Filmmaking as a Collective Work—Negotiations between the Film Producer and the Film Director instead of Dichotomized Roles

In the critics of auteur theory in film science I can identify parallel thoughts for seeing art as an agent and art work becoming into being in the aesthetic play. Several authors have asked if the influence of a director of a film can be traced in a specific film. Is it possible to view a film director as the author, or "auteur", of a film text when thinking about the collective work of perhaps hundreds of people behind a film (Andersson, 1999; Hollows, 1995; Koskinen, 2002; Lapsley and Westlake, 1988; Stoddart, 1995)? These opinions draw even more attention to the role of the producer.

The relation between the producer and the director is, however, not unproblematic in practice. In my interviews with participants in varying professions in the film business, it has been quite common to hear about differences and controversies in opinions concerning this relation. For instance, some directors want to produce their own films because they don't want any intervention in the artistic process. On the other hand, there are directors who want the producer to have the responsibility for finances and the overall organizational procedures, in order to be free to concentrate on the artistic process.[54] Most of my informants expressed, however, the wish to work with a creative producer who is interested in the creative/artistic project and not one who only wants to get the production "out of hands". That was a description a director used in order to characterize a producer, who, according to her/him only cared for the economic aspects of the film without interest in the artistic quality. Consequently, the reasoning behind my choice of interviewees can be seen as a strategic selection (Eneroth, 1984). It has been interesting to listen to the stories of especially those producers, who are interested in the creative process.

The following is an example, told by Bo Jonsson, of how this creative, relational process can take gestalt in the important manuscript phase:

We are working with a Swedish novel, which will be directed by a person who is going to make his debut as a director. The author, me [producer Bo Jonsson] and the director have been working together for a very long time. During the journey, the script has totally been worked up. We have started with the novel and the aim has been to meet the director in order to get him to understand what he is doing. It has been a very special process. The scriptwriter and I are old friends. We know everything in the text, which is about the 1980s. We imagined that everything was clear, but the director, who belongs to a younger generation, has been wondering around several questions that what do we mean. Fortunately, there has been a good cooperation in our team. We could have done a break, said: "He doesn't understand anything," and chosen another director. However, we have had a successful communication. The director has taken the script to him, and we know that he is able to make this film. So, the author and I have stepped back, and the director has climbed in. (Bo Jonsson)

---

[54]An example of this controversy between art, decisionmaking and finances is a debate, that occurred in Swedish media during the summer of 2004 (one of the references DN 20040707) .It concerned the decision of some television producers to engage a specific film director in a new drama production. The problem was that the scriptwriter was annoyed over the producers' choice of the director. He didn't consider the director's artistic potential high enough to realize the project.

Film Producers and Their Work Practices—Listening, Intuition, and Attunement

In my conversation with Lars Jonsson we talked about his everyday working practices as a film producer. One of the questions was about *cooperation* between the director and the producer. Lars stressed that he is actively seeking new talents who could possibly work as directors and with whom the production company could develop a long term cooperation:

> *It is a great decision when you commit yourself to cooperation with a specific person. You then say no to work with others. It is a big risk, too, which you take. Your time goes to this person. The production company is staking several millions on it, and it is our responsibility to run home the project, which perhaps takes three years as a whole.* (Lars Jönsson)

Lars prefers to work with long-term relations. That includes accepting that all the films may not be successful. For instance, if a director has an experimental phase in his/her development, it is not sure that the film will be a public success. But at the same time, hopefully, there will be something new coming out:

> *It is my job to present a specific project, with the director and the actors, to different financers. The industry is a bit conservative and we have now and then come with some spectacular projects. Everybody has opinions and attitudes concerning the film, like "The script is too long", or "The script is too short." Then, I see it as my responsibility to be a kind of safeguard to the director so that the director doesn't need to meet all the financers and all these opinions. I make a kind of filtering on what goes on to the director and at the same time try to convince the financers with words about the potential of the project.* (Jönsson)

Concerning *the contents of the film*, Lars told me that much of his time goes into working with the *quality of the film*:

> *I want to work as a hands-on producer to a film, near the artistic process. I look at the takes every night during a shooting and spend much time in the editing room, which we have here in the same building in the attic. The editing phase is crucial for the final result.*

> *You commit yourself to that film and don't have time to have too many films going on at the same time. The director has a final cut but I do my job in mutual understanding with her or him. We want to have full control in the company, not make compromises with distributors or cinema owners. It is important that the directors we work with can feel that they have full artistic control, but I trust in my intuition and it is my responsibility to tell if I feel that some actor, for instance, doesn't function well, or if it is not fun when it should be. Because the director has the final cut, I can be quite direct and forthright in my opinions.* (Jönsson)

Lars thoughts about the *team dynamic* was that different kind of films and crews need varying approaches, some need an authoritarian one, others not. As an example, he told me about the filming of *Show me love* (Fucking Åmål, 1998) with Lukas Moodysson as the director:

> *We chose to have a little team with an antiauthoritarian atmosphere. Several of the actors were young girls. The protagonist was only fourteen years old. Then we chose to have several young persons in the crew, too. For instance the make up person and the costumer, just to create a trustful atmosphere. There was much of laugh, play and fun. Lukas spent much time with the actors. For instance, some evening they went to bowling, instead of watching at the takes with me. Things like that. It wouldn't have worked with middle-aged male fellows. The producer must be sensitive to this kind of situations. It is necessary in filmmaking* (Jönsson).

What, then, about *motivation*? We were talking about motivation as a force in one's identity construction. The inspiration for my question comes from Deleuze (Deleuze and Parnet, 1987), who suggest that, rather than being focused on some unachievable "lost " object, desire can be seen as the primary force in life. It requires no focus, but can be channelled. The self is a reflection of desire, and channelling desire actively moulds it. Motivation, then, is about the search for identity, for a positive valuation from the Other (Jackson and Carter, 2000). I wondered how Lars saw the distribution of work between the producer and the director. He told me that he has an education in filmmaking, but continued that when he has an idea for a film he thinks mostly about who could be the most suitable director for the film. Consequently, he decided to work as a producer and let others do the directing:

> *But it is important to work with people who have "that some-*
> *thing," some kind of auteur quality, a will to tell something. Integ-*
> *rity. Playfulness, serious and funny at the same time. Much hu-*
> *mor. It is like love, you can't tell exactly what it is. Every direc-*
> *tor comes with a universe around him or her. There is a great*
> *pleasure to work with people who I like* (Jönsson).

I asked Lars whether he would like to be in the searchlight, like actors
and directors? Lars maintained that he wouldn't like it. He tries to be
anonymous. What he appreciates is the whole filmmaking process with
its different aspects, from starting with the idea, to creating the international contacts, to selling the film abroad. He emphasized that it is motivating to be wellknown in the Swedish film industry, where he can
feel that his job is appreciated.

Obviously, these practices describe a good strategy. There are several Memfis films that have been very successful. The film *Dalecarlians* 2004 (Masjävlar), directed by Maria Blom, her debut feature
film, recieved three Guldbagge Awards and was a box office hit in
Sweden in 2005. The film *Zozo*, directed by Josef Fares and Anna An-
toni as a hands-on-producer (Lars colleague at Memfis film) was
nominated for an Oscar in 2006 in the category for best foreign film.

In a marketing magazine for Swedish film 'Made in Sweden' it is
told that a Swedish business newspaper 'Veckans Affärer' has earlier
the year 2005 characterized the Memfis team as "the Swedish champions at spotting new talent and turning it into a box-office hit". Lars
comment to this was:

> *It may seem hard to believe, but we never really think in such a*
> *calculated way. If you want to make a good film, you just have to*
> *trust your own tastes. And then work really hard and try to be true*
> *to your original vision.* (Jönsson in Andersson, 2005:9, "Made in
> Sweden" magazine for Swedish film)

Film Producer and Aesthetic Entrepreneurship— Concluding Remarks

The production of art and the whole experience economy have attracted a lot of attention in economic policy discussions since the
1990s (AMS rapport 2001:80); in relation to the question of, for instance, how to create growth in regional economies and find solutions
to labor market problems. With film production as my focus I have
wanted to show examples from art and culture production as possible

inspiration for entrepreneurship in different contexts. Film production has a long history of handling questions of relating art to commercial interests (Björkegren, 1992, 1994), which, perhaps, could also lead to proposals for everyday practices in other kinds of artistic/creative enterprising and entrepreneurship. I do not argue that the practices garnered from a specific film production can necessarily be applied to another film project or other kind of business. They could possibly be, however, seen as examples of the variety of human action, and could lead to different, maybe new, ways of organizing in our "world creating," both in the art field, but also, more generally, in enterprising.

In order to give attention to the aesthetic dimension, in both the organizing of a film production and in the final product, I have wanted to show how artistic creation has become in a kind of aesthetic play in relational processes. In that play, passions, pleasure, and adventure are important driving forces. They give the energy to start and run through these entrepreneurial events, not only in the artistic creation in front of the camera, but in everything surrounding it, including the circumstances behind the camera. A film is created in a team where the team dynamics depends on each person who is participating in it. The identity of the producer, and motivation behind it, is created in these "negotiating processes," in these aesthetic plays. They are not always harmonious, but fun and pleasure are also important aspects.

I have not discussed the particular marketing or financial aspects in this text; it could be a topic for some further research. What I have wanted to point out is the importance of the role of the producer in the whole filmmaking process. Although a Swedish film production can't be compared to a huge American production in quantity and variation in the organizational performance, there exist different types of producers in Sweden, too: There are those who concentrate on the economics; There are those who have long experience in the industry and have more or less "slipped" in to the job; and there are those who want to participate in the creative process. A varying degree of cooperation between producer and director exist in different constellations. I argue, however, that the producer is always involved in the artistic process, if we want to see it from a relational entrepreneurial perspective. I have emphasized the relational aspects with regard to the creative process and, consequently, in constructing the producer identity. I argue that these intuitive, relational processes also have influence in financing, although the effect can be difficult to measure in dimensions other than the number of tickets sold. "How to measure the beautiful?" as Eneroth (1984) asks. But why not take inspiration from Lars Jönsson. He tells that he and his team in Memfis film do not try to make calculated film successes, but to be sensitive to what is happening around in the world and, consequently, be true when realizing ones visions.

PART III

THE MEDIATED EXPERIENCE

CHAPTER 3

ESCAPING AND RECREATING EVERYDAY LIFE
THE EMERGENCE OF THE SARAJEVO FILM FESTIVAL[55]

SENADA BAHTO

Introduction

Film festivals are commonly presented and understood according to the model-image provided by big, "mega-festivals" such as those in Berlin, Cannes, or Venice. According to that model, film festivals are "events (usually annual) which invite films into competition and offer prizes." (Blandford, Grant and Hillier, 2002, p. 96, as quoted in Stringer 2003, p. 16) Apart from these two—we can call them basic functions—film festivals also include activities that celebrate films, fa- cilitate deals that lead to the production and distribution of films, and arrange social activities of interest to the international mass media (Stringer, 2003). As an event happening in a certain time period and at a certain place (actual or virtual), the experience of a film festival is by necessity local and temporal, contingent, indivisible from its context and individuals taking part in it (i.e., experiencing it). Expressing or translating those experiences (e.g., "feeling of festivity and potential […], the excitement" or being "exhausted, deluged by more movies more often than I wanted to handle" as Turan [2002, p. 4–5] puts it) into verbal or written communication is yet another complex process through which new means of (re)presentation and understanding occur. This chapter, however, tells about a film festival that might be consid- ered more special and unique than most others. It is the case of the Sa-

---

[55] The author wants to express her gratitude for insightful comments from an anonymous reviewer of an earlier draft and a special thanks to Daniel Hjorth for suggestions and constructive editorial interventions.

rajevo International Film Festival, "Beyond the End of the World" that took place in besieged Sarajevo in October 1993.

The question most commonly raised by the foreign commentators and reporters interviewing the Festival's director during and after the event was "Why a film festival during the war"? (*BH Dani* 05/04/2002) Building on my own experience of the siege and the Festival and using conceptual and analytical tools developed by Mikhail Bakhtin (1965/1984) and Kenneth Burke (1945/1969), I will develop my thoughts and reflections in an attempt to provide answers to this question. The purpose is further to give a contribution to entrepreneurship research by showing how Burke's method for analysis and Bakhtin's concept of carnival admit a disclosure of the societal-creative force of entrepreneurship. The kind of experience hereby focused is accordingly much broader than the consumer-oriented one foregrounded by Pine and Gilmore (1999). The accounts of the Festival at the time by attendees and others justify, legitimize and explain it, and are a solid basis on which to build an understanding of the complexities of "experiencing an event". Accounts of an event are inevitably a key to responding to the *why* question, because they provide more or less coherent testimony to the intentions of organizers and participants. This is in accordance with the credo of the narrative mode of knowing (Bruner 1986) and its characteristic special type of explanation: "Narratives exhibit explanation instead of demonstrating it" (Polkinghorne 1987, p. 21 as quoted in Czarniawska 1997, p. 19). Narrative explanation leaves aside the search for the one-and-only answer to the question of what "caused" and determined the course of events. It does not explain an event in terms of recognizing it as an instance of a general law, or a category. To the contrary, the accounts presented and analyzed provide an explanation by linking the actions to the narratives of the individuals and to the context in which they were happening.

As a point of reference for describing the particularities of the Film Festival, I will rely on Bakhtin's concept of carnival, as opposed to everyday, normal life and official festivity. I will posit a context in which war and siege appear as opposites to normal, everyday life before the war, and where the Film Festival itself appears in opposition to what normal life became in the context of the siege. Another parallel with the carnival is that the Festival was not ordered and arranged by the official authorities, but spontaneously evolved from the passions and commitment of (everyday) people. The dramatist model, as developed by Kenneth Burke (1945/1969), is a helpful tool for possibly explaining the actions and narrated intentions of the actors who made the

Festival happen. Using Burke's model, we can read the making of the 1993 Sarajevo Film Festival as an example of a reversal of the drama of the siege from a tragedy into an epic one, where the victims become heroes. But this, by no means, explains why that reversal happened. Czarniawska's (1997) "control philosophies" need to enter the model in order to provide an explanation of "the determining factor" (ibid.) for the reversal of the drama. The intention is to analyze different accounts on the Film Festival using Burke's model and different control philosophies. Explaining different actions-scene-actors ratios will shed light on the question: "Why a film festival during the war?"

This chapter proceeds in the following way: First, film festivals and film consumption are discussed in the analytical framework of staged experiences, introduced by Pine and Gilmore (1999). In the next section, the concept of carnival is introduced, in order to offer a different and broader perspective on the creation and experience of a film festival (here suggested as a manifestation of the creative-societal force of entrepreneurship). Narrative accounts of the organization and attendance of the 1993 Sarajevo Film Festival are presented in the following section, which are then discussed in terms of Burke's pentad: first using the control philosophy, where the primacy is given to the scene, and then employing, instead the concept of carnival, thus providing for a "dramatist-carnivalesque" analysis. This is linked to the concluding section where creation of the Festival is discussed as an illustration of an entrepreneurial event, as an experience of the possible.

Film Festivals as a Specific Form of Film Consumption

You can see a film in different forms: You can buy or rent a film on videotape or a DVD, and watch it at home; you can watch a film on TV, paying a subscription fee to the operator of the television channel; in the case of a commercial channel, you can pay to see a film with forced exposure to commercial advertisements; you can go to the cinema and see a film there, paying for the experience by purchasing a ticket; and finally, you can attend a film festival and watch a film, or a myriad of them. Every form of access to seeing a film has its particularities, in terms of the nature and characteristics of the viewing experience. Looking at these forms from the perspectives of the experience realms offered by Pine and Gilmore (1999) we become aware of how these four realms for viewing film differ in the experiences they offer.

Pine and Gilmore (1999) argue that in staging an experience the central issue is the level of the customer's engagement with the event experienced. The degree of engagement in experiencing an event (or staged consumption of a product) can be assessed in many different ways, but two of the most important dimensions are the level of participation in the event and the nature of the connection, or environmental relationship, between a customer and the event. The intensity and extent of participation varies and ranges from passive participation (reception) to active involvement as depicted on the horizontal axis of figure one. The vertical axis represents the level of connection with the event, ranging from absorption to immersion.

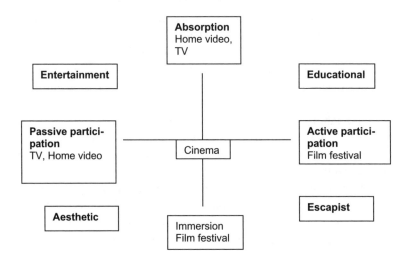

Figure 3.1 Dimensions of Engagement With the Event Experienced. Adapted from Pine and Gilmore (1999) Figure 2.1

Application of this organizational principle to film viewing experiences allows us to note some of the specific aspects of each experience. The level of participation gradually increases with seeing a film on TV as the most passive form in terms of choice of film, as well as timing of the experience. In the case of seeing a film at a cinema, the participation level is increased, because we choose which film to see and when. Attending a film festival is, then, the most active way to experience a film. The selection of films is broadest, both in terms of the number of films and the exclusivity of the occasion to see them. Home video is somewhat problematic to classify because consumers are actively engaged in choosing both what and when they want to see. The location of experience is however limited to the private sphere and most of the aspects of a public event are missing, making it a passive form of participation. From the perspective of the relationship between the viewers and the film, a similar pattern can be noticed. Moving from the TV and home video to cinema and film festivals, the viewing experience qualitatively changes to become more absorbing and immersive culminating in the experience of attending a film festival.

When linked together, the degree of participation and the nature of relationship between a customer and the event define the four "realms" of an experience–entertainment, educational, escapist, and aesthetic (Pine and Gilmore 1999). These four realms, or domains of experience, are complementary and can overlap in every individual instance of experiencing an event. The film viewing experience, in every form, combines all four dimensions/domains. As figure one suggests, however, the intensity and focus of different dimensions differ as we move from one to another form of staging that experience. A film festival, as a specific form of film consumption, combines different means in order to enrich the film viewing experience in all four dimensions. In this way, visiting a film festival becomes more than a way to consume films.

Blurring the boundaries between these four dimensions increases "the realness of the experience" (Pine and Gilmore 1999, p. 38). This brings, from the point of view of a festival goer, the experience of a film festival closer to the ideal of an experience, or, in other words, the Mikhail Bakhtins' image of carnival. Despite more recent criticism and distancing from Bakhtin's understanding of medieval culture and his concept of carnival (Humphrey 2000), it can be argued that it is exactly this ideal (necessarily simplified and romanticized) image of the carnival that we try to enact in contemporary festivals, because carnivals were "the second life of the people, who for a time entered the utopian realm of community, freedom, equality and abundance" (Bakhtin, 1965/1984, p. 9), and they remain so for us today.

Realms of experience	Means by which film festivals enrich a realm	Final result: a quality of experience specific for a (film) festival
Entertainment	selection of films; games for the audience; sightseeing tours; parties.	Building a sense of belonging; sharing common interests;
Education	selection of films; seminars and workshops; interaction among festival goers.	being a part of a community /fellowship.
Aesthetic	selection of films and venues; creation of a memorable atmosphere; glamour.	
Escapist	selection of films; concentration and intensification of experience in time and space.	

Table 3.1 Four Realms of Experiencing a Film Festival

Every film festival strives towards its own continuation and expansion; to grow bigger and better every year. What would a film festival look like beyond the end of the world? Here comes such a story, which announced the Film Festival in Sarajevo in 1993.

Bakhtin, the Carnival and Entrepreneurship

For Bakhtin, carnivals celebrate "the temporary liberation from the prevailing truth and from the established order" (1965/1984, p. 10). It is the time of inside out, of constant shifting from high to low, profanity, crowning and uncrowning, moving from front to rear, and from the sacred to the grotesque. This is the folk humor of the medieval carnival; the source of analysis and discussion in Bakhtin's development of the concept of the carnival(esque). The purpose of the carnival is not negative, rather, it is precisely a way of saying *yes* to the creative forces of life: The multiplying of human creativity, the bubbling and swarming, and the growth-like-fungi of the endless variations of the heterogeneous becomings of life (de Certeau, 1997; Deleuze and Guattari, 1987).

> *The carnival spirit offers the chance to have a new outlook on the world, to realize the relative nature of all that exists, and to enter a complete new order of things.* (Bakhtin, 1965/1984: 34)

The fool and the clown of the carnival bring us laughter, which unites high and low, and in so doing punctuates the lofty auras of the authorities and their ceremonies. Everything is possible as the reigning order of the life outside the carnival is put on hold.

The carnival is also the time of the "material-bodily". We are brought into connection with that which is changing–through eating, dancing, and making love. The structuring forces of society and the official order are shaken by this movement. The carnival time manifests clearly that human freedom is the basic condition upon which power operates in order to achieve control. "In carnival, the body is celebrated for its capacity to express joy and irreverence; it overflows its own limits, refuses confinement and order, and functions as a site of excess and extravagance." (Michelson, 1999: 143) The battle between carnival and lent, which is central to the formation of the European mind (Findlen, 1998), is of course part of this creative tension.

This chapter draws on the Sarajevo Film Festival, draws upon the possibilities for using the concept of carnival to highlight the entrepreneurial element of an event. How can we conceive of this relationship between carnival and the entrepreneurial? I suggest that entrepreneurship, as process of a social creation (Hjorth and Steyaert, 2003), especially in the case of creating a festival which is also a *case* of creating life, can be understood by the use of Bakhtin's carnival. It is this joyous affirmation of the possibilities of life's creative force that breaks through all skeptical questions of sound rationality. Entrepreneurship is always poaching from the official order; making use of the dominant/strategic thinking (de Certeau, 1984; Hjorth, 2005) in order to create space for play/invention in places structured for the purposes of production (as in the company) or by war (such as in Sarajevo in 1993).

Accounts of the 1993 Sarajevo Film Festival

Picture is Awareness of Darkness

> *The film. The twentieth century. The new art form. Sarajevo. The end of the twentieth century. The end of the world? The end of film?*
>
> *For already nineteen months, a city has been under brutal siege. It is no more important that it is a European city, that it is a city where cultures of the East and the West have been crossing each other for centuries; not even that the city has always been open to the new and different, always curious and keen to change itself.*
>
> *It is important that a city is under siege in the time of high technology, enormous human knowledge and experience. In the*

era of speedy transfer of information, and, I used to think, in the era of reason. All the attributes of civilization, which I used to believe were mine too, are being annihilated by the everyday deaths and severe injuries in the streets of Sarajevo; in the apartments, schools, and hospitals of Sarajevo; and in the graveyards of Sarajevo. And all of us in Sarajevo are aware that it is but only a part of the catastrophe that is taking place in Bosnia and Herzegovina, which in other towns of Bosnia and Herzegovina is assuming even more dramatic dimensions.

Not so long ago, the genocide against the Jews devastated the world. Now the genocide against Bosniaks is happening. It is completely irrelevant whether we like the national feeling a person has, or whether he or she has any national feelings at all. What is striking the eyes are the facts. Two, among the many countable, are enough to mention. First, a city has been under siege for more than a year and a half and everyday people are being killed in it. Second, thousands of people are dying everyday only because of their names and family names. Sarajevo is the city in which the world of the twentieth century, the world to which we were born and brought up, has died. In other places the dying is taking place. Here, we live beyond the end of the world. In spite of the horror, a new spirituality is being created in Sarajevo; a state of things not evidenced yet. The character of that spirituality is unspeakable. Everything is now other.

When addressed by the curious journalists from other world cities with the question "Why a film festival in Sarajevo?" most often I used to answer with another question "And why are they killing us?" Almost always there was a smile of embarrassment; an unspoken excuse for neglecting the most fundamental questions. Never had a Sarajevan asked me "Why a film festival?" Most of the film artists from all over the world did not ask why. First to answer was Wim Wenders saying, "Of course, I'm sending you the films you're asking for!" Then Lina Wertmiller said, "I support you!" Then Dana Rothberg appeared in Sarajevo on a private visit. She said "We will make an excellent film festival!" Then Vanessa Redgrave came for another art project. We told her about the Festival. She did not say anything. She left, but on the basis of what she already had done for the Sarajevo Film Festival, it seems as if all this time there is nothing else for her but Sarajevo and the Festival.

Why do Sarajevans and film artists from all over the world understand this need for film maybe better then the others? Simply because we feel that the art is a fundamental human need. The same as food, sex, and sleep. Because being constantly close to death means desiring love in the strongest way. Because being unfree means to understand the greatness of freedom.

Here, of course, I talk about the film as art, not of the film as media, which can be so terribly misused. I am talking about film pictures, that make understanding possible, not the ones that destroy it.

The picture is not important. The reality behind the picture is [important]. A brighter picture does not mean a clearer insight into the reality behind the picture. Because of that, I do not worry that the screenings via electronic machines are going to be somewhat blurry, colors shineless, or that the edges of the pictures will be somewhat sloped. The sound is not important. The silences between the sounds are important. I am not worried that the quality of sound is going to be below the general standards. The silence is always the same.

We are inconsolable. It is terribly sad beyond the end of the world. (My translation)

This is how its director, Haris Pašović, introduced the Sarajevo Film Festival in October 1993, in a letter printed in the Festival's program in the form of a special appendix to a Sarajevo daily *Oslobodjenje* on Friday, October 22, 1993. I was living in that Sarajevo "beyond the end of the world". At that time I was not reading newspapers, watching television or listening to the radio. I hardly had access to any media at that time. I did not have access to most of things that formed my everyday life before April 1992.

Just to give you an idea of what it (my everyday life before April 1992) was like, I will present myself briefly. In April 1992, I was 23 years old. I had just graduated from the university with a major in marketing, learning it from books written by American gurus like Philip Kotler. I had done my bachelor thesis work in a Volkswagen joint venture company that was producing spare parts and assembling Volkswagen cars. There I was supposed to start working for real (any day). I lived with my parents and siblings in a family house on the periphery of Sarajevo. I had several so called spare-time interests including: reading, music, theater and film. Sarajevo offered a rather diversified range of opportunities to satisfy them. I was born in Sarajevo and during those 23 years I collected a considerable number of friends with common interests, and we use to spend a lot of time together. Back in 1992, I would not consider myself a film freak; however, films were available anytime and watching them, preferably in the cinema, was an activity that constituted an important part of my everyday life.

What was it that made me not wonder "Why the film festival?" in October 1993 and, not ponder the pros and cons of attending it? What was the driving force for a 24 year old person to expose her life to more then unavoidable risks, in exchange for experiencing a film festival? To see some films?

The Dramatist Analysis

It is possible to understand the driving force or motive for someone's actions by applying the approach of Kenneth Burke (1945/1969) in *A grammar of motives*. This approach is known as Burke's pentad and is often used in the social sciences when interpreting human conduct (e.g. Czarniawska, 1997; O'Connor, 1995; Johannisson, 2005; Kostera, 2005). Burke suggests that every human action/human conduct can be formulated and analyzed in terms of five elements: scene, act, agent, agency and purpose:

1. Scene relates to the settings of the conduct, answering the question "where is it happening?"
2. Act identifies the action, answering the question of "what is happening?"
3. Agent is the actor, person or actant (i.e., the one who acts).
4. Agency refers to the means the actors use in accomplishing the purpose, answering the how question.
5. Purpose answers the why question of the actor's conduct.

Element	Description	Answers the question
Scene	Context in which action takes place.	Where?
Act	Identifies the action	What?
Agent	Actor or actant.	Who?
Agency	Means the agent uses to accomplish the purpose.	How?
Purpose	The aim of the action.	Why?

Table 3.2 Model of Dramatist Analysis. Based on Burke (1945/1969)

Burke called the application of these five elements to the formulation, explanation, and understanding of human conduct *dramatism*. The dynamic dimension of the approach is secured by analyzing the mutual relations among these five elements: what Burke calls *ratios,* where the most important, according to him, are the *scene-act ratio* and the *agent-act ratio*. His assumption is that the principles of drama are valid not only for the theater but for everyday human conduct as well, where those principles call for balance among the five elements of the pentad. The explanatory potential of the model is, however, not absolutely generalizable, valid for every time and space. The model needs to be contextualized into cultural tradition and social history where the principles of drama are defined. Additionally, as Czarniawska (1997) points out: in order to explain the effects of applying different ratios, or the assumed priority of one or another element of the pentad, control philosophies need to be added to the model. "Control philosophies differ in their underlying belief about what is the determining factor" (Czarniawska 1997, p. 39).

Dramatist Analysis of Accounts of the 1993 Sarajevo Film Festival – Number One

How could a model of dramatist analysis help to answer the question of, "Why a film festival in Sarajevo, a city that has been besieged for 19 months?" In order to be able to apply this analysis to this question, it needs to be reformulated and new additional questions should be asked, so as to be able to identify all five elements of the pentad and establish the relationships among them. Some additional clues from the Festival director's letter are also of help, such as:

- The question was posed to the director of the Film Festival.
- Foreign journalists were asking the questions.
- The inhabitants of Sarajevo (i.e., potential, and prospective festival goers) did not wonder.
- The [film] artists (even if coming from different parts of the world) did not ask why. They engaged and made the festival happen.

Scene:	Sarajevo, October 1993; a city under siege.	October 1993, in the city where I was born and have seen many films.
Act:	Organizing a film festival.	Attending a film festival.
Agent:	Festival director, volunteers, friends of the festival, and film artists.	A Sarajevan; a 24 year old woman.
Agency:	Multiple activities and means: Improvisation and commitment are the most important.	Overcoming the fear of going out and then walking, running, queuing, waiting, sitting, watching....
Purpose:	To satisfy the need for film.	To satisfy the need for film.

Table 3.3 Dramatist Analyses of the Festival Director's and My Account of the Festival.

If we employ the control philosophy where primacy is given to the scene, the scene will determine the actions, the agents, the agency, and consequently the purpose. This is the control philosophy of the modern project (Czarniawska, 1997) of a rational human being. When war is going on, and a city is under siege, its inhabitants are given the option/role of being the besieged: Their purpose is then to survive. The agency could be: to stop the siege by fighting; to escape the siege, or to endure by minimizing exposure to the risks related to the siege. I did not mention surrender, as an option it simply did not exist. An individual in Sarajevo did not have anyone she could submit a statement of surrender to. Suicide might have been a way to make a similar announcement, but who knows why, or for what strange reason—no matter how absurd it seems to be—I had respect for my life, in spite of being aware that at any second I could die. But I can put this in another way, too. Surrender was not an option available as one could not position actively against it. Being killed or dying of starvation, for example, were the only probable outcomes, no matter what you chose to do, or even if you chose not to do anything. The awareness of death is, of course, part of the human condition, but "Since the discovery of death ...[h]uman societies have kept designing elaborate subterfuges, hoping that they would allow them to forget about the scandal [death is the scandal of reason]" (Bauman 1992, p. 1). This "elaborate effort of society" (ibid, p. 2) is usually successful because "in normal times we move actually without ever believing in our own death, as if we fully believed in our own corporeal immortality" (Zilboorg, 1970, in Bauman 1992, p. 2). Sarajevo under siege was not a normal time; it is an example of the failure of (ordered, official) society. It was the end of the world. Although some of our policies of survival that Bauman discusses—God, common cause, love and self-care—probably had been helpful in channelling the horror of death, none of them was able to make us forget it, or to legitimize and justify the way and the context in which we were to die.

How, then, does the organization of a film festival fit into a story of war, siege, and survival? For a modern, rational human being—let's say a foreign journalist—it does not, and this necessitates resorting to Burke's method of analysis. In a city where the conditions for life barely exist, organizing a film festival is both impossible and absurd. Who would put her life on risk in exchange for seeing a film? For an insider, however, the control philosophy, the drama, and its principle changes. Life beyond the end of the world is not the same kind of drama as life before. Pašović wrote:

Why do Sarajevans and film artists from all over the world understand this need for film maybe better then the others? Simply because we feel that the art is a fundamental human need. The same as food, sex, and sleep. Because being constantly close to death means desiring love in the strongest way. Because being unfree means to understand the greatness of freedom. (Oslobodjenje, October 22, 1993)

What other control philosophy (apart from that which gives priority to the scene) could then work from the perspective of an insider?

I don't really remember how I came to know about the Festival. Anyway I had no excuse to miss it. For a week or so, each day in two locations, which were once cinemas, a film or two were supposed to be shown. Each film takes 90 minutes at least, multiplied by 20 (in appr. ten festival days) makes 1800 minutes of escape, of forgetting who and where I am, of what is going on outside in the reality—"Behind the End of the World", as the festival was named along one of the Wim Wender's new movies shown during the Festival. (Bahto 2002)

This excerpt from my retrospective account establishes a somewhat different purpose for my attending the Sarajevo film festival in 1993: "…1800 minutes of escape, of forgetting of who and where I am, of what is going on outside in reality…" A year ago, when I asked my brother why he was attending the Festival back in 1993, when he was a 14-year-old boy, he had a hard time putting this into words. He kept repeating, "it was important", providing no explanation. Going to the festival was the aim in and of itself. Seeing the movies was maybe only the means. What might be so special about a festival that it can be an end in itself?

Dramatist Analysis of my Festival Account – Number Two

Scene: the carnival.
Act: living according to the principles of play.
Agency: attending a film festival.
Actor: a human being.
Purpose: to feel alive.

In his recent work, long-term student of entrepreneurship Bengt Johannisson (2005) sets out to describe, perform, and write about the essence of entrepreneurship. After a summary of his enormous, rich knowledge and experience in entrepreneurship Johannisson gives an account of an event he initiated: bringing together participants from the world of art and science with the aim to renew the life of a region/community. The insights he gained from this event demonstrate that entrepreneurship is far more than an expression of rational human nature, of *homo oeconomicus,* where one seeks and seizes market opportunities as they strive after economic and material gain. Entrepreneurship is neither a pure expression of extraordinary (superhuman) personal traits, nor restricted to bringing to the market innovative products, services, or modes of organizing. Entrepreneurship is more of an existential drive through which individuals express different potentialities inherent in being human. Through entrepreneurship, people are seeking to express the complexity of their identities, to explore and confirm their potentials. Entrepreneurship expresses human playfulness as well (Hjorth, 2001). Whole new worlds and new ways of living are created (Spinosa et al 1997). The perspective of an entrepreneur, argues Johannisson (2005), is to perceive every action and every coincidence as the "eventness" of an opportunity. Time and Being are not closed and finally defined. The ontological perspective is one of becoming. Whether personal character, or identity of the actor, nature of the scene, or means available. The purpose is recognizing and acting upon the possible becoming(s). Here I use Burke's dramatist analysis of an entrepreneurial event, which stresses the event as a specific form of organizing: in-between a project typical for formal organizations and a fellowship "Gemeischaft."

	Project	Event	Fellowship
Activity	Reducing uncertainty and ambiguity	Acknowledging and exploiting uncertainty and ambiguity	Creating sustainability via bottom up and indigenous forces
Actors	Individuals playing appropriate roles	Individuals as carriers of different resources and relations	Equal but different individuals
Purpose	To balance goals and resources	To enact together, to co-construct reality and self	To be together
Scene	Functional/physical space	Space to be made sense of	Social space
Agency	Hierarchy	Heterarchy	Network

Table 3.4 Entrepreneurial Event Compared to Other Forms of Organising. Based on Johannisson (2005) Table 5.1. and Kostera (2005) Table 2.

Applying the suggested frame as the control philosophy to the director's account of the 1993 Sarajevo Film Festival makes another pentad possible. Let us now turn to this.

Dramatist Analysis of the Festival Director's Account – Number Three

Purpose: To express/make manifest; perform the new spirituality.
Act: Enacting a film festival.
Agency: Inspiring, acting unprofessionally, commitment, and passion.
Scene: A city beyond the end of the world, where all and nothing is possible, a space to be made sense of/a space to be filled with sense.
Agents: Committed individuals contributing the best they can to the event's enactment.

People in Sarajevo could not watch films because the cinemas were closed, most of them devastated and destroyed. There was no electricity to run them. Houses and apartments were without electricity so no films could be seen on television either. People could not meet because going out on the streets was dangerous. Those few cafes and restaurants still operating had no money. Traditional spaces for concerts, theaters, and art exhibitions were impossible to use. There were no opportunities to live a normal, organized cultural life. The impossibility to do normal things opened a way for doing something else, for *creating* another normality. Bringing the electricity that the city needed in order to run the existing cinemas regularly was impossible. The idea came to make a film festival; to concentrate the film watching experience in ten days as a way to make up for the lost months, but also to make up for much more than film viewing.

This festival would not be possible to make without support and extraordinary engagement of large number of people and institutions in Sarajevo as well as all over the world. (Text from the Festival's program)

The list of organizations and individuals that supported the Festival is long. In 1993 the city of Sarajevo and its film festival had many friends. Without their energy, passion, commitment, and endurance it would not have been possible to make the Festival happen. For them, setting it up was not a job; it was not mere entertainment for its guests. On the last page of the Festival's program, where an orderly schedule was presented, the Festival's organizers "proudly announced" that they, honestly speaking, could not and did not promise anything. The only promise they made was to do their best to make it happen. They believed and they hoped.

The Festival did not follow the schedule. Many of the films and guests announced never appeared. So like any "real film festival" it had its share of scandals, as Pašović (ironically) commented in a more recent interview (Turan, 2003). There were no seminars, no workshops, no parties, no red carpet, and no glamor. The foreign reporters, though, were there. After all, a story of a film festival in a besieged city "sells" well, because it is demand. Given the inconsistency of the "ratios" from an outsider's point of view the story needs to be told in order to make a sense of such a festival. "The function of the story is to find an intentional state that mitigates or at least makes comprehensible a deviation from a canonical cultural pattern." (Bruner 1990, p. 49–50, quoted from Czarniawska 1997, p. 20) Those who lived the festival did not read the stories written about it. For them the festival made sense from the very beginning. No story needed.

Festivals between a Managed Project and an Entrepreneurial Event

The Film Festival in Sarajevo in 1993 was a unique event and, hopefully, such an event will never need to be reenacted. A dilemma is, however, posed to the organizers of today's film festivals in Sarajevo, as well as anywhere else. As indicated at the beginning of this paper, there seems to be a tendency of institutionalization and commodification of film festivals as a specific, but not less competitive, form of film consumption. Managerial discourse with phrases such as, need for differentiation, targeting, competitive edge, and so on produces, although in perhaps a more sophisticated dialect, the vocabulary of the experience economy. Festivals are seemingly competing for money, attention, films, stars, and audiences, as they expand and strive to get bigger and better. Film festival organizers appear to be a new type of professional/manager (Stringer, 2003), whose role is to balance goals and resources by working against uncertainty and ambiguity, which inevitably follows any type of event (Eldridge and Voss, 2001). On the other hand, the (romantic) ideal of a festival, which should be "the second life of the people, who for a time entered the utopian realm of community, freedom, equality and abundance, (Bakhtin, 1965/1984, p. 9) is a dear image for most of festival goers who either gave up, or never believed in the possibility of feeling fellowship and a sense of community in ordinary life. Using Bakhtin's concept of carnival, we can describe entrepreneurship in the case of creating the Festival, creating space for living, creating experiences of the possible–actualized within the realm of the impossible/war–which contest the dominant normality (the usually not normal) of a besieged city. Entrepreneurship, well illustrated by this case, belongs primarily to life and is a process of creating sociality, and societies (Steyaert and Hjorth, 2006). The experience of a festival, as of a carnival, and perhaps also of entrepreneurship, is the experience of a possible life–a life to come, hitherto missing.

The hope we have is that there will be a festival once a year where we will be able to escape and feel alive for a while. It is up to the festival's organizers (entrepreneurs) to make those moments—when the lights turn off and we enter the world of moving images—last a bit longer than an average screening. Otherwise, we need no film festivals but yet another Disney-, Lego-, Nike- or xyz-land with a mass-customized, but guaranteed high quality "experience". I hope I have indicated that this, however, would indeed be a very different kind of experience.

CHAPTER 4

OF ANGELS, DEMONS, AND MAGIC ITEMS
THE EXPERIENCE ECONOMY OF EVERYDAY PROJECTS

JERZY KOCIATKIEWICZ

The Experience Economy

The phrase "the experience economy," as presented by Pine and Gilmore (1999), has been used to describe the economy based on peddling experiences. In this chapter I would like to propose—without abandoning the label— a slightly different reading: The experience of an economy, or rather, the experience of the work environment. The reversal is not just a flippant gesture; it underscores the issues of human experience involved in the production processes of the experience economy and, ultimately, the entrepreneurial aspects of the construction of everyday experiences.

The overarching theme of this book is the development and opening up of the idea of the experience economy, and in that spirit I would like to look at the workplace construction of reality as precisely the experience of economy at its most basic level. I endeavor to see the social situations examined here not as subject to some overarching laws of economics, or within any framework grounded in economics, but rather through the perspective of organizational (working) life as the foundation for the set social relations usually subsumed under the name of an economy. More specifically, I look at the issue of how a relative newcomer to the social scene of the workplace is mediated and integrated into the experiences of more established social actors. Through such inquiry, I hope to shed some light upon the translation processes central to the most local levels of operation of the experience economy.

The newcomer in question is the personal computer, an actor whose role I studied in the late 1990s in Poland. While somewhat similar inquiries have been conducted many times since at least the early 1980s—most famously by J. David Bolter (1984), Sherry Turkle (1984) and Gary Downey (1998)—I believe my own research presents a particularly interesting insight into the issue of the active experience of the technologized workplace environment, and not just the construction of technological agency.

Because my study was conducted in the late 1990s and focused on personal computers, the examined technology was perceived more as a part of everyday life and less as a novelty (unlike in most of the earlier studies); this in turn helped me research the experience of an established institution, and particularly one important to working life. At the same time, through presenting the construction of the computer's role as an entrepreneurial act involving active participation of all the social actors involved, I would like to pinpoint such acts as they occur in everyday, habitual situations.

Myth

In this chapter, I turn towards myths to provide a scheme for analyzing the workday experience of interacting with computers. I looked for myths and archetypes that represented the experiences of computers described by my interviewees. This approach allowed me to anchor my analysis in the symbolic realm, and thus, hopefully, to reach beyond a purely functional interpretation of their expressed behavior and opinions. I hope also to point to both the ritualistic and spiritual aspects of social experience (Sievers, 1994), and to the social construction (or perhaps creation) of meaning inherent in the process of making sense of computers (Weick, 1995). Also, as mythology comprises the narrative element of religion (Margul, 1989), it is ideally suited as a metaphor for analyzing stories, which collectively build an image of the protagonist—in this case the experience of the computer's social role.

The Computer

Information technology, and its foremost symbol, the computer, continue to involve ever new spheres of human activity. Life in the Western world is becoming increasingly synonymous with computers. This sentence would form a powerful argument in Poland, where the drive towards the West, which officially started with the fall of communism in 1989, remains a strong political and social force, of which joining the European Union is but a single stage. Computer literacy, especially in the bigger cities, is high, and available personal computer technology is on par with that in western European countries. Poland's transition into the computer era has been, perhaps, more abrupt than in the West. It was only after 1989 that new technologies became widely available, although a considerable home computer market existed before that time. At this point, I do not have access to any data comparing the level of Internet utilization in Poland and in other countries, though I suspect that Internet access is somewhat less widespread than in western Europe, mostly due, perhaps, to the obsolete Polish phone network. Other means of connecting to the Internet were not popular in 1998, when I conducted my research.

Against this background, I have attempted to examine how computers are experienced in workplace conditions in the Polish context. This study shares some similarities with previous studies examining the social roles of computers, but there are a few differences as well—not only the background of rapid changes (both technological and social) taking place in central and eastern Europe, but also my emphasis on both casual and enthusiastic users. The latter point serves additionally to assuage Macgregor Wise's (1994) criticism that constructivist studies of technology concentrate on the already empowered system builders. At the same time, I treat the users as taking active part in constructing their workplace experience, and in particular, their experience of computers as social actors. I can, thus, focus on the nuanced and creative interplay between technology, organizing, and the processes of sensemaking.

The Study

My research took the form of 13 unstructured, anthropological interviews with professionals who, as social actors, were in positions allowing for extensive contact with computers in their workplace. Twelve of the interlocutors actively used computers in their work, and one was chosen because of her refusal to use computers. The interviewees ranged in age from 23 to 59; five of them were female. Their professional backgrounds included six civil engineers, four computer scientists, a photographer, a translator, and a teacher. Becasue my basic agenda was to "follow the actor," (Latour, 1987)—in my case, the computer—I was trying to talk to people who, I believed, could provide me with interesting insights into the roles played by the computer. This focus was further enhanced by concentrating solely on how the computer figured in the working environment. I did not seek out people using computers (purely) for entertainment. I did not attempt to form a comprehensive picture, and my interviewees are not by, any means, representative of anything. They are the people I believed had interesting insights into the social roles played by computers, and I trust that my findings justify this belief. Throughout the research, I have treated the computer as a "black box" (Latour, 1987)—an undisputed social fact or institution. I have thus not tried to gain an understanding of what a computer is, and what it is not; where the computer's boundaries are, or how it came to occupy the present position. I tried only to concentrate on discovering the bundle of roles it played in Poland, in 1998, in working life. This does not mean that I attempted to describe the *state of affairs*. Like Barbara Czarniawska (1992), I prefer to look at processes rather than structures, because the process of constructing reality is much more interesting than the resulting construction. The current role played by computers still remains an act, or a process, and the study need not be historical in order to examine this role dynamically. This makes my approach close to a "window study" (ibid.), except that in the center of my research stands an actor rather than an organization.

I would like to explain my use of the term *social actor* to conceptualize the role of the computer. After Michel Callon (1991: 140), I take the actor to be "any entity able to associate texts, humans, non-humans, and money." This definition does away with the traditional division between active humans and passive objects, concentrating instead on positioning all participants in an action (i.e., the actors) according to their involvement in the events. Such an actor obviously does not have to be human, and indeed, the most important actor in this story is the computer. This decision to speak about the computer as an actor creates a problem: Are all computers to be treated as one actor, or should each computer be treated as a separate actor? Obviously, both decisions are possible, since a group of humans and non-humans can also constitute an "entity," according to Michel Callon's definition. I wanted to look synthetically at the social role of computers, and thus felt it useful to group them together, although with the full understanding that this should not lead to formulating any *laws* pertaining to *all* computers. At best, I could hope to find some tendencies for computers to be cast in particular kinds of roles.

In the actual retelling of the tales, I have attempted not to silence the interlocutors, striving instead to leave as much of their voice as possible in the stories they have told me during the interviews. I tried to include lengthy quotes illustrating my points, thus giving the readers at least some possibility of judging the validity of my inferences for themselves. For the same reason, I have attempted to keep the language editing in these quotes to a minimum. Although the need to translate the interviews into English required some drastic interference on my part, I have tried to preserve the spirit of their original form, including nonstandard grammar and wording. Having said this, I also understand that even choosing and grouping quotes equals mutilation of the original utterances, and that in this text, I can speak only at the price of silencing others (Behar, 1993). The myths presented here are, all things considered, my retellings of the stories I have heard. But then, retelling lies at the heart of mythology, and the role of a storyteller is by no means a shameful one.

The Demon

One frequently encountered myth I would like to touch upon portrays computers in fairly extreme roles, perceiving them as either demons personifying the ills of the modern society, or as angels offering transcendence on earth. This myth illustrates Barbara Czarniawska's (1993) observation that people tend to either romanticize or demonize modern technology. While my interviewees evidenced the existence of two totally opposed views towards computers, they tended to do so in a somewhat different light than might be expected– not as their approach, but observed often in others. This is similar to the role of the opponent to change, as described by Kristina Genell (1997). The label of opponent to change was given by her interlocutors to others, never to themselves. My interviewees, however, used two labels to describe this dichotomized view of technology—that of the technophobe and the technophile. Let us first look at the role played by the computer in its demonic incarnation.

This point of view is nothing new, and neither is the practice of ascribing it to others also is not. Bernward Joerges (1994) describes the example of a possibly apocryphal expert opinion detailing numerous dangers of building new railway lines, often cited by proponents of technological progress. Pushkala Prasad (1995), while writing about anthropomorphization as a tool usually used to ease the acceptance of computers, notes that the depiction of computers as highly intelligent, and sometimes even as higher lifeforms can lead to human users feeling shy and needing to keep their distance. Let us also remember that the story of the computer as demon is a depiction of the point of view of another by someone who may describe their own experiences, behavior and motivations in a quite different way. My interviewee, who claimed to have almost no contact with computers whatsoever, stressed that:

[11] It seemed to me, that they [computers] somehow "machinize" our lives and dehumanize it lightly, and partly the computer starts to replace humans. Contact with computers becomes for some people more important than contact with other people.

She pointed mostly to the negative social influence of the role computers play by rather than to their uselessness or the difficulty of using them. Thus she did, as might have been expected, join the group of people who criticized the fanatics of computerization, but she did not exhibit the characteristics ascribed by my other interviewees to the technophobes:

[1]: And I never had an opinion, that it [computerization] should be discarded, that it is some kind of a devil. I remember a big meeting some ten or fifteen years ago, when there was a discussion whether to buy computers. There were some design engineers, whom to this day I respect, because they have great knowledge, but they thought that it is throwing money away—a person is a person, a machine is a machine, and a machine will never do right everything that needs to be done.

[2]: Even today there probably are some people who do not want to touch this junk at all, because they never got to know it before—and now it seems it is too late for novelties.

[6]: There are some people here, who... I have a friend here, who has a computer at home. His son uses it there, but he, well...he doesn't even try pressing the keys. And he is probably not going to change. He is around fifty now. So, a person who doesn't know it is somewhat afraid: doesn't know how to use it, doesn't know its capabilities.

[3]: If there are no computers somewhere—computers only start to enter—then people usually are greatly afraid; there is such danger even among the young people. But those who did not have anything to do with computers before, [that] they are simply afraid that suddenly somebody, somebody younger and inexperienced, knows much more about it than they do. And they often do

not know the simplest things. Sometimes there are situations such that there is a computer and somebody needs to send a fax, then the secretary does not type it on the computer, but writes it by hand, or has a hidden typewriter which she uses for documents. She is afraid. She doesn't know how.

The computer here is shown as a demon, the personification [sic!] of the fear of the unknown, or as a danger to one's position or one's power. It is also worth to noting how speaker number one stresses knowledge of the opponents to computerization, which leads us to think that the decision of whether or not to buy computers was not so obvious at the time, and that one's commitment to computers back in those days was an act of courage to be proud of.

It is also interesting to note, in light of the discussion of the difficulty of describing the social actor's boundaries, that the technophobes were supposed to be certain of the clear line dividing humans and computers. This may be taken to mean that now one can see this division as much more problematic, or at least that in this organization the dividing line lies in a quite different place than it did fifteen years ago.

Age was often cited as the major criterion for dividing technophobes and technophiles. Older people were supposed to be the former:

[7]: There are people who cannot get accustomed to it. Especially people who encountered computers for the first time—were mobilized to work with computers at the age of around 50 and the younger—to like computers and to want to work with them.

[1]: And the young people, yes, they probably drink it with their mother's milk and are taught at school. In high schools there are computers. At the universities there are computers, and these people want to learn.

This division is also mentioned even by those who did not agree with it. Speaker number three, in an excerpt quoted above, points out that there are technophobes "even among the young people," and that there are older people who like computerization:

[5]: ...at some point I worked almost at the same time with a quite young enthusiast, an atmosphere ecology specialist, and with a person who was past retirement age, who all the time pushed me to expand the program for lighting design.

Both speaker number three and five are computer scientists experienced in introducing computers to companies, which does not by any account mean that the correlation between age and affection towards computers does not exist. Having encountered other similar situations they can more easily quote examples that go against the general trend, which does not necessarily mean that there is no such trend. Of course, the argument can go the other way as well: Having more experience, these people can more easily spot the appearance or lack of any trends. Even though it is impossible to prove or disprove this idea based on the analyzed data, it is clearly manifest among computer users (in Poland, in 1998), as opposed to, for example, the idea of a correlation between feelings towards computers and gender.

The Angel

On the opposite side of the spectrum to technophobes there is, according to my interviewees, a group of computerization fanatics, who can only see its plus side and who perceive computers as the solution to all the world's problems. This group is necessary for championing any kind of change. Bruno Latour (1993/1996) describes the fate of Aramis, an automated underground transport system that was supposed to be built in Paris, and which failed because of a lack of enthusiasts ensorcelled by the project (or the design process and the emergent research possibilities). For my interviewees, however, it was important to keep a certain distance from new technology; superfluous enthusiasm was not gazed upon favorably:

[1]: And also, I do not identify with computers in any way, nor am I a fanatic like they show in the movies, that I would get inside the computer and start to work in it. No, nothing of the kind.

[2]: For me, [the computer] is also [helpful]. It helps me so as to save quite a lot of time with such tasks as spreadsheets, but I am not blinded by their abilities. I don't think they will do everything for us, because they won't. They will do only what we tell them to do. That's how it works. My contact with computers is, let's say, superficial.

[3]: There is also the other group of people, who are perhaps somewhat too much fascinated by it, and who perhaps overdo it the other way. They try to do everything on computer; to store

everything in it, which can end in different ways, because its such a blind faith in computer; that it can do everything well.

Apart from keeping a distance from the technophilic attitude, my interviewees presented themselves as positively disposed towards computers:

[1]: Anyway, I say, I was always a computer enthusiast.

The characteristics of technophiles were used mainly to show the rationality of one's own standpoint, safely located in the "golden middle," and thus impervious to any accusations of radicalism. Only one of my interlocutors valued the technophilic with enthusiasm, and who saw himself strongly among the champions of computerization:

JK: Were you enthusiastic about the idea [of computerization] right from the beginning.

[5]: Because of my being lazy, yes. It appealed to me a lot that a computer can accomplish a task impossible for an engineer because of its labor intensity, or that it can do such a task in an unbelievably short time.

Most of my interlocutors, however, although subscribing to an idea similar to that of Bernward Joerges (1990)—people tend to see computers either as "bats," that is, the epitome of evil, or as "butterflies," that is, beauty, progress, and the hope for the better future—placed themselves somewhere between these two extremes, in a place where, according to the logic of dichotomization, there should be only a few people. Perhaps more accurate theses would include Pushkala Prasad's claim that people seldom have clear and unambiguous relations with computers. They do not either love them or hate them. Quite often, people can, at the same time, abhor technology and long for more of it.

The Trickster

The trickster (Kempinski, 1993) is a mythical figure common to many Indo-European mythologies as an opponent or as a sidekick to the main hero, who exhibits a set of conflicting characteristics, both positive and negative. His merits usually include knowledge, intelligence, and oratorical skill, while his flaws include mischievousness, unreliability and, the inclination towards lying. As I introduce an analogy between the trickster and the ambiguously judged computer, I would mention the following as corresponding to the trickster's positive qualities. Computers provide easier access to data:

[10]: What else [does the computer allow me to do]? The access to a whole lot of data—dictionaries and encyclopedias—[is] very handy.

The offer a wonderful capability for data processing:

[1]: I was a design engineer and the computers were also helpful for me. One could do so much more. One could calculate the exchangers where it was so easy to make mistakes, for which SPEC [the water authority] would get angry with us; that something was wrong. And if there was a computer program, accepted by SPEC, it was just plain easy.

Finally, there are the graphics and multimedia functions:

[8]: And one could paint with this program. But there is another program, which is much more interesting for painting—Painter 5.0, the main function of which is painting. One can change brushes there; build one's own paint structure...one can do lots of things; paint with metal—quite an interesting program.

And as far as the equivalent flaws go, I would (or rather my interviewees did) list the difficulty of usage:

[6]: They gave me a very difficult computer program—horrible, which nobody in the company could use. The person who did was fired and I got two months to get to know the program.

They also mention the errors and unreliability of software:

[5]: Software is an unreliable factor. It works not according to the manual, not according to one's intuitive expectation, not according to, or let's say, not compatibly with the previous version. It does not work like we expect it to. Sometimes it contains obvious errors.

The mythological trickster, such as Loki in the Nordic mythology, is at the same time a benefactor—he invents the fishing net; helps Thor reclaim Mjöllnir, his magical hammer; and participates in the creation of the first humans—and the spirit of evil. He steals golden apples from the goddess Idunn, causes the death of the good god Baldr, and then prevents his resurrection:

His merits long balance out his flaws ..., and even make him indispensable for the functioning of the community ..., in the end, though, they do not save him from the deserved punishment (Kempinski, 1993: 422).

Although the history of computerization, so far, seems to refute this pessimistic diagnosis, it does not mean that we have to abandon the whole metaphor; not only because all social institutions, including technology, are reversible—even though at a particular moment they may seem untouchable (Latour, 1987)—but also because we do not have to look at the metaphor prospectively. We are, after all, talking about the role the computers play today, and in the tales I have collected the computer acts according to the archetype of the trickster.

My interpretation of the myth of the computer as trickster does not speak to an approaching punishment for all of its shortcomings, but to the ambiguity of its today role as the source of both substantial help:

[2]: I have used and I use computers as a typewriter and as an archive; as something that has helped me to clean out the file cabinets and to throw away all those dusty files where the cockroaches roamed, because now I have my whole archive in the computer and it is very positive.

as well as considerable woe:

[2]: When somebody's disk gets wiped by mistake, that person is in deep shit, and this has happened twice in this room. Then it all really vanishes if there are no printed archives, and if the computer breaks down, then there is a problem, because some work, some achievement, goes to waste.

The current trend seems to point toward further and ever more dynamic development of computerization, but this is not the subject of this particular myth. Donald McCloskey's (1986) point that economies is a historic science and not only cannot, but also need not predict the future, pertains to other social sciences (which certainly includes economies as presented by McCloskey) as well, including management and organization studies.

There is one other aspect of the trickster archetype that makes it an interesting analogy for the computer. Sometimes, in different retellings of the myth, the trickster character vanishes from the protagonist's entourage, and then the hero often starts to exhibit the trickster's qualities (Kempinski, 1993). This correlates nicely to Latour's (1993) point, that in the case of a human being using objects, we deal with the emergence of new aims, different from the original aims of either the human or the object.

If we stop looking at the computer as a separate actor from its user, either treating it as a tool of the latter, which I will deal with in a moment, or assuming that together they form a more complex organizational actor, we do not have to deem the computer's social influence as negligible or unimportant in comparison to that of its user. This influence will manifest itself either in the actions of the newly established actor, or in the changes in the behavior of the user (if we believe that it is still the same actor after the appearance of the computer).

Furthermore, the end of a trickster story is never unambiguous or ultimate. Loki gets captured and imprisoned, but sets himself free before Ragnarök, the battle at the end of time. But while he is supposed to die, this part of the myth deals with the far future and, as I just argued, determinism (particularly in the social sciences which, is where, I guess, we should classify mythical cosmologies) is not very much in favor nowadays (Joerges, 1994). I will, thus, propose another story as an illustration. It is a story by Philip K. Dick called "The Great C," about a powerful computer that endured the third world war. Because of damage to its original power source, it gains the energy to function by eating travellers who are unable to ask it a question for which it does not know the answer. In the first version of the story (Dick, 1953/1995), the main protagonist cannot ask such a question and so has to die. When over twenty years later Philip K. Dick used the same motif in a novel cowritten with Roger Zelazny (Dick and Zelazny, 1976/96), the same answer to the same question ("How did the world come to be?" and the reply, "There are a few theories…") no longer suffices to satisfy the questioning protagonist who thus manages to get through unscathed.

The Frankenstein Monster

The computer in "The Great C" is but one of a number of notable, characters cast in roles reminiscent of the trickster myths, starting with the legend about the Prague Golem who breaks out of the control of the Rabbi who created it, and leading up to the HAL-9000 computer from Stanley Kubrick's film *2001: A Space Odyssey*. This last iteration deals directly with the main theme of this study: computers, and its importance in cultural terms can be seen in the University of Illinois' organization of a birthday party for HAL in 1997, as this was the time and place where the film claimed it was constructed (Latour and Powers, 1997).

However, arguably the most culturally vivid symbolic depiction of the ideas of technology and progress, their role and their boundaries, is the story of *Frankenstein* by Mary Wollstonecraft Shelley (1818/1989), which is culturally present both as a novel and in numerous film adaptations (including the most famous one of 1931, boasting Boris Karloff as the monster). This tale does not promote a single interpretation, but shows the dilemmas of science unbound. It leaves the final judgment to the reader.

Two controversial characters form the axis of the story's symbolism. The first one is the title hero, the scientist Victor Frankenstein. He is the archetypal mad scientist, a genius who loses control over his invention. In the subtitle of the novel he is called *the modern Prometheus*, evoking associations with the hero of Greek mythology. The mythical Prometheus is a positively valued character. He is the creator of the first humans, but he also defies the gods (most importantly by stealing fire for the humans) for which he is sentenced to eternal torment. Frankenstein also suffers for his transgression against nature, though the value of his gift is much more problematic.

The second important character is the Monster itself. An innocent being at first, who is then abhorred and rejected by his master, he exacts terrible vengeance leading to the death of not only his creator, but also many innocent people. Let us look at the reference given in the title. If Victor Frankenstein is Prometheus, then perhaps the Monster is not only analogous to the first human, but also to fire as well. And the role of fire is, of course, deeply ambivalent: it is the lifegiver as well as lifetaker, bringing warmth and light, as well as destruction. If we follow this link to the technology represented by the Monster, we are faced with a vision of great possibilities entwined with mortal danger.

The relationship between Victor Frankenstein and the Monster can also be viewed as a symbolic description of the connection between a computer and its user, where the fear of technology competes with the delight at the wonders it offers. There is yet another promethean analogy—the Greek hero did not invent fire, after all, but only disseminated it, like the users, who bring the computer's abilities into their own work. This is the theme that Isaac Asimov (1991) saw in Goethe's poem, about *The Sorcerer's Apprentice*. In this poem the hero tries to use the magic of his master, for which he lacks the skill, and ends up in serious trouble. This story is even easier to treat as an allegory of the meeting between humans and computers.

The Magic Item

Whereas the archetype of the computer as trickster, or as a Frankenstein style monster, was used by my interviewees primarily to describe its appearance to others, in their own relations with a computer they tended to give it a much less important role, objectifying it and stressing that it is, after all, "only a simple tool" (cf. Turkle, 1994) for them:

[1]: I do not belong to such fanatics. I believe that it is a normal work tool, such as the slide rule I was taught how to use, which I then changed for a calculator. It is yet another such asset.

[7]: At this moment, all of both the design engineers and the assistant designers has a computer at their desk and this is like the slide rule for many years, as were calculating machines. Nowadays, of course, for the simpler tasks there are still calculators, but if there is something more complex, one just sits and enters data into the computer. There is only a question of the appropriate program.

[3]: I see not a lot of people who have this, I would say, appropriate attitude towards computers. They either are afraid, or they idolize this computer. They would use it at all times. They would do everything on a computer, or browse the Internet. But they cannot usually treat a computer as such tool, which is used for some tasks—that one does not work with a computer, but one does something, and the computer is only a tool for making this task easier.

Yet even as a "simple tool" the computer does not only ease the operations that were tedious without it, but it also provides new abilities, unattainable before, to its users, giving them a creative power they had no access to before. This example from the realm of photography is a good illustration:

[8]: At some time these programs were used mostly for retouching photographs and for setting the colors, for which only few actions needed to be taken. Then there was this craze of collages, transformations, isolating of particular fragments of the photo, pasting objects which did not exist in reality or on the photo, electronic-digital processing of the image, inserting things into the picture, montages—something that before was very tedious, for example, in photography, because it could only be done with professional cameras using masking and multiple exposures. Now nobody bothers with it anymore; just snaps different pictures, scans them separately, and then cuts out bits and pastes them onto the other picture—this is much simpler and easier and cheaper, because such complicated montage could take a few days in a studio, and now one does the separate elements and it takes just a short time. But in such realist photography, as it is, the image processing really does not take place. This is a quite different branch of photography and, like at one point photography approached painting and created a new path for itself, so now digital image processing or digital paintings are just a quite different path and should not be compared with realist photography. The spectrum of possibilities becomes ever wider. One can find a technique to suit one's needs. And with a computer, one can consciously create lots of kinds of very different montages. This is like a quite different branch, though one needs to do it according to established conventions, obviously.

I have decided to include this rather lengthy excerpt because it seems to me that one can see in it the various interesting aspects of the computer's role. First, this change that a tool causes in the actor using it (Latour, 1993) not only transforms the user's work day, but also causes the user to change:

[8]: I have grown used to computers more than to the photographic equipment. I do mostly that—90% of the time. At one point the proportions were opposite—90% was photography—documentaries and commissioned work and advertisements, and the so-called industrial photography—this is the photography of

> *industrial objects, mostly for the industry, for companies, who want to document technological processes or objects.*

but also the user changes—new branches of photography emerge, which work by their own rules and conventions that one needs to observe. Even the photographer that decides to stick to the old subject matter and methods, stops being simply a photographer and becomes a realist photographer instead.

Secondly, with the increasing importance of the role of the computer, there appear new customs, conventions, and social norms, which describe the extent of its usage—less in realist photography, more in digital image processing or digital painting. As similar situation is found in engineering and design, where, a few years ago, custom (because it was not codified in any technical form) called for checking calculations, which is now deemed unnecessary:

> *[7]: There used to be an assumption that calculations were supposed to be checked with two distinct and unrelated programs. Now there is no time to do this and practically [all] the programs are so large and complex—I'm talking about analytical programs—that the design engineers usually get used to just one program, which they get to know well, because one needs to know the program very well and somehow faultlessly, because each program has some mistakes, some weak points, which one simply needs to know. This is why, in most cases, the design engineer gets used to one, two programs, and uses them, and the verification means checking the assumptions and input data, and not the calculations, because one believes that programs are well designed and tested and one does not check the functioning of a program; even something like six years ago, I remember using two different programs for calculation and to compare the results.*

Where, a few years ago, custom (because it was not codified in any technical norm) called for checking the calculations, which is now deemed unnecessary. This change is hard to dismiss with the simple statement that people finally got used to the infallibility of computer programs and so distrust towards its results evaporated. As far as this distrust goes, let us just say that it is not only speaker number seven who claims that computer programs now have at least as many bugs as they did before, and perhaps even more:

[5]: [At one time] programs were different, they were of a much higher quality. A result coming from a computer generated from appropriate data was really totally correct, which we cannot be so sure of nowadays.

JK: The fact that a new program is less predictable than an old one, already tested, is one thing. But there is another: Was it easier to understand a program for Amiga [a computer popular a few years ago] than for a contemporary Personal Computer?

[9]: No, this is something different—a question of volume—that checking a few mega[bytes] of code—Windows now have how much? Probably at least thirty something mega[bytes] of code—the working stuff, not pictures and such nonsense...this is simply—a person cannot check it.

Thirdly, and finally, the way to execute particular tasks changes, as well as the time needed for their execution and their ascribed importance. Montages and inserts, attainable at one point only in very costly studios, and so highly valued, have become very accessible, consequently losing a lot of their prestige. An extreme example—that of realist photography—has actually become unwelcome.

Let us, however, return to the issue of time, because saving time seems to play an important part in the role my interlocutors ascribed to computers:

[2]: The main gain [in using computers] is foremost in time.

[6]: [Using computers] in clerical work undoubtedly wonderfully orders activities and speeds them up, and this is very useful organizationally.

[10]: [Working with computers] in an obvious way affects speed. Everything takes place faster, more efficiently.

At the same time, only one person admitted that this speeding up of work thanks to computers has given him more free time:

[10]: I have more effects...yes, yes, I do a little more, although I have become lazier. So I gain something because I can rest for a while and also I have more effects.

Perhaps it is important to note that speaker number ten is self-employed as a translator. And in the case of other people, this gain in time does not look so bright:

> *JK: How did your work day change with the appearance of computers?*

> *[2]: This work day has simply stretched a lot, because there is more work since privatization. One simply has to put more time in.*

> *[6]: In my case it is hard to say, whether I have saved a lot of time—in different circumstances somebody else would be doing some of the work I do, and as I know these things a little bit better, I am interested in it, so I do things other people could have been doing for me. So it is hard to speak about saving any time.*

> *JK: I will return once more to the possibility of better data exchange; the possibility of doing things. Does it increase the available free time, or only the work load?*

> *[3]: The work load. It is like this with free time—unfortunately?—this is a private company, where the capitalist relations are clear to see. They are important, even though this company is nice in that is pays a lot of attention to its employees and social matters, but let us not deceive ourselves—it is the profit that matters the most, so all the free time is practically consumed by the company.*

Time gains are redefined as gains in efficiency, although it does not necessarily follow that the positive effects of greater efficiency achieved with the help of computers affect only the employers, for example, speaker number three continues:

> *[3]: Perhaps the speed with which information circulates means that there is more time which can be used for example for learning—as progress is so swift in this field in which I work. One has to learn all the time; has to find new things; look for them; and there is more time for that and less time for routine tasks. Those which can be largely automated.*

> *JK: Did the work get more interesting, then?*

[3]: Probably, yes. Perhaps because of that, in the case of this company, that we have the knowledge that we are working with cutting edge, world class technology, this has such positive effect on people.

Apart from the gain in time, there appears here one more important positive aspect of the computer's role: They are a symbol of progress, and they give their user a feeling of power associated with having command over such potent and complex technology:

JK: So what does computerization give you, most of all?

[4]: It gives me satisfaction that at my age, not so young anymore, I [can] do this work, that I have learned to use the computer. It gives me such satisfaction, that I can work with a computer.

Is this only about the social prestige of working with a computer? I do not think so. I believe it is a question of the aforementioned power of creation, given by the computer, as well as some power over time.

Let us try to bring together the stories of computer as a source of power and as an agent of change for the user and their sense of time, as a tool speeding up the execution of tedious tasks and setting ground for quite new undertakings, unimaginable only a few years earlier. Such a wide area of influence seems to go far beyond the abilities ascribed to normal tools, which is why, in my opinion, my interlocutors speak of the computer as a magic item. It has both its obvious functions associated with the whole class of similar objects (*Olla,* the magical cauldron of the Celtic god Dagda remains, after all, a cauldron) and supernatural abilities, gained because of its magical origin or due to sorcery woven upon it (*Olla,* the gift of Samias the druid is at the same time a vessel of abundance, impossible to drain of its contents; the Celtic version of cornucopia) (Kempinski, 1993). Such abilities allow the performance of magic: actions that would have not only been impossible, but often also unimaginable without the wondrous powers bestowed by the traditional magic item, or the computer.

I would also like to point out that numerous inconveniences, or even outright flaws, pointed out in computers do not invalidate the magic item metaphor. After all, Mjöllnir, miraculous hammer of the Nordic thunder god, Thor, is supposed to have a handle that is obviously too short. This proves to be quite a serious flaw (caused, incidentally, by Loki the trickster, who intervened in its making), as it leads to Thor's demise in the Last Battle, where he dies poisoned by the fetid breath of his opponent, Jörmungandr, the world serpent (whom he will, however, manage to kill before his demise).

We can find one more interesting aspect of a magical item such as computer by comparing it to a magic ring not sourced from an actual mythology, but from J.R.R. Tolkien's famous *Lord of the Rings* trilogy (1955/1990). This ring exerts considerable influence over its owners, causing them to use it more and more frequently. Although my interviewees ascribed considerably less diabolic character to computers, they, too, tended to make them more and more indispensable:

[1]: I cannot imagine that computers could disappear.

[5]: The engineers can no longer design a construction by hand, and they need a computer to do it.

[7]: Although three years ago there was one computer per four-five people, now practically everybody...every person has a computer, and now it is practically impossible to work without one.

Another parallel between magic items and computers is that they both have changing context and properties, as well as history independent from that of just one user. Both are created, later change hands, and can be stolen, given, or sold, and, finally, broken, like *Excalibur,* or destroyed.

A criticism against this interpretation could be, according to Bruno Latour's (1993) account, that these characteristics do not make the computer stand out from the crowd of other tools used by human beings. These also leave their distinct mark upon the social actors they meet, and together create new aims and programs of action. This is still not, however, a standpoint reflecting the usual approach to objects (even in academia) and so, perhaps, in this context, I am more inclined to agree that all the items are magical, which perhaps serves as a contemporary answer to Max Weber's "disenchantment of the world."

Experiencing Economy

The notion of attempting to reenchant the world is by no means unique or revolutionary. George Ritzer (1996) criticized the attempts by McDonaldized (the term he uses to describe importing modes of operation from the fast food industry into other economic spheres) companies to infuse consumption with a sense of wonder and enchantment. It is my belief that my perception of objects, and particularly complex machines such as computers, as magical draws upon a somewhat different understanding of experience than that espoused by Ritzer. In his analysis, the sense of wonder is seen as a flavor added to the otherwise dull act of consumption (cf. the critique in Martin Parker, 2002). In the context of this paper, the sense of wonder is inherent to the acts of sensemaking, regardless of how mundane the setting appears to be. To see and, more importantly, to use a computer as a magical item is to draw upon the pleasure of reinterpreting (that is, experiencing) the surrounding reality.

The American psychologist George Kelly (1955), in describing Personal Construct Psychology—his vision of the human condition—used the image of each person as a scientist, actively constructing (or inventing) his or her own environment. I would argue that an image more fitting to organization and management studies, and to the study of the experience economy in particular, would be that of each person as an entrepreneur, using the available tools (and magic items) to create and negotiate an environment for sharing with other social actors. An entrepreneur can be understood as one who acts upon social, technical, and economic networks (and as John Law, 1991, argues there is no appreciable difference between the three) in order to realize aims that might, or might not, be economic in nature. It should be noted as the example of the computer as angel or demon demonstrates, that such an entrepreneur can attempt to stabilize networks involving the worldviews of other human actors as much as his or her own, possibly crafting a set of experiences that can, indeed, be peddled to those other actors.

CHAPTER 5

THE DESIGNER AS THE CREATOR OF EXPERIENCES IN THE POSTMODERN ECONOMY

ULLA JOHANSSON AND LISBETH SVENGREN HOLM

Every human being is a designer. Many also earn their living by design—in every field that warrants pause, and careful considera-tion, between the conceiving of an action and a fashioning of the means to carry it out, and an estimation of its effects. Norman Potter (1989:13)

Design is a value-driven activity. In creating change, designers impose values upon the world—values of their own or those of their client. To be a designer is a cultural option: designers create culture, create experience and meaning for people. Rachel Cooper and Mike Press (2003)

What is a coffee maker? It could easily be defined as a product or an object that makes coffee. Beyond this obviously functional aspect, a coffee maker could also represent a sense of nostalgia or even the source of an experience. An unidentified person, reflecting upon the expensive coffee maker he just bought, said:

It's just a coffee maker! A water tank in plastic, glass jug for the coffee, a plastic filter holder, and some heating elements. OK, it makes a very good coffee, but that's due to the exclusive quality of the beans and the excellent water quality we have here. The coffee maker is of course of a very good quality, too. Actually, it reminds

> *me of the coffee maker I saw in Italy where we were on vacation a couple of years ago, so maybe it's a little bit nostalgic. That was a very nice holiday and Italy was so cool. Looking closer at it, it actually has some of the aesthetics of the Italian ones'. Maybe that's why I bought it.*

In a narrow sense, a product such as a coffee maker, is just parts put together for a functional purpose, solving needs or problems: heating water, filtering coffee, or making a hot beverage. Smart solutions make the product easy to use and maybe also easy to manufacture at a desired cost, while the form of the product makes it look appealing. An engineer probably came up with the solution for the heating elements, and an industrial designer came up with the concept for the form of the water tank and the jug. On an elementary level, the industrial designer could be defined as an engineer with an aesthetic mind. This is, however, a one-dimensional definition of industrial design that is quite ignorant. Industrial design is more than form and aesthetics; more than problem solving and smart solutions. (Industrial) design is first of all a value-driven, culturally related process with a purpose that relates to the experience we have when using or buying a product. By relating design to experience we claim that design *is* experience on two levels: a process level and a product level. Experience is omnipresent both in the design process itself and in the goal of the process.

The core act of design is to infuse experience into products or service offerings. Design has always been concerned with increasing the experience and value of HIT everyday products like cars, furniture, household equipment, communication articles and so on. Gregor Paulsson's *Beautiful Everyday things* was published by the Swedish Crafts Association in 1919 in order to educate people about design qualities, or the combination of functionality and aesthetic form. In his book *Alessi The Design Factory* Christopher Frayling quotes Alberto Alessi, who stated his design philosophy at a seminar with postgraduate students at the Royal College of Art as:

> *to dream, to play and to satisfy, with the designer as lyric poet rather than storyteller...not a question of craft versus industry, but of craft with the help of machines* (Frayling, 1998).

Through the inspiration of art and poetry, designers try to make products and services more beautiful, funny, simple, complicated, or whatever is needed in order to inoculate in the things an increased experience. This experience dimension—and thereby the design—is more and more important when we analyze the quality of a product or service. We no longer buy clothes, cars, houses, books and CDs because of their technical performance or function. We buy them because we are seduced by them, we like them, we love them—and the liking and loving is of utmost importance (c.f. Julier, 2000; Thornquist, 2005).

Design and experience are inseparable dimensions. The heart of design is to appeal to our heart and senses. This concept was implicit in modernist thinking, where "form follows function" was part of a broader ideology with both social and aesthetic ambitions. Having a beautiful and ergonomic chair designed by Marcel Breuer or Bruno Mattson gives me a wonderful experience every day. It is like a piece of art that, at the same time, provides me with a function.

In postmodernist design, the experience value may be exaggerated at the expense of the function depending on the type of product, or sometimes the function is just taken for granted; the product works. The playfulness at the heart of postmodern design is almost identical with experience—or rather, the playful design is aimed to give the user, or the viewer, an experience.

Historically, experience has been almost identical with design, or rather; design has embraced experience as the forefront of the purpose of design. But this is not the case in the relation between the economy (or economics or economic value) and experience. The term "quality" has traditionally, in economic discourse, been understood not as quality in experience, but rather, quality from a durability and technical perspective. In the postmodern era, this rather simple relationship has been questioned and abandoned in innovation and product design development. The concept of experience has been introduced as something that goes beyond the traditional quality dimensions; instead, experience has a rather loose relationship to both cost and quality.

The origination of postmodernism in the realms of art and design preceeded the postmodern discourse in management. Relating postmodernism to the notions of design, experience, and economics, therefore, means adding the concept of "economics" to what was already there. Postmodern design means breaking up the tight functionalist relationship between form and function, and looking for the experience more as a play with forms than as a consequence of function. Adding "economics" to this means submitting the values embraced by postmodern design, where a liberated experience is at the forefront, to a business perspective.

The Experience Economy as a Stage for the Designer

Above we discussed a design perspective on how design and experience are inseparable concepts. The concept of "the experience economy" comes from Pine and Gilmore's book *The Experience Economy: Work is Theatre and Every Business a Stage* (1999)[56]. Their main message is that *the experience economy* is a new transformation with distinct qualitative changes similar in character to what happened when the focus on products was transformed into a focus on service and the place where the service was consumed, or experienced, to use the words of Pine and Gilmore. Service, accordingly, came to embrace products and the environment of their delivery. In the experience economy, it is the experience that is the focus, not the product or the service as such. Experiences are what we, as consumers, are attracted by and willing to pay for, even if products and services are what we receive.

We do not only enter into the experience economy in the sense that the experience dimension is increasingly more important. Pine and Gilmore particularly stress the importance of communicating the experience. Communication is both part of the experience, as such, and a way of making the consumer aware of the distinct qualities of the product or service. Marketers need to communicate the experience not only to describe the qualities, but also to start the experience, and to distinguish the offered experience from other offerings. The consumer wants more and more experiences, and the augmented experience cannot always be expected or self-evident for the consumer, but has to be communicated.

Communication, such as Pine and Gilmore talk about communicating the unexpected in a way that makes the communication as such an experience is at the core of a designer's competence. Looking at this communication from a design perspective, it can be orchestrated through the design of products, environmental design, graphic design etc. Creating a combined message through these different channels is the very core of design management (Olins, 1989). This design discourse peaked in academic studies in the 1980s when the goal was to create such a message—one in accordance with the mission of the company.

Designers are trained to communicate so that all five senses interact with each other in a total experience. They know that communication

---

[56] A library search for "experience economy" shows that books and articles of Pine and Gilmore and book referees of these books count for 9 out of 10 references.

by words is only a small part of the communication, and that communication can be accomplished by artefacts, colours, shapes, and symbols which interact with each other to give a specific message that is then interpreted and experienced by customers according to their specific situations, values and backgrounds.

The concept of the experience economy, therefore, embraces the designer, and puts the designer on centre stage. The designer becomes, through her or his competence, the one who ultimately shapes and constructs the reality of the experience economy; the one who through colours, textures, sounds, and form makes the product or offering into a holistic experience.

Experiencing Design as Product and Process

Within professional design discourse, design is normally defined in a much broader way than in the popular discourse:

First, when referring to design as a product it does not, contrary to a common belief, have only to do with forms. It also has to do with texture and feelings, sounds (opening a car door, for example), sights (and, accordingly, form and colour); in other words features that deliberately influence all our senses. The focus on sensual dimensions gives design a self-evident relation to experiences (Norman, 1988).

Secondly, it is not only the result that defines design, but the process, or the designer's methods, that constitute the design concept. The process of designing is a specific process alternating between analytical and creative moments in the creation of new concepts (Lundequist, 1995).

The Design Concept when Related to Artefacts/Products

When you open a newspaper or look at Television you will find many features of design. In these articles or programs design seems, however, to be more or less equivalent to beautifully shaped *artefacts* like clothes, furniture, vases, cars, home decoration, and so on. Design seems to have to do solely with forms, colours, shapes and "good taste". As stated above, this is, however, a very narrow description of design, and one that Donald Norman refers to as "Everyday things" (Norman, 1988). In the creation of products, there are many dimensions that are important to the designer. Functional or ergonomic aspects have always been at the core. Aspects of technical production create limitations that the designer needs to be aware of, and environmental and ethical considerations are part of the design agenda beyond the aesthetic aspects. In all these considerations, it is the sensual experience of the user, be it a user in the distribution chain, or the end user, that is the basis for the design and what often is seen as the constitution or core of the designer's competence.

In the following text, we will argue that there has been a shift in priority among the above variables. In the postmodern era, the more playful, sensual aspects of design have been upgraded while the more technical functionality has been downgraded. These changes make the experience dimension, always present in the design agenda, even more exaggerated in the postmodern world.

Design When Seen as a Process

Within the last decade, design has been highlighted as a process rather than as a result. Focus has been on the designer's specific method of working as the core of his or her competence, rather than on the capacity of creating artefacts (Lundequist, 1995). The designer is seldom an expert in any of the specific fields that are related to the creation of the product, but rather an expert on the coordination of different kinds of knowledge, thereby being simultaneously a translator and a coordinator. Lundequist (1995) defines the core of design as handling intertwined processes: artistic processes, information processes, negotiating and decision making processes, etc. Since these processes are of ultimately different epistemological character, the handling and coordination of them makes the designer to a combined translator and creator rather than a mechanistic coordinator.

Within this coordinating role the designer uses his or her capacity to move between a holistic and a detailed view of the situation, almost as if there was a zoom camera in his or her eyes. This capacity to alternate perspectives is part of the designer's learned skills, and also the way s/he combines more analytical skills with artistic creativity. The designer, thereby, reconciles the different characters of knowledge that separate the humanities, art, and technique. Many design researchers have noted this capacity as specific to design knowledge and methods (Ramirez 1987). Another specific feature of the design method is that it starts with the user's requirements, the user context, and the experience from the user perspective (Monö, 1997).

This creative role of the designer is further defined through the important skill of visualization, which makes the designer an illustrator of the goal of the group, but also moves one step further. Illustrating means conceptualizing and concretizing at the same time. And this, in turn, makes the designer a creator of common goals and concepts. The designer puts together and reformulates entities from different profes-

120

sional worlds. He or she translates and re-creates what exists in these other worlds, and wedges him or herself in between them in order to create room for his or her own interpretation. By rendering and further concretizing what exists in the other professional room, the designer engages in a creative act that both relates to and separates from the other professional worlds. These characteristics are also those of the entrepreneur.

The Design Process Seen From Entrepreneurial Perspectives

Entrepreneurship can be understood as organizational creativity; creating new businesses by breaking the existing rules. Traditionally, entrepreneurship research has been either oriented towards the macrofunctions and the structural nature of entrepreneurship as the innovative force of economies (Schumpeter's view), or toward the psychological dispositions of individual decision makers, influenced by McClelland (1961). More recent research in entrepreneurship has emphasised growth-willingness, entrepreneurial orientation and opportunity recognition as ways to form a steady basis for a theory of entrepreneurship, thereby reading entrepreneurship from a constructionist point of view. Hjorth and Steyaert (2003) have tried to move beyond the conceptually limiting horizon of *homo economicus* that also seems to underlay the academic entrepreneurship tradition. Opening towards a more playful, social approach they urge us to try to keep the vibrant and vivid adolescence of entrepreneurship research, keep its movement qualities. Hjorth has introduced the construction of the entrepreneur as *homo ludens*, the playing person, rather than *homo economicus*. A novel reading, entrepreneurship is described as a form of social creativity, as a tactical art of creating space for play/invention, for actualizing new practices (Hjorth, 2003).

Two similarities exist between the designer and the entrepreneur. One similarity is that both belong to the art of *homo ludens* rather than *homo oeconomicus* in their way of acting and creating value for the organization. Also, it is the creation of new rules rather than the application of existing rules that is at the core of their actions.

The Character of (Industrial) Design in the Modern and Postmodern Era

When talking about design and experience, a distinction between design in the modern era and the postmodern one needs to be made. Design was born in the age of modernity although interest in it reached a peak during the time referred to as postmodern, or at the time of transition from high modernity to postmodernity. Design seems to flourish in the different fields of postmodernism, changing meaning and aims like a chameleon.

Design in the Modern Era

The separation between design and technique, between art and technical aspects, is taken for granted in the modern world. This separation is, however, a modern concept itself and the result of the industrialization process. In the premodern world, as far back as ancient Greece, the artistic and technical side of design were inseparable. This was symbolized in the word *techne*, which is the root "technique" but referred to both technique and art at the very same time (Johansson et al 2003). Thinking and making were seen as inseparable processes.

In the industrialized era, design has been divided into a number of subdisciplines such as graphic design, web design, fashion design, and industrial design. This way of dividing design is both pragmatic (it relates to ongoing professional educations that differ from each other) and a result of modernist systematization. The borders between different design professions are about to dissolve. The area of retail design, for example, integrates graphic design, product design, packaging design, and interior design. These different competencies have to cooperate in such a way that a coordinated message is given to the customer. Similar tendencies of integration of different specialities are seen in other design areas as well. There is a paradoxical tendency of further specialization and merger of the borders at the same time.

Another well-known way to construct industrial design is to regard it as a coordination in equal terms of form, function, and production/technology. A common philosophy for the modernist industrial designer is that "form follows function." The concept of functionalism is closely related to modernism and the resulting fragmentation of both processes and organizations. The industrial designer, therefore, can be regarded as a coordinator trying to reunite the separated dimensions, creating a holistic process, and to do it in new ways (Johansson et al 2003). The designer is a product of modernity. Yet he or she is, at the same time, an alien figure in the logic of modernity, because in modernity art and technique are separated logics, contrary to the holistic approach that permeates the designprofession. The designer, therefore, becomes somewhat of a tightrope walker between the different logics in the modern organization, trying to combine and coordinate them into one product.

Part of the ideology of "form follows function" was that things should be "simple," and that they should have no extra ornaments. The reason for this was twofold: First, an adjustment to production was a goal in itself, because it enabled lower costs and lower prices and set the stage for mass production and consumption. One could say that the early industrial designers were part of a radical political movement aiming for the masses to have a better life. Secondly, this social ideology led to an aesthetic ideal where simplicity was desired.

The goal of simplicity did not mean that the experience or emotional dimension of the product design was neglected in modernity. "To make people happy when they used the things" was important for the modern designers (Dreyfuss, 1967). Tthis goal was realized, however, through detailed ergonomic studies and consideration of the technical and production possibilities. Adjustment of the form to technique and function was a matter of being honest. Since honesty regarding material and form was important, form was expected to follow function in the simplest way possible. A Swedish example of functionalist design are Bruno Mattsson's chairs—made in the 1930s and after, built with contours that follow the body, and which differ remarkably from the earlier heavy armchairs in both form and material. Mattsson's chairs were, indeed, an entrepreneurial way of making chairs that functionalism made possible.

High Design – a Modernist Concept that Bridges into Postmodernism

The concept of "high design" (Dormer, 1990) refers both to a specific, exclusive design and to an expensive design. High design is a cultural and market phenomenon with strong correlations and similarities to "high culture" (Bourdieu, 1993). Dormer (1990) divides "high design" into two categories: heavenly goods, and tokens. The former are the objects that are designed for, and affordable by, the very rich, whereas the latter are objects with an exclusive design and affordable by the "wish-they-were-rich."

A classical example of "high design" is Philippe Starck's Alessi Salif juicer. The juicer is not a product of a strong coordination between functionality, production aspects, and form. In fact, it is less functional than many juicers that cost just a fraction of what this one costs. Juice often spills over. Nor is it as easy to produce as many others. The value of Philippe Starck's juicer is that of experience, one that is close to art. It is the considerable artistic and symbolic value of the juicer that gives it its market value. If you buy it, you do not (only) buy an artefact to press lemon juice, you buy an experience, a belonging to high culture, and a story about the product that is part of the product. All this makes the act of making lemon juice different; it turns the act into an experience. It is this experience that constitutes the design and the reason for buying the artefact, not easy production or good functionality.

Postmodern Design – When Experiences are the Core

In the postmodern era, where the logic of the experience economy flourishes, the equal co-ordination of form-technique and function becomes an obsolete construction. A logical optimizing of the three dimensions of function, technique, and form no longer exists. Rather, the access to high design, that in the modern era was a privilege for the few, is now accessible to many. An example of this is, IKEA, whose vision is "to create a better everyday life for the many people." The concept "is based on offering a wide range of well-designed, functional home furnishing products at prices so low that as many people as possible will be able to afford them" (www.ikea.com). At least in Scandinavia, IKEA has become a concept synonymous with this idea.

Within the postmodern era, a new relationship between art, function, and production has emerged. Having the simplest and optimized relation between the three dimensions is no longer the main point sometimes, not even a point at all. Instead, the symbolic experience value has an enlarged importance. The experience has become the core, not only in "high design" for the rich, but also in design for broader groups of consumption. This liberation in the relation between form and function gives an extended place for the play dimension and, thereby, a stage for the designer to take an entrepreneurial role. When the traditional model of the relationship between form, function, and technique dissolves, design takes off and leaves an empty space, really an entrepreneurial space for the designer to grab.

Postmodern Design as Experience Design

Making a helmet for welding in the modern era would probably be a matter of finding a form that follows function and production; however, in the case of the very popular helmet made by Ergonomidesign and Hörnells (now owned by 3M) (see below) the postmodern characteristics are obvious. The helmet is not only a helmet protecting the workers from heat and made in such a way that workrelated injuries are minimized. It is also a helmet of pride, a helmet connecting the traditional craftsmanship of welding to other worlds of glory and respect, for instance, the knights or the world of astronauts and spaceships. For workers, used to being devalued in their work, this really matters. When they can chose, they chose the experience of having a helmet that refers to ideas that can be made into a story, rather than a helmet that is "plain" ergonomically, and where form equals function. Workers want the added emotional experience. At least, this is the interpretation we make of the great success that this helmet has had on the market.

In this example, as in many others, experience is at the core of the design. It is not the *only* dimension. Rather, the experience dimension is integrated into other functional dimensions. But this integration is *not* done with the ideology of "form follows function." It is, instead the *play* with symbols, and symbolic value and identity that is important. A design is a playful creation of something that touches the emotions, while at the same time, it is functionally and technically interesting.

In postmodernism, the aesthetic dimension creates a value that is independent of and in addition to the functional value. The value is not a consideration of production technique, but rather the other way around. The triangle, accordingly, is no longer an adequate metaphor for the relationship between form, function, and production. The relationship is no longer as close as it was, and also, it is not a matter of optimizing coordination, but a more free relationship where the form and the experience are the core that is anchored in function and production.

Our conclusion from these examples is that design in the postmodern era can still be said to deal with a combination of form, function, and production, however, the relationship between the three dimensions and the requirements of form has undergone a metamorphosis. Function and production have become basic requirements, and form has evolved to become more important as it determines the character of the product, or the essence of its value. Optimizing the triangle is no longer a matter of importance, rather the character is the design, and the function and production become requirements to be taken under consideration.

As a consequence of the postmodern turn, form, function, and price are now decoupled. The design process becomes increasingly important since it has to deal with both the coordination and the decoupling of these different dimensions. Furthermore, since the aesthetic dimension is increasingly important, design will also take a driving role in the experience economy, where perception is at the core. Cooper and Press (2003:6) state, "Design is a value-driven activity. In creating change, designers impose values upon the world, values of their own or those of their client. To be a designer is a cultural option: designers create culture, create experience and meaning for people."

The designer, through his or her holistic view and method of analyzing societal trends, sees and creates new possibilities. These new possibilities are created at both a more abstract, conceptual level and at a concrete, artefactual level. The functional, artistic, and technical aspects have been put at the forefront of modernist design. In the postmodern concept, however, the designer is identified as a creator of experiences and of business opportunities (Press and Cooper, 2003), thereby, necessitating an acknowledgement of the similarities between designers and entrepreneurs.

Taking this definition of design seriously imposes a heavy burden on the shoulders of the designers. Therefore we might argue that we cannot leave all of this to the designers alone. They need partners from the management world who understand design and who can see how a design process and design thinking can contribute the entrepreneurial thinking needed by industrial organizations, as well as to the creation of products and services that give customers and consumers the experience they are willing to pay for. We need to develop management and marketing theories so they include the more substantial notion and definition of design, both as a process and a result.

Concluding Remarks

In this chapter we have reflected upon the relationship between design and experience and the role design can play in the experience economy. We have found that the concept of design and the concept of experience are in many ways so intertwined that they are inseparable, specifically in the postmodern notion of design. Yet this tight relationship between design and experience is totally absent in the discourse created by the concept of an "experience economy", a concept derived from the business school context where design is mostly absent.

Yet, the design competence needed to create experiences is discussed in the experience economy discourse. Design *is* the creation of experience, and participation by a designer is needed because designers are those who work with creating products, services, or experiences that relate to our senses. Just as social science, to which both marketing and management belong, works conceptually and analytically, design works with sensuality and creativity. Sensuality and creativity are at the core of the designer's work and the definition of the design profession.

Because of this, it is worth noting that the design perspective, the design profession and the designer's part in creating the design society are never mentioned in Pine and Gilmore's influential book. This is remarkable for many reasons. Not only does it leave out a perspective that is central to the creation of an experience, it also takes away the process of dealing with the integration between design, marketing, and management in this creation. And since this relationship is known to be problematic (Johansson and Svengren, 2003; Bruce and Bessant, 2002; Press and Cooper, 2003), it leaves out both problems and possible solutions.

The conclusion of our analysis of the relationship between design and experience economy, therefore, is that it is time to invite the design perspective to be part of the intellectual discussion on the experience and experience economy. Or, to paraphrase Pine and Gilmore, it is time to let design enter the stage!

CHAPTER 6

FROM BECOMING ENTERPRISING TO ENTREPRENEURIAL BECOMING
TOWARDS THE STUDY OF ENTREPRENEURSHIP AS ETHICO-AESTHETIC PRACTICE

RICHARD WEISKOPF

"Experience…is something you come out of changed"
(Foucault 1991a, 27)

The Big Secret of Success

Increasingly, entrepreneurial qualities are not only demanded from proper "entrepreneurs" but also from organizational members who are expected to behave *as if* they were entrepreneurs or *as if* they were the owners of the company they work for (see Peters/Waterman 1982, Kanter 1990). The traditional "employee," who has been constructed in various ways over the last century (see e.g., Jacques 1996, Rose 1990), is seemingly being reimagined as an entrepreneur of a special kind: as a strange hybrid, or mixture between an "employee" and an "entrepreneur," or an "entreployee" as this monstrosity has been called by the sociologists Voß and Pongratz (2003). Entrepreneurs "who form an extremely important group of people in the workforce" are seen as "major creators of employment and catalysts of change." (Kets de Vries 1996, 856) Personality traits like the need for achievement (Johnson 1990), an internal locus of control (Duchesneau/Gartner 1990), self-reliance and extroversion (Lee/Tsang 2001) are attributed to this "extremely important group of people" (Kets de Vries 1996).

The development of entrepreneurial skills is prescribed as a panacea that seemingly cures anything.

Some empirical studies have shown that "personality traits in general are not important factors affecting venture growth" and suggest that "the focus of previous studies on the impact of psychological characteristics on performance may have been misplaced" (Lee/Tsang 2001, 597–598). A similar conclusion is reached by Chell et al. (1991) who reviewed research attempting to identify entrepreneurial qualities and found that many entrepreneurs did not possessed the qualities attributed to them and that these qualities seem to vary historically. Curiously, quite a few entrepreneurs even appeared to lose entrepreneurial qualities after an initial success. On the whole, the review shows that the causality of the abilities in question could not be demonstrated. These arguments lead to the suspicion that "the trait approach as a whole is obsolete" (Armstrong 2001, 543). Despite this critique and despite the critique of a misleading essentialism (see e.g. Gartner 1988; Hjorth/Steyaert 2004; Jones/Spicer 2005; Jones/Spicer forthcoming) in entrepreneurship studies, it is quite common to assume there are specific personality traits that characterize successful individuals in general, and successful "entrepreneurs" in particular. The assumption that these traits are given and can be *identified*, once the appropriate methods have been developed and applied correctly (Kets de Vries 1977; McClealland 1987; Gartner 1989), has constituted a specific mode of thinking.

This mode of thinking has also infiltrated managerial practice, consulting and the popular press. It is frequently argued in this context that "Entrepreneurial organizations need employees who regularly demonstrate entrepreneurial characteristics". Consequently, the prescription is that "management of entrepreneurial companies must work diligently to recognize, identify and attract this type of employee." (Hadzima/Pilla 2006, 1) Some time ago, the Austrian newspaper *DER STANDARD* (2003, 11–12) reported an interesting story. Under the heading *Das große Geheimnis des Erfolgs (The big secret of success)* the author describes rather enthusiastically how modern management realizes competitive advantages and mobilizes "human resources." In the article references a consulting company that can, seemingly, provide the necessary expert knowledge to allow companies to uncover the secret and the necessary technology to identify this special type of employee. This silver bullet is called "Discovery of Natural Latent Abilities" (DNLA). So, what is the mystery behind this identification code? According to the description of the consulting company (http://www.dnla.de), it is a "scientifically proven", "practice tested" procedure that builds on "scientifically proven models of modern occupational psychology", and identifies the "latent abilities" which supposedly slumber in each employee, in order to optimize human resources. The following description makes it even more clear what is sold under the label of DNLA: "A precision instrument for measuring, evaluation, transformation and control."[57]

Figure 6.1 DNLA method (Source: Company Brochure)

The procedure produces knowledge about employees and potential employees. The supplier promises that the application of these "scientifically proven methods of modern occupational psychology" allows for the identification of "natural latent abilities" that are clandestine and that can only be seen and made visible by adequate expertise. With the help of the procedure, it is possible—so it promises—to measure "abilities" precisely; to select and distribute employees "optimally." It is also possible to make some "objective" comparisons: between single employees, between teams, and even between whole companies and populations.

Producing the "Managerial Entrepreneur"

I selected the example of DNLA rather randomly. The "continued failure to *find* the character of the entrepreneur" (Jones/Spicer 2005, 235, emphasis added), the warnings of Human Resource-experts against the

---

[57] Translation of the text: "*A precision instrument for measuring, evaluation, transformation and control.* In every employee there are slumbering potentials. However, practice shows that many of these potentials are never discovered or are even destroyed by ignorance and false leadership. *The other side*: missing potentials. Often, these are not even noticed, even if they are the cause for a lack in performance. This is true for both newcomers and for employees of the company."

numerous "pitfalls on the road to measurement" (Pfeffer 1997), and even the warnings against the possible destructive implications of the tendency to "measure everything" (Power 2004) have not stopped the search for the entrepreneur as if he or she would be some*thing*, out there, waiting to be discovered. On the contrary, the call for "[r]enewing the hunt of means of identifying potential entrepreneurs by personality characteristics" (Hull et al. 1980) seems to have been followed widely over the last decades. A plethora of procedures and technologies, like the DNLA-technology mentioned above, promise to identify and measure the "most important asset" in the knowledge economy. Even though these technologies are heterogeneous and different in detail and concrete form, they also represent a certain method. It is thus useful to read this and other similar technologies symptomatically.

This means that we are not to engaging in "renewing the hunt", but rather look at the technologies of the hunters; we do not attempt to improve technologies in order to hit the target but, rather, we problematize the technologies themselves in order to create a reflexive distance that moves us beyond "managerial governmentality" (Hjorth et al. 2003, 97). In the remainder of this section, I will develop categories that allow us to understand the production the "managerial entrepreneur" (Hjorth et al. 2003, 97) as a version of the "governable person" (Miller/O'Leary 1987). In section III I will engage in "enterprising up" (Strathern 2000) and illustrate how managerial technologies implement the urge to "become enterprising," and how they create the "enterprising self" as a very specific mode of experience that is restricted and limited rather than open and productive. In the final section I open with a line of thought that understands entrepreneurship as an ethico-aesthetic practice that attempts to move beyond the limits of established ways of doing and seeing things.

In particular, the work of Michel Foucault allows us to understand the process that constitutes a specific experience, and to open it to discussion. Throughout his work, he was concerned with this process of production and with the various technologies that have been invented over the course of time. His aim was to "create a history of the different modes by which, in our culture, human beings *are made subjects*" (Foucault 1983, 208, emphasis added). His work was, and continues to be, a major source for reflecting on the constitution of the "enterprising self" (see du Gay 1996, 2000, 2004). The entrepreneur is certainly "one of the fantasies of economic discourse" (Jones/Spicer 2005, 382) that has become hegemonic in recent times. Discourse does more, however, than create a mere fantasy. It says that "what the subject is only in a certain, quite particular game of truth" (Florence 1998, 462). Such games of truth, as Foucault suggests, under the pseudonym Maurice Florence (ibid.):

> *open up a field of experience in which the subject and the object are both constituted only under certain simultaneous conditions, but in which they are constantly modified in relation to each other.*

One of his central claims is that the individual is not a given, but rather is an effect, or product, of technologies of power. In contrast to traditional views, Foucault emphasized the "productive" nature of power. Power, in his view, does not primarily work as a negative, or limiting, force but rather as a productive force that creates rather then represses a certain reality. Power "produces reality." It "produces domains of objects and rituals of truth. The individual and the knowledge that may be gained of him belong to this production" (Foucault 1977, 194).

When Foucault talked about the "productivity" of power, he wanted to overcome the traditional view, which saw power mainly as limiting and restricting those subjected to power. He also rejected the position, that power and knowledge are in a relation of exteriority to each other, and contradict and mutually exclude each other. "We should admit rather", he argued "that power produces knowledge (and not simply be encouraging it because it serves power or by applying it because it is useful), that power and knowledge directly imply one another; that there is no power relation without the correlative constitution of a field of knowledge, nor any knowledge that does not presuppose and constitute at the same time power relations" (ibid., 27). Power/knowledge or power-knowledge (*savoir-pouvoir*) express this indissoluble entanglement in shorthand. "Practices," that Foucault increasingly put at the center of his work, are the sites of entanglement (cf. Florence 1998, Foucault 1991). This also corresponds with the methodological principle and "style" (Gordon 1991, 4) of Foucault's analyses. The attempt is "not the discovery of true things" (Florence 1998, 460) but, rather, the analysis of the interconnection and mutual development of the processes of *objectification* and *subjectification* that bring them into being. The question is not: What is power? Who has power? Where does it reside or come from? but rather *how* is power exercised? The question, then, is not: What are human beings doing and why are they doing what they do? But, rather, the study of:

> *methods and techniques used in different institutional contexts to act upon the behaviour of individuals...so as to shape, direct, modify their way of conducting themselves.* (ibid., 463)

What then does the DNLA method "do" when we look at it as a technology of production rather then as a technology of "discovery"? *How* does it contribute to the production of the governable person?

A first step in this process consists of making human beings objects of a specific knowledge. In this way, human beings are constructed as objects that can be handled and managed. Only when human beings—just as any other "object" to be governed (the population, an enterprise, a university, the psyche, etc.)—are described in a certain language can they be governed. "All government depends on a particular mode of 'representation': the elaboration of a language for depicting the domain in question that claims both to grasp the nature of that reality represented, and literally to represent it in a form amenable to political deliberation, argument and scheming" (Rose 1991, 80). It is therefore important to draw attention to language and discourse. As long as one follows a nineteenth century philosophy of language, and views language as a "transparent window" to the world, or as ideally representing the world out there, one is concerned with developing clear-cut categories, systems, and so on, that adequately represent the real. This is, however, completely different once we recognize that language, or discourse, constitutes reality. This is not to take an idealistic position; to reduce the world to language, as it is sometimes falsely claimed. As Robert Chia put it, "[t]here is not *nothing* outside of language, but *nothing*. There is no thingness about the material or social world except when comprehended through the codifying structure of language" (Chia 1996, 37–8; see also Chia 2000). It means, rather, to understand discourse and the power of discourse in its materiality and in its material effects. Attention must, therefore, be given to the categories used to "describe" and "represent" reality and, to the "truth-effects" (Foucault 1980) that are generated by the acceptance of these categories. Technologies of measuring and "representing" human capacities and "resources" have long been seen as necessary aids to government. The utopia of having a perfect overview of the "things" to be governed was already articulated as early as the seventeenth century.[58] The modern

---

[58] "Would it not be a great satisfaction to the king to know at a designated moment every year the number of his subjects, in total and by region, with all the resources, wealth & poverty of each place; [the number] of his nobility and ecclesiastics of all kinds, of men of the robe, of Catholics and of those of the other religion, all sepa-

tendency to "measure anything" (Power 2004) is associated with this utopia. Given the infinity of the "real," this is, of course, an impossibility and remains an illusion. This is particularly the case when it comes to the attempt to represent subjectivity. Paul du Gay (1996, 73) explains this in Lacanian language: "The 'Real,'" he says, "always escapes attempts to govern it because there is always a 'surplus' separating the 'Real' from its symbolization" (see for a critical discussion also Jones/Spicer 2005). Nevertheless, these technologies have real effects. This again is illustrated by the example of DNLA.

Leistungsvergleich:
Mitarbeiter<>Mitarbeiter

Figure 6.2 Comparison of Employee Performance (Source: Company Brochure)

Heini and Klaus, the two model-employees in figure two above, are constructed as objects, using criteria of modern psychology and the Harvard leadership model. Obviously, the dimensions of *Leistungsdynamik* (performance dynamics), *Interpersonelles Umfeld* (interpersonal surrounding), *Erfolgswille* (will to success) and *Belastbarkeit* (resilience) are considered as relevant and selected from the universe of possible criteria. Heini and Klaus only come into existence after the procedure has been applied to the concrete persons. They are made comparable, classifiable and manageable. Heini and Klaus are of course *fictions*. Obviously, they are not real persons but rather inventions. Nevertheless, these fictions are also real in their effects; "Visibil-

---

rated according to the places of their residence? [...] [Would it not be] a useful and necessary pleasure for him to be able, in his own office, to review in an hour's time the present and past condition of a great realm of which he is the head, and be able himself to know with certitute in what consists his grandeur, his wealth, and his strengths?" (Marquis de Vauban, proposing an annual census to Louis XIV in 1686, quoted in Scott [1999], 11).

ity is the trap" (Foucault 1977, 200). This becomes obvious when we look at the effects, which are associated with the procedure. Comparison and differentiation creates rankings and orders individuals along a norm, and introduces them into a double system of gratification-punishment.

In *Discipline and Punish* Foucault describes the various procedures of "disciplinary power". This is a form of power which orders, classifies, categorizes, measures, and judges. At the very heart of these procedures is the "examination." This "tiny operational schema that has become so widespread" (Foucault 1977, 185) manifests the "subjection of those who are perceived as objects and the objectification of those who are subjected" (ibid., 184–5). All objectifying sciences—and also those "modes of enquiry which try to give themselves the status of sciences" (Foucault 1983, 208)—took the examination as their model, which is basically a model of testing material:

- The "object" is observed form a distance;
- from the background of a specific grid, which organizes perception;
- according to the categories of perception, the object is created;
- the complex human subject is turned into a "case;"
- it is made comparable and calculable;
- it is subjected and integrated into a "power of writing" (Foucault 1977, 189).
-

The individual is "fixed" and inscribed into documents and files. Objectification allows collecting and storing "information." This is, of course, not a neutral process; rather, it brings the unformed into form. It brings it in a form that allows the real to be handled and managed (Cooper 1990).

Information systems thereby, have reality producing and reality forming effects. They demand that the "real" be formed according to the image inscribed in the grammar of the systems (Kallinikos 1996, Zuboff 1988). They also demand that the real be ordered and trimmed in a way that allows it to be proceeded via information technology, and to be coupled to an "apparatus of writing" (Foucault 1977, 190). From the point of view of governing this offers a series of possibilities and gains in efficiency. (In)formations can be worked with as soon as they are collected. They can be correlated, connected, and aggregated. They can easily be transported and moved to "centres that calculate" (Latour 1987). In work organizations, for example, both the "qualitative" and "quantitative" method can capture and manipulate the "stock of personnel". "Human resource pools" can be created and so forth. There are hardly any limits to fantasy and imagination. Even moral and ethical considerations, emerging in the face of concrete persons, can be made volatile. Decisions can be made at a safe distance. All this, and much, more is possible on the basis of this little technology and its "an- anesthetizing" effect (see Carter/Jackson 2000). As soon as "human resource pools" are created and related to modern technologies, there is the tendency to shift from examining individuals to checking files.

Objectification is only one side of the process. *Subjectification*, the process by which individuals are made subjects in the sense of being "subject to someone else by control and dependence" or of being "tied to his own identity by a conscience or self-knowledge" (Foucault 1983, 212) is the other.

How, then is it that Heini and Klaus come to constitute themselves as subjects? How is it, that they come to *see* themselves as a *Gutermann* (good man) or *Schlechtermann* (bad man)?

First, this happens when "real" persons start to define themselves in categories provided by discourse and to conduct themselves accordingly. To put it another way, they reflect and observe themselves in pregiven categories. The individual, who observes herself, also objectifies herself. She turns the means of power against herself and disciplines herself. The individual forms herself according to the normative images and historically specific imaginary ideals (*ideal speculatif*) (see Butler 1997, 90) [59]. '

The production of the governable person relies, however, on a variety of mechanisms and technologies of power, that go beyond the disciplinary procedures of categorizing, classifying, etc. "Pastoral power" is a form of power that cannot be exercised "without knowing the inside of people's minds, without exploring their souls, without making them reveal their innermost secrets. It implies a knowledge of the conscience and an ability to direct it" (Foucault 1983, 214). The roots of this form of power lie in early Christianity, which served to "govern"

---

[59] "He who is subjected to a field of visibility, and who knows it, assumes responsibility for the constraints of power; he makes them play spontaneously upon himself; he inscribes in himself the power relation in which he simultaneously plays both roles, he becomes the principle of his own subjection." (Foucault 1977, 260)

individuals and their conduct with respect to salvation in the next world.[60]

This form of power is mainly exercised through the technologies of confession and avowal. Even if the roots of this form of power can be found in the realm of the church, the technologies have been increasingly secularized. "The truthful confession was inscribed at the heart of the procedures of individualization by power" (ibid., 58–9). The confessional has been built into a series of worldly and institutional contexts. "One confesses in public and in private, to one's parents, one's educators, one's doctor, to those one loves; one admits to oneself, in pleasure and in pain, things it would be impossible to tell to anyone else." (ibid., 59) One first, perhaps, confessed one's sins at confessional, then on the psychoanalyst's couch. Humanistic psychology has integrated the technology of confession into various technologies of interviewing, that where designed to reveal the truth about the inside of the individual: her wishes, desires, needs, and anxieties. Like all other technologies, confession has also been integrated into the practice of modern management (see also Townley 1994, 1998).

For example, self-assessment questionnaires are designed to help the would-be manager/entrepreneur to judge and evaluate her suitability for a career or her potential to become a successful manager/entrepreneur. Self-reflection on pregiven categories promises to help the individual, and in a certain sense, it really does. At the same time, however, the questionnaire is also a subtle technology through which one is subjected to the categories that are inscribed in the forms organization. Like the examination, the confession is "judgemental" (Townley 1998). It is a technology that attaches the subject to an identity, and ties him or her to it through conscience or self-knowledge. "Confession, then, is the diagram of a certain form of subjectification that binds us to others at the very moment we affirm our identity" (Rose 1990, 240).

What characterizes the confessional discourse, and what makes it a productive technology of power, are the effects it produces.[61] This

---

[60] It is important in this context to see the historical dimension. Pastoral power is associated with the figure of the shepherd. This figure for example is distinguished for example from those concepts of government that are associated with the figure of the captain who directs a ship. The shepherd governs a herd. Pastoral power, is in principle "beneficent" and is acted upon a "moving multiplicity" (see Foucault 2004a, 173-200).

[61] "What secrecy it presupposes is not owing to the high prices of what it has to say and the small number of those who are worthy of its benefits, but to its obscure familiarity and its general baseness. Its veracity is not guaranteed by the lofty au-

does not only mean that one who confesses, or is forced to confess, reveals secrets and truths that allow the other to manipulate and influence them. This is, of course, an important aspect of the production of *governability*, as the long history of the systematic picking out employees' brains demonstrates. This extends from the "listening posts" of the Human Relations to modern forms of attitude surveys, interviews and mentoring programs (see Townley 1994, 1998) that are designed to find out "what the employee thinks" (Houser 1927) in order to govern enterprises in an "employee-oriented" way. The manipulative potential of these forms of questioning has often been criticized (e.g. Adorno 1979). The effects of power, associated with the confessional discourse, are, however, deeper and more subtle. It takes effect, "not in the one who receives it, but in the one from whom it is wrestled" (Foucault 1981, 62). As with any discourse, the confessional discourse is performative. Whoever confesses does much more than give a message or information about herself, or reveal a possibly "hidden truth." The confessing subject constitutes herself as inferior and deficient, measured against pregiven criteria. The confessional discourse not only transforms and constitutes the relation to oneself but also the relation to others.[62] One always confesses in the presence of another, even though this other might be physically absent, and is integrated into an asymmetrical relational arrangement. "The agency of domination does not reside in the one who speaks (for it is he who is constrained), but in the one who listens and says nothing; not in the one who knows and answers, but in the one who questions and is not supposed to know" (Foucault 1981, 62).

The difference between the constructed ideal and the (inferior) real not only constitutes the power of experts but also creates the possibility of "governing the soul," which "depends upon our *recognition* of ourselves as ideally and potentially certain sorts of person, the *unease* generated by the normative judgement of what we are and could become, and the *incitement* offered to overcome this discrepancy by fol-

---

thority of the magistery, nor by the tradition it transmits, but by the bond, the basic intimacy in discourse, between the one who speaks and what he speaks about." (Foucault 1983, 80)

[62] "Through self-inspection, self-problematization, self-monitoring, and confession, we evaluate ourselves according to the criteria provided for us by others. Through self-reformation, therapy, techniques of body alteration, and the calculated reshaping of speech and emotion, we adjust ourselves by means of the techniques propounded by experts of the soul" (Rose 1990, 11).

lowing the advice of experts in the management of the self" (Rose 1990, 11, emphasis added).

Even desire, which one is inclined to think of as the innermost and private *kern* (kernel); as "authentic" expression of human personality; as purely private or "subjective" region, is given a specific direction. It is attached to objects that are discursively constructed as desirable. We do not desire what we wish in our innermost regions, but rather those things that "machines to showing you desire" (Barthes 1978) present as desirable and valuable.[63] Also, we do not suffer from natural lack. Lack, rather, has to be produced. The human being who feels lack of plenitude, who experiences lack as a condition of her own desire, and who masters the art of failing, is perhaps the epitome of the governable person (Vogl 2002, 345). She is not purely rational and free of desires, longings, and passions, and has not substituted passions for interests (Hirschman 1997). *Wer immer strebend sich bemüht, den können wir besteuern* (Whoever strivingly endeavours, can be taxed by us) could be said in a slight modulation of Goethe's saying (quoted in Vogl 2002, 346).The one who endeavors in that way cannot only be taxed but can also be governed. Insatiable desires and passions are exactly what make him calculable, useful, useable ("employable"), and governable.[64]

"Become Enterprising!: The Enterprising Self as a Historically Singular Mode of Experience

The logic of the production of the "governable person" (Miller/O'Leary 1987), just as the arts and technologies of government, changes historically. Disciplinary regimes, which Foucault

---

[63] However, desire moves "rhizomatically." It, therefore, can never be fully "captured" and poses limits to government (see Deleuze 1995, Deleuze/Guattari 2000). See also Brewis/Linstead (2001) for a review of theories and concepts of desire. Fenwick (2002, 705 quoting Forrester 1999, 194-5), for example, has shown in a study of self-employed women entrepreneurs that "new energies of desire and work seem to emerge that resist "the master discourse: economic competition and employee performance and productivity within a neo-liberal framework."

[64] As Hirschman has shown in his historical study, leading philosophers of the eighteenth century welcomed capitalism amongst others, for the reason that it would be able to tame the wild, dangerous, incalculable and unpredictable passions, and transform them into material interests that were seen as innocent. "In this way everything was well: an activity such as the rationally conducted acquisition of wealth could be categorized and implicitly endorsed as calm passion that would at the same time be strong and able to triumph over a variety of turbulent (yet weak) passions" (Hirschman 1977, 66).

(1977) analyzed in *Discipline and Punish*, reached their heyday at the beginning of the twentieth century. In these regimes, the problem was to construct the individual as part of a machine and to adapt the individual to more or less stable "moulds" (Deleuze 1995, 178). Taylorist forms are almost paradigmatic of this style of organizing work. Distributing individuals in space, detailed regulation of movements, and processes and prescriptions (in the sense of "one best way") and the construction of (visibility in the sense of "scientific selection of workman") are central principles. Typically, the factory was characterized by a strict regulation of time, which ensured the continuity of production. The factory as a spacio-temporal concentration of production typically was constructed after the model of a technical machine. The individual is supposed to function in a predictable and calculable way, whereby the principles of functioning are modelled according to the imperatives of a technical algorithm. In a sense, it can be argued that "scientific management" was an application of disciplinary power "to greater organizational depths" (Townley 1998, 195).

In the contemporary regime, which Gilles Deleuze (1995) has described as the "society of control" the conditions of production are fundamentally changing. Deleuze noticed a general "breakdown of all [the] sites of confinement" (Deleuze 1995, 178) that characterized the disciplinary regimes. Labor is increasingly organized outside of the confined spaces of the factory. It is more and more "spatially diffuse [*ortsdiffus*]" (Beck 1986, 225) and deterritorialized (eg., Bocklehurst 2001; Kallinikos 2003). At the same time, labor is itself re-imagined and discursively reconstituted as an enterprising activity.

The model of the factory is increasingly replaced by the model of "business" or "enterprise," which, as Deleuze remarked, has less the character of a solid body, but rather that of a gas, which intrudes through all rifts of the social texture. With the "generalization of the *form of enterprise* within the social body or texture" (Foucault 2004, 333, emphasis added)[65] in the course of the neo liberal reformation of society, the conditions of life and work are changing fundamentally. "The life of the individual is not to be integrated as an individual life in the frame of a big enterprise, which would be the company or the state in the end. Rather the life of the individual is to be integrated in a multiplicity of convoluted and entangled enterprises" (Foucault 2004, 333–4). This is the context in which a new social model of the working subject appears: the "entrepreneurial subject" (du Gay 1996), the "new

---

[65] Quotes from Foucault (2004) are my translations from the German edition.

employee" (Storey et al. 2005), or "entreployee" (Voß/Pongratz 2003). In contrast to classical economic discourse, the working subject is now portrayed less as a purely cognitive-rational individual who is mainly motivated by the cash-nexus. The (good) working subject is rather portrayed (and prescribed) as being enthusiastic, and even passionate. With this reconstitution however, the character of the entrepreneur changes. In classical economic theory [e.g., in Schumpeter] she was described as an "irrational destroyer of existing economic orders" (Jones/Spicer forthcoming) in contrast to the manager who was concerned with rationally calculating input/output ratios. Now she emerges as a version of the governable person. At the same time, the "workforce" is "enterprised up." Passion is no longer excluded form work organizations and banished to the private realm. It is, rather, mobilized, channeled, and prescribed (Krell/Weiskopf 2006). The discourse of enterprise does not reject (irrational) passion but rather stresses "what a wonderful force passion is" (Chang 2002, 215) and even sees passion as "the single, most important factor for realizing profit" (ibid., 245). It reconstitutes work as a passionate activity and relates it to an immediate bodily experience. In this sense, it constitutes a specific *economy of experience* which might be called a "restrictive economy of experience"[66] that limits and streamlines passion, and excludes the darker, and potentially transgressive, dimensions of human passion. "Passion heightens performance: Increased energy, focus, and creativity all contribute to one end: heightened performance. Passion drives improvements in both the quality and quantity of work performed" (ibid., 14).

---

[66] I use this term very loosely with Bataille's (1989) distinction of "restrictive" and "general economy" in mind. These categories are elaborated with respect to entrepreneurship in Jones/Spicer (2006).

Figure 6.3 The Model of the Future (Source: Own Photography)

This model is embodied in neo-liberal theories of "human capital" (Foucault 2004, 305) in which human labor turns from a passive factor of production, which has to be *exploited* according to economic calculus, into capital which is to be selectively invested. Theories of "human capital" provide a further basis for the unfolding of biopolitics and bio-power.[67] The state is interested in the population from the point of view of securing national competitiveness. All the conditions that may cause variations, health, longevity, birth, and mortality, are of interest from the point of view of securing national competitiveness and become the target of bio political interventions. According to Foucault, this has been an indispensable element in the development of capitalism (see Foucault 1990, 140–144), however, it took a new twist under the neo-liberal regime (Foucault 2004; see also Gordon 1991; Lazzerato 2004). Care for the "fitness" (Bauman 1995) of the population finds its correlation on the level of enterprise as well. It is the care for the quality of the "Human Resources" that leads to further analytical penetration of the workforce in order to realize the principle of adding value and to moving the spiral of productivity in the direction of hyper-productivity. The "human factor," which has been explored in classical economic theories with respect to "productivity" turns into a "strategic human resource" who's potentiality is to be optimized by linking individual interests and selfactualizing impulses to strategic goals. The laboring subject—the subject who labors—turns into a

---

[67] Foucault uses the term bio-power in order "to designate what brought life and its mechanisms into the realm of explicit calculations and made knowledge-power an agent of transformation of human life". (Foucault 1990, 143)

"competency machine" (Foucault 2004, 319) in whom resources are invested and from whom income must be produced.

The individual is called a flexible, adaptable, open, and selfresponsible subject who is able to continuously adapt to ever changing conditions. Subjectification here does not take the form of adaptation or "analogical" reproduction of stable moulds, but rather the form of a "permanent modulation" (Deleuze 1995), in which the individual has to be adaptable in the sense of a "flexible normalism" (Link 1998), and continuously has to work on herself. The contemporary "enterprising up" (Strathern 2000; du Gay 2004, 45), which aims at constituting this subject, is affected by a complex assemblage of technologies of power that "determine the conduct of individuals and submit them to certain ends or domination, an objectivizing of the subject" (Foucault 1988, 18) and "technologies of the self, which permit individuals to effect by their own means or with the help of others a certain number of operations on their own bodies and souls, thoughts, conduct and way of being, so as to transform themselves in order to attain a certain state of happiness, purity, wisdom, perfection, or immortality" (ibid.). "Government" is what Foucault calls the point of contact where these technologies are connected and interplay (Foucault 1993, 203).

The so called "360 degree feedback" is an example that illustrates this interplay and connection of technologies, in the sense of a "form of entrepreneurship considered *proper* managerial *governmentality*" (Hjorth et. al. 2003, 97). This standardized procedure of performance appraisal and evaluation, which has received considerable attention in HRM and organizational psychology, is also an example of what Paul du Gay (ibid.) calls "administratively imposed Enterprise." It has been developed mainly in big companies in cooperation with expert consultants, and is considered an appropriate technology that reassures responsibility, openness to the demands of customers makes this procedure distinctive compared to classical forms of appraisal as well as readiness of constant (self)improvement. These evaluations and appraisals come do not only from "top town," but rather from "all sides." The individual is subjected to a "multi-perspective supervision" (Bröckling 2003, 85). Proponents of the procedure usually see it as a superior medium that allows finding out the truth about the individual by removing and eliminating "blind spots." By making reference to the ideology, which suggests that four, or even forty, eyes see more truthfully than two (Adorno), the procedure is a very effective truth-machine. Since the procedure potentially includes all people, and makes anyone both an object and a subject of appraisal and "gives everyone more of a sense of participation" (Newman 1993, quoted in Townley 1995, 277), it is often seen as genuinely "democratic."

In this procedure:

- The individual is called to self-evaluation/assessment in terms of pregiven categories (self-objectification);
- Appraisals/assessments of others are collected—in principle at least—"from all sides" (multiple objectification);
- Usually, evaluations take a written form and are connected to information technology;
- Assessments of others are condensed to a profile, which serves as the basis for "feedback" and self-assessment;
- Feedback and appraisal are connected to the task of "permanent learning" which is constructed as the (self)responsibility of the individual.

The procedure subjects individuals to permanent control and observation. It keeps them in a continuous condition of readiness and suggests that one always has to be "open" to demands and expectations that are articulated from different sides. One has to be permanently aware of the possibility of being catched out red-handed. The process of subjectification thus seems to become more and more "proto-paranoide" (Zizek 2001, 356).[68]

The individual is evaluated and judged permanently. Via "feedback," one is constructed as a "permanent learner"; one is called to be permanently open and to be permanently ready to adapt to ever changing expectations. In the society of control, "one never finishes anything" says Deleuze (1995, 179). This means that the task of self-perfection and self-optimization, to which the individual is subjected, are incomplete and, above all, can not be completed at all.. The technology prepares, and opens, the individual for a continuous process of retraining. It produces the appropriate individual for the experience economy, where "Work is Theatre and Every Business a Stage" (Pine/Gilmore 1999). The "worker mannequin" (Baudrillard 1982, 35)[69] who has to present herself on the stage of performance advanta-

---

[68] Zizek (2001, 256) relates the "proto-paranoid mode of subjectification" to the storing of detailed information and personal data in the files of the "corporate cyberspace." This mode, he says "constitutes me as a subject, who is inherently related to data-information which is elusive; it is related to a file to which I have no access, but in which my destiny is written large."

[69] My translation from the German edition.

geously to the audience is a sort of model built in the technology. Effective self-presentation is more important than substantial skills. According to Baudrillard, at the "aesthetic stage of the political economy", "one no longer works, but celebrates an act of production." (ibid.) In this context he also talks about a "re-feudalisation of work." (ibid.) Work is transformed into a "total service", in which the "service provider" is more and more personally involved.

360 degree feedback also illustrates that the effectiveness of these technologies for governing does not simply rely on repressing and limiting the individual. The effectiveness of the "make-you-better feedback" (O'Reilly 1994, 94) relies, rather, on a subtle entanglement of positive incitements or promises, and open or latent threats. The promise of success and recognition is coupled with the threat, and ever present possibility, of losing status and recognition if the judgments and evaluations are "bad," or insufficient, in the next round. The "work on oneself" turns into a an experience of combined pain-pleasure, as the technicians and experts of evaluation well know:

> *What your boss, your peers, and your subordinates really think of you may sting, but facing the truth can also make you a better manager.* (O'Reilly 1994, 93)

In many respects it is plausible to see 360 degree feedback as almost paradigmatic for the production of the governable person in postdisciplinary regimes. It represents a sort of micro-laboratory, in which contemporary technologies of governing are systematically connected. Similar to Bentham's Panopticon, it is hardly ever realized in its ideal form. However, like the Panopticon it may be seen as "the diagram of a mechanism of power reduced to its ideal form" or "a figure of political technology that may and must be detached from any specific use" (Foucault 1977, 205). Seen as such, it represents a diagram of subjectification in the post-disciplinary regime. It, thus, represents a diagram of a specific mode of governing that constitutes the "enterprising self" as a:

> *historically singular mode of experience in which the subject is objectified for himself and for others through certain specific procedures of "government."* (Florence 1998, 463)

"Refusing Who We Are": Studying Entrepreneurship as Ethico-Aesthetic Practice

The various arts of government have invented—and are continuously reinventing—technologies and procedures that aim to make humans calculable, predictable, and governable, and to link individual aspirations and desires to the aims of government. This should not be understood, however, as a simple and linear story of "success." As Miller and Rose noticed (1998, 50), the mentality of government is fundamentally "optimistic." However, government is a "congenitally failing operation." This is exactly the reason why technologies of government are continuously reinvented. Just as the "entrepreneur" can never be finally "found" and "captured," the enterprising self can never be fully or finally constituted. Additionally, there is "a creative and transgressive impulse in enterprise, which somehow unfolds within and sustains itself alongside market discourses and global competition" (Fenwick 2002, 705).

The "arts of governing men" are accompanied by critique, which is the art "not to be governed like that, by that, in the name of those principles, with such and such and objective in mind and by means of such procedures, not like that, not for that, not by them" (Foucault 1997, 28). The *art of critique* as an "art of voluntary insubordination" does not consist of rejecting government all together, for example in the name of an "autonomous subjectivity" (or in the name of some authentic entrepreneurial passion). It affirms a *historically* given without accepting it as invariable, and experimentally searches for possibilities of transgressing historically specific limits. In other words, it is "a practical critique that takes the form of possible crossing over [*franchisement*]" (Foucault 1997c, 315).

From this point of view, we could understand *entrepreneurship* differently; in fact, as a critical—that is an *ethico-aesthetic*—practice that implies a "straying afield of oneself,"[70] a detaching oneself from what is given and defined as necessary, normal or natural *and* simultaneously a practice of creating and organizing relations to self and others differently. In this sense it is not an attempt to create organizations (as a substantive) but rather a *practice of organizing* (see also Rehn/Taalas 2004, 146). To put it another way we can say that entrepreneurship is

---

[70] *Égarement* is the French term which has been translated to English as "straying afield of oneself" (Foucault 1992, 8). According to the Robert Dictionary the primary meaning of *égarement* is "an action of getting a distance form what is defined as morality, reason, and the norm, and the state that ensues" (Rabinow 1997, xxxix).

an ethico-aesthetic practice that "result(s) in the creation of new styles (of living), that is, of new bases for everyday practices" (Hjorth 2004, 223; Hjorth, Johannisson, Steyaert 2003). As such, it is not restricted to profit making or even to economic activities in the narrower sense. It is also not restricted to any specific group of people; rather, we can say with Hjorth et al. (2003, 102, emphasis added) "ordinary people perform 'real' entrepreneurship in their creations and initiatives *as they pass beyond the habitual, the passive and the docile*, in which consumerism, work life, and education attempts to slot them."

The subject of entrepreneurship is a (historical) form rather than a timeless substance. It has both a history and a future, and is open to (trans)formation (see also Jones/Spicer forthcoming). The self is better understood "as a form-giving practice that operates with and upon heterogeneous parts and forms available at a given point in history" (Rabinow 1997, xxxviii). Reorienting studies of entrepreneurship, in this sense, implies that we follow Foucault, who writes that the "target nowadays is not to *discover* what we are, but to *refuse* what we are" (Foucault 1983, 216, emphasis added). This does not mean that we should take a self-denying attitude; rather, what we should refuse is the representation of entrepreneurship as the domain of the "enterprising self". We should refuse those technologies of managerial government that bind us to these predefined identities that, by way of administrative inquisitions, seek to define "who we are" or prescribe what we should become. What we should refuse are the forms of individuality and subjectivity that delimit the space of our possibilities. This refusal is—paradoxically—a "non-positive affirmation" (Foucault 1998, 74).

Critique, in the form of *problematization* and *eventalization* (événementialisation) aims (O'Leary 2002) to "refuse who we are" by creating a *distance* from established ways of seeing and doing things. This very distance is a necessary precondition that allows a variety of answers, and it assures that "to one single set of difficulties, several responses can be made" (Foucault 1997a, 118). Problematization is a "critical analysis in which one tries to see how different solutions to a problem have been constructed; but also how these different solutions result from a specific form of problematization" (ibid., 118–9). Eventalization, on the other hand, "means rediscovering the connections, encounters, supports, blockages, plays of forces, strategies and so on which at a given moment establish what subsequently counts as being self-evident, universal, and necessary" (Foucault 1991, 76).

Both problematization and eventualization are procedures of analysis that introduce *thought*. Thought, it is important to note, is not calculation. It is not limitation or restriction; rather, it is "freedom in relation to what one does, the motion by which one detaches oneself from it, establishes it as an object, and reflects on it as a problem" (Foucault 1997a, 117). Thought opens a crack in all we routinely accept as necessary or natural. Thought is a widening and a deepening of that crack and an increase in potential responses. It creates the in-between space of entrepreneurship; an "opening between what exists and what could become" (Hjorth et al. 2003, 91; see also Engelman/Steyaert 2002).

What, then, are the consequences of refusing the idea of an essential or timeless subject? Foucault spelled them out: "I think that there is only one practical consequence: we have to create ourselves as a work of art." (Foucault 1982, 237) The idea to *create* oneself as a "work of art" is fundamental to a Foucauldian ethics, which is at the same time aesthetic.

Ethics, in the Foucauldian sense, is not a system of rules and regulations, or a prescriptive apparatus that defines what is morally right or wrong. It is not restricted to moral codes, nor is ethics concerned with the foundation of what constitutes good or bad behavior; rather, ethics concerns self-relations and a specific attitude that one takes towards self and others. For Foucault, freedom is the "ontological condition of ethics" and ethics is "the considered form that freedom takes when it is informed by reflection" (Foucault 1997b, 284). Ethics, in this sense, is precisely a "practice of freedom."

At the same time ethics is "aesthetic" in a special sense. It is neither an objectivist aesthetics, in the sense of being a property of some object (and thus external to the individual subject), nor is it subjectivist, in the sense of referring to the emotional response experienced by an individual in relation to some (external) object; rather, it is *practical*. It focuses on *practices* of (self)formation and (self)creation. More specifically, it focuses on practices of "stylization," of *giving form* to one's life.

Foucault uses the term "*work* of art," sometimes in the sense of "oeuvre" and sometimes in the sense of "travail." In some ways, he seems to have been attracted to the idea of "beauty" (of existence) as oeuvre. With respect to the formation and organization of the self, a "*work* of art" is rather a continuous process (a "travail") that never comes to an end. The creation of the self is never a completed *work-in-progress* (see also Cooper 1976). This is not a linear process of a step-by-step advancement to some predefined goal or end. It rather includes being *errance*—to err; to wander; to stray from the norm, or from the predefined path—as a permanent possibility. It is also not self-realization or self-actualization in the humanistic sense. It is inventing and creating, rather than "discovering" new modes of relating to self and others. This creation, or dis/assembling, highlights the material and relational aspects of the process.

The subject of entrepreneurship is always a subject of *experience*. It does not simply exist. At any point in time, it can only be said to exist in the "embryonic form of its future becoming" (O'Leary 2002, 120). This experience is constituted in the space *between* historically specific discourses and practices of governing that delimit and circumscribe the field of possible action and the space of freedom, which lies always within and in-between them. The subject of experience is also the subject of the line of flight, which is a *becoming* rather than a being. As Ron Day explained:

> *the becoming agency of the subject along lines of flight is not due to the will of the subject, but rather to the transversal engagement of heterogeneously located bodies, assemblages and lines of production. Subjective agency is not an essential property of the subject, but appears at certain moments for the organism, empowering it to disengage form standard production machines and to re-engage and make active and real transversal trajectories running through various levels of production. Such flight engages and re-encodes productive bodies through their cuts and furrows which open them to the world of materials and which form their genealogical tracings form the past and into the future. Nomadic flight is precisely possible because of the historical graftings, limitations and openings of productive bodies to one another in a negative space.* (Day 1988, 102)

Managerial government is a practice of "structur(ing) the *possible* field of actions of others" (Foucault 1983, 221, emphasis added). It is, to put it in another way, an "art of the possible." Entrepreneurship, as a practice of critique, is related more to what Derrida (1998) has called the *Im-possible*.[71] Put another way, it is government as the art of the possible; a practice of territorialization that is accompanied, subverted, undermined, limited, transformed, and so on, by processes and practices of "deterritorialization" (Deleuze/Guattari 1990).

---

[71] The *Im-possible* is not an Utopia and does not refer to a transcendence. Rather it is of this world. "This im-possible is nothing negative, it is an affirmation. This affirmation allows us to resist the pseudoactions, the pseudodecisions and the pseudoresponsiblities in a critical way" (Derrida 1998, 49, my translation).

"The line of flight is a deterritorialization" (Deleuze/Parnet 1987, 36). It is a line of creation, a line of change, variation, and transformation. It is a line of experience (that comprises both experience in the (more or less) ordinary sense *and* experiment. It is a practice—an experience/experiment—of/in organizing differently. Entrepreneurship, as an art of organizing together, becomes a creative process in which the stylization of existence—*giving form to one's life*—is a generically collective process[72] of what Nietzsche called "inventing new possibilities of life" (Deleuze 1995, 118).

Entrepreneurship, understood in this way, is a work of organizing. It is the work of giving form to matter. As an ethico-aesthetic practice, entrepreneurial organizing is both formgiving ("artful making") and the creation of reflective distance to demands and precepts. Understood in that way, it is an embodiment of a philosophical ethos that is a "historico-practical test of the limits that we may go beyond, and thus a work carried out by ourselves as free beings" (Foucault 1984, 47). Entrepreneurship might then be seen as an experience of doing things differently, which cannot be restricted to a certain "extremely important group of people in the workforce" that are conventionally called "entrepreneurs." It is a line of flight to a more creative, artful, and ethical economy working against the enterprise economy's standardization and limiting of experience.

---

[72] It is interesting to note some parallels to Schumpeter's reflection of the "entrepreneurial function." He writes "the entrepreneurial function need not be embodied in a physical person, and in particular in a single physical person. Every social environment has its own ways of filling the entrepreneurial function…again the entrepreneurial function may be and often is filled co-operatively… Aptitudes that no single individual combines can thus be built into a corporate personality… In many cases, therefore, it is difficult or even impossible to name an individual that acts as 'the entrepreneur'" (Schumpeter 1991, 260-1, quoted in Hjorth/Johannisson/Steyaert 2003, 100).

PART IV

MASSEXPERIENCE

CHAPTER 7

ARTISANS OF THE SPECTACLE
ENTREPRENEURSHIP IN THE EVENT INDUSTRY[73]

MARJANA JOHANSSON AND
LOVISA NÄSLUND

These days [companies] invest in events – it's part of the market-
ing mix. And why do they organize events? It is the meeting: talk-
ing and experiencing something together, and doting on people
without other competing impressions.

According to Petter Andréasson, founder and CEO of Andréasson Public Relations and quoted above, corporate events are no novelty. He
has seen many a kickoff and launch in his day. What is different, however, is the increased packaging of and focusing on the event as a significant business activity. An aestheticized business discourse has
gained ground, bringing forward event organizing as a central feature.

In the following chapter we intend to study the event as it is staged
by the entrepreneur in the experience economy. Events are planned,
staged, and carried out in order to convey an intended message. In order to understand how the event is produced, we examine how it can
be understood through the concept of *theatricality*, and how techniques
from the theater are translated into the sphere of business to create a
spectacle. Theatricality denotes the conditions of production of theatrical performances. It uncovers how theatrical effects are achieved in the
theater, means which may also transcend to social life outside the
stage. In this chapter, we will analyze how the production process is
designed and executed in order to create a desired set of meanings.
Through the concept of theatricality, we can demonstrate how the en-

[73] The authors would like to thank Guje Sevón, Willmar Sauter, Thomas Lavelle,
and Karin Darin for comments on earlier drafts.

trepreneur seeks to gain from the techniques of theater when it comes to providing an experience, while trying to avoid the potential pitfalls of being perceived as inauthentic. We seek thereby to demystify the "magic" of the experience. Examples are drawn from two Swedish Public Relations/event companies.

A Theatrical Perspective on Organizations

To view social life—including that of organizations—through the lens of theater is a fairly extensively explored approach. Theatrical models or metaphors have been drawn upon—commonly in reference to Kenneth Burke and Erving Goffman—to study organizational action, lately with an increasing attention to theater as a technology used in organizations (see e.g., Schreyögg and Höpfl, 2004 for an overview). The increased interest in a theatrical approach may be linked to a general "aesthetic turn" in organization theory, emphasizing an aesthetic perspective on organizing and organizations (e.g., Ramírez, 1996; Strati, 1996; 1999; Linstead and Höpfl, 2000) and focusing on the cross-fertilization of art and business (e.g., Jacobson, 1996; Guillet de Monthoux, 1998; Guillet de Monthoux and Sjöstrand, 2003). Organizational action has been described in terms of theatrical performances (e.g., Mangham, 1990; Jeffcutt, 1996; Jeffcutt, Grafton Small, and Linstead, 1996; Höpfl, 2002), differing from the more common use of organizational performance to denote a strategic concept of operationalized success criteria. Although an attractive device, there are limits to applying a theatrical metaphor, both to an organizational context (Cornelissen, 2004) and to social phenomena in general (Carlson, 2002). To merely infuse organization studies with the language of theater is not fertile. Although we are borrowing from the conceptual realm of theater studies to further our understanding of event organizing, our purpose is not to view organizations as theaters.

The Stage is set for the Experience Economy...

In an experience economy, value is primarily attributed to experiences—ephemeral instances designed to produce an emotional engagement. In a world saturated with gadgets, offerings are differentiated by being given immaterial qualities that focus on the envisaged experience of the prospective consumer. George Ritzer points out that consumption not only concerns goods, but also extends to human relationships that are established for the consumption of services. Human interaction is commodified and "emotions and personal relations ... are carefully orchestrated" (Ritzer, in Baudrillard, 1970/1998:13).

Business offerings are to be planned and packaged so as to provide memorable experiences, which will enrich a product or a service by giving it a further emotional content (Jensen, 1999). Customers are enticed to consume by means of having "their movements ... choreographed, their moods managed and their senses triggered" (Löfgren, 2005:289). Places and spaces are created for the purpose of consumption. They constitutes, Ritzer's terms, fantastic cages, which are phantasmagoric yet restraining: "The new means of consumption offer the consumer fantastic, mythical images (signs) *and* they are objective structures that constrain the behaviour of consumers" (In Baudrillard, 1970/1998:17, original italics). The means of consumption grant the consumer the opportunity to experience things that had been hitherto, impossible, but they simultaneously require a consumerist compliancy. To further follow Ritzer (1999), the spaces of consumption are enchanted through the means of spectacle (cf. Debord, 1967/1995), either by creating extravaganzas à la Las Vegas, or—resonating with Baudrillard—by simulation.

It is easy to dismiss theatricalized offerings as feigned and set apart from real life. Baudrillard, however, argues that this is a false dichotomy. These simulations and performances constitute our reality; intertwining with, and shaping "real life" as we perceive it; shaping a form of neo-reality. A tempting neo reality it is, too, for it has become the immanent obsession of the modern society, which constantly craves an even more rapturous surface and a more moving experience. Theatricality could, therefore, be regarded as one of the mechanisms by which this neo reality is constructed, and is thus set to become an increasingly prominent aspect of organizational life. The postulation of the experience economy favors theatrical presentation over reality, sending to oblivion the pejorative connotations of theatricality, described by Jonas Barish as "a kind of ontological malaise, a condition inseparable from our beings, which we can no more discard than we can shed our skins" (1981:2). The theatrical—formerly negated and excessive—is now positively defined and included in an economy.

In accordance with a fascination for spectacle, the theatrical and the spectacular have been hailed as key value creating qualities of the experience economy. Guy Debord's much deplored "general gloss on the rationality of the system" (Debord, 1967/1995:16) has not lost its attractive power. Whether conceptualized as a gloss, an aura (Björkman, 2002), or a story (Jensen, 1999), consumption is, to follow Baudrillard further, "governed by a form of *magical thinking*" (1970/1998:31, original italics) by which offerings are consciously endowed with fantastic qualities.

One central quality is uniqueness. Baudrillard's consumer society is based on an accentuated role of differentiation. Agency and identity are established through consumption, as we are left to the means of consumption to seemingly stand out through our "individual choices and preferences". Identity construction, where the self is presented partly through consumption, is a central feature. Goods and services present a wide range of identities and displays of difference (Knights and Morgan, 1993). Indeed, the main role of consumption, Mary Douglas argues, is to signal our lifestyle and identity. What we own and experience becomes part of who we consider ourselves to be (Douglas, 1992), and it also shows others who we are.

...and the Entrepreneur Takes the Cue

As a result of the increased focus on identity and experiences, the smartly staged event now forms part of the successful company's market strategy, through which the company aims to convey a desirable image of itself to customers and others. Aptly staged, events provide a powerful way to reach customers—not only those that take part, but also others who will learn about it afterwards through media. However, if the event goes wrong, there will still be a result, albeit not a positive one, for now there will be added negative connotations to the brand name. The event, although potentially a good thing, also carries an inherent risk, and there is little room for trial and error. It must work perfectly the first time around.

Arguably, it is here that the entrepreneur enters the stage, like a Fowlesian magus of experiences, providing his or her expertise in making an event the sought-after success. According to Joseph Pine and James Gilmore, "companies stage an experience whenever they engage customers, connecting with them in a personal, memorable way" (1993:3, original italics). The event is presented as a central tool for connecting through engaging the senses. Memorability is paramount, as the value of the experience lies in what "lingers in the memory of any individual who was engaged by the event" (ibid, p. 12); thus, aesthetic and emotional engagement as well as memorability form the fundamental characteristics of the event.

Following Chris Steyaert and Daniel Hjorth, we characterize entrepreneurship as "the search for an elsewhere, for another moment to use" (2003:19). We share their view of the entrepreneur as one who is able to see opportunities and to grasp them, appropriating and creating spaces where they can be made to happen. "Entrepreneurship moves with an aim to depart from places exhausted by the normalizing routines of settled worlds" (ibid, p. 10), so the emerging event market provides fertile grounds for entrepreneurship. How, then, is the entrepreneur's enactment of the event to be understood? We argue that events are planned and staged with a dramaturgical approach similar to the one employed in theater productions, immersing the audience and inviting their interpretation. The entrepreneur introduces theatrical techniques into a business setting, and is thus able to offer the business customer a novelty.

Borrowing techniques from the realm of theater does not, however, come without complications, for that which is considered theatrical is often deemed inauthentic and exaggerated. It may be discarded on the grounds of "its tendency to excess and its emptiness, its surplus as well as its lack" (Postlewait and Davis, 2003:4). It is excessive yet empty, abundant yet lacking. In the contemporary economy, however, "where work is theater & every business a stage" (Pine and Gilmore, 1999), this tendency to excess is not necessarily a disadvantage, but, rather, a necessity if one is to accrue a profit. Jensen (1999) argues that in today's market it is precisely the added emotional content of a product that we are willing to pay for—the experience has become a critical asset. Indeed, one might argue, as do Orvar Löfgren and Robert Willim, that "[c]onstant talk of the shallowness or superficiality of the 1990s ... may blind us to the fact that much of what is dismissed as 'cultural icing'—like aesthetics, style and performance—reaches deeply into management and production processes" (Löfgren and Willim, 2005a:13). Aesthetically oriented practices are not to be dismissed as mere trompe l'oeils. To further follow Baudrillard, the event is not to be regarded as separate from reality but as constitutive of it. This aspect is appealing to us, and, therefore, has dire consequences for business logics. William Gartner, Nancy Carter, and Gerald Hills (2003) define entrepreneurship, not so much as discovering opportunities, as enacting them, regarding the entrepreneurial enterprise as something subjectively seen rather than an objective truth. The successful experience entrepreneur is the one who is, arguably, able to understand and develop the workings and mechanics of the experience.

The Workings of the Event

The magic[74] of the event, which makes it such a central feature of the experience economy, lies in its emotional and aesthetic potency. The event becomes a medium for creative cross-fertilization between the logos of business rationality and the pathos of playfulness. The notion of creating new and exciting crossovers is a major feature of the experience economy. What has transpired is a "culturalization" of the economy, to follow Orvar Löfgren and Robert Willim (2005a), or, inversely, a commodification of culture, to follow Ritzer (in Baudrillard, 1970/1998).

We would like to view this culturalization, as well as other crossovers, in the light of translation, regarding the translation of ideas into practices in a Latourian sense. When ideas or artefacts spread, is not simply a matter of diffusion, but a continuous transformation where "everyone shapes [the token] according to their different projects" (Latour, 1986:268). The thirtieth actor in the chain is as powerful and able to influence the token as the first. Furthermore, it is not a question of the movement of the token being slowed down by inertia and friction; rather, it moves continuously, changing form and content on its way, and is given new energy by everyone who takes it aboard and makes it their own. In this context, it is the matter of the aesthetic and the theatrical, which, translated by the entrepreneur into a business context, creates the event, and makes it something more than a corporate gathering. What, then, constitutes an event?

An event can be defined as a set of activities bounded by time and space (Handelman, 1990; Berg, Linde-Laursen, and Löfgren, 2002). Events are also said to be governed by "event-time" and "event-space," constituting an alternative realm to that of everyday life (Ristilammi, 2000). Events may be perceived as having varying degrees of ability permeate boundaries and seep into everyday reality. The event is, however, not limited to its actualization on the spot. Events are remembered and narrated afterwards, thereby having their boundaries extended and blurred.

The purpose of an event is to immerse the spectator, to make one lose reflective knowledge of participating in a staged occurrence by attentively focusing on the performance at hand (Crary, 1999; Ristilammi, 2000). The event is, to follow the popular event management literature, an aesthetically and emotionally engaging technique (Pine

---

[74] Magic, of course, is another notion that has surfaced during the past few years in a management context. See e.g., Berg (2003) and Löfgren and Willim (2005b).

and Gilmore, 1999; Bowdin, McDonnell, Allen, and O'Toole, 2002). The reverse characteristic of the event is its potential to obscure. That which is not bathing in the spotlight lies hidden in the darkened wings. The immersing quality of the event is simultaneously an enslaving one, directing our attention in the desired direction.

Events entail a plot so as to produce a holistic experience. A plot is generally characterized by sequentiality, which, argues Donald Handelman, "is often associated with goal-directed activity and so is informed with intention." (1990:12) An event is expected to "do" something; it has an intended, performative purpose. It is precisely this performative aspect that invites us to look into the logics of performance, and hence turn to the concept of theatricality.

Notions of Theatricality

Theatricality is often primarily thought of in semiotic terms, or how signs are employed. Erika Fischer-Lichte takes such a semiotic perspective, saying that "theatricality may be defined as a particular mode of using signs or as a particular kind of semiotic process in which particular signs (human beings and objects of their environment) are employed as signs of signs—by their producers, or their recipients" (1995:88). The semiotics of theatricality applied to a social context relates to "what makes [a performance] recognizable and meaningful within a certain set of references and codes" (Féral, 2002:5). The grounds and rules of such performances were the focus of Goffman's (1959) much quoted work on the presentation of self, and we would also like to point to Elizabeth Burns's (1972) notion of theatricality and conventions. Theatricality, Burns argues, operates according to a grammar based on historically and culturally contingent rhetorical and authenticating conventions. "Theatricality' in ordinary life consists in the resort to this special grammar of composed behaviour; it is when we suspect that behaviour is being composed according to this grammar of rhetorical and authenticating conventions that we regard it as theatrical" (Burns, 1972:33). Theatricality thus resides in the eye of the beholder. Josette Féral concurs, stating that '"theatricality is the result of an act of recognition on the part of the spectator" (2002:10). Joachim Fiebach (Fischer-Lichte, 1995) contests Burns's view by arguing that theatricality is not only a mode of perception, but also one of behavior and expression. Josette Féral refers to Fiebach's definition of theatricality as "first and foremost a process of production geared toward a spectator who consumes it, and once it has been consumed, it

161

disappears" (Féral, 2002:7). Theatricality in Fiebach's words is an interactive, ephemeral instance of expression and perception.

A second, equally fundamental, take on theatricality concerns time/space constructs as conditions of theatricality (Féral, 2002). According to Féral, theatricality arises as a result of cleavages being identified by the spectator. These cleavages allow the (theatrical) event to be perceived as separate from everyday reality, creating tension between reality and fiction, and existing in a space where the two counterexist and interplay, similar to the way event-time and space interrupt everyday routine. To further follow Féral, the first cleavage arises from the spectator's gaze, separating "the observed event or object away from its everyday surroundings" (2002:10). Thus isolated, the event or object is made into a representation—it is theatricalized. The second cleavage, or condition of theatricality, has to do with the tension between reality and fiction. While the presentation occurs in reality (actual people perform actions), it may simultaneously refer to a fiction (the actions and events are simulated representations). Theatricality is, thus, the result of cleavages "between everyday space and representational space, between reality and fiction" (Féral, 2002:11). There is tension and constant movement in between. At the heart of the debate about the status and implications of theatricality is a proposed (or rejected) irreconcilable duality between life and theater, authenticity and falsity, reality and simulacrum. Siding with Baudrillard in this matter, we regard theatricality as a process of constructing reality, rather than of representing it. The means by which theatricality is produced are also the means of event organizing.

The communicative aspect of theatricality—that something is performed for someone, who perceives the performance and interprets it—is something we want to stress. To conceptualize the interaction process, we wish to point to the notion of the theatrical event as defined by Willmar Sauter (2000; 2004), which signifies a "description of the interaction between performer and spectator, the nature and mutuality of this interaction and its relation to various contexts within the life of the theater and outside it" (Sauter, 2000:31). Experience is a key word when it comes to the theatrical event. What does the audience experience during a performance? To try to define a general experience is futile, as experiences are subjective. There are, however, some points of similitude in our experiences, one of which Peter Eversmann calls a "peak-experience," where the spectator is immersed in the performance and often "deeply moved on a personal and emotional level, which causes the performance to have such an impact that it is stored in memory for a long time" (2004:139).

To conceptualize the theatrical event, Sauter (2000) outlines three layers of interaction: the sensory, the artistic, and the symbolic. The sensory level refers to the audience's emotional and cognitive response to an actor who is physically present, being observed and evaluated. The artistic level concerns preconceived notions of style and genre, which, for example, tells us to expect singing in the opera and (mostly) talking in the theater—or a business-like performance by the CEO at an annual general meeting. Here, we may also draw parallels to Burns's authenticating conventions and Goffman's region behavior. The symbolic level refers to the actors' creation of fictional characters and a fictional plot, which is collaboratively created with the audience. It is through this mutual agreement that we experience Hamlet on stage, while still knowing it is an actor portraying a character. As members of an audience, we let ourselves be knowingly suspended from reality for the sake of an entertaining or thought-provoking experience. The fact that what is present on stage are real people portraying fictive characters does not interfere with our ability to be enthralled by the performance. The audience deals with the different layers simultaneously.

We have discerned three central elements as conditions for the production of theatricality, which form the basis for our exploration and understanding of the process of event organizing: sign, cleavage, and interaction. To reiterate, we wish to regard the organization not as if it were a theater, but rather to analyze the communicative, performative aspects of corporate events, achieved through the means of theatricality. As with a theatrical performance, the outcome of an event is always uncertain. The unmanageable, which rigorously dissected or possibly transformed into a recipe in event management handbooks, is both the potential and the peril of an event. Unmanageable does not, however, necessitate unknowable. We would argue that, armed with an understanding of theatricality, we are able to analyze the experience and demystify the label of "magic;" thereby, moving from understanding *that* aesthetics, style, and performance shape management and production processes, to *how* this is done.

In the following, we will present two cases of events employed in a business context. The companies in question are Andréasson Public Relations, one of the oldest PR-companies in Sweden, and Heart of Stockholm, a small, young event business that provides "a meeting platform" called So Stockholm. While Andréasson Public Relations offer a wide range of PR-functions, and different ways for a company to re-represent itself, So Stockholm's offer is somewhat different: Rather than a director who can stage an experience, which will alter others' perceptions of you, they provide a space, or arena, that allows you to present yourself. So Stockholm offers a space of self-realization through the consumption of human relationships (cf. Ritzer, in Baudrillard, 1970/1998:15). These cases present two different settings for event organizing. The first concerns a temporal, theatricalized presentation of the company in question, while the second concerns creating a lasting, enchanted space for felicitous crossovers between business and culture.

Andréasson Public Relations go Liljevalchs

In late November 2004 Andréasson Public Relations invited former employees, clients, family, and friends to a bash to celebrate the fifteenth anniversary of the company, as well as the fiftieth birthday of its founder, Petter Andréasson. It was to be held at Liljevalchs' art gallery, which was featuring an Andy Warhol exhibit. The invitation playfully, but perhaps purposefully, displayed the portraits of Andréasson and Warhol in juxtaposition, casually naming them Petter and Andy (see invitation). Guests were invited to drop in between 6 and 9 P.M. to have a glass of wine, sample the buffet, be entertained by a disk jockey, and view the exhibition. The authors of this chapter participated as invited guests.

Figure 7.1 Invitation from Andréasson Public Relations

Event Time and Space

The invitation establishes this instance as an event according to our general definition of an event as an occurrence occupying a given space at a given time. The setting is different from the company's everyday office space, office activities, and office time. We are told that the event is in celebration of the company and its founder; it marks a milestone. This is further enhanced by the choice of venue. Liljevalchs is located in an impressive and well-known building, situated on Djurgården, a recreational island in central Stockholm, inhabited by the well-to-do. Strictly speaking, it was not necessary to rent such a large facility for the occasion: We notice that most guests remained in the first hall and did not venture into the exhibition halls, even though guides were provided by the art gallery. The space might, thus, be regarded as displaying both the excess and (quite literally) the emptiness that Postlewait and Davis (2003) speak of. Not only was the venue too large, but the guests did not seem to take much interest in the art which is main attraction of Liljevalchs. The galleries remained empty for most of the evening.

However, this only holds true if we consider the art gallery as just a space for the display of art. One could argue that this is an example, instead, of the entrepreneur appropriating a space, transforming it from "the normalized routines of the settled worlds" (Steyaert and Hjorth, 2003:19), and creating something new. It becomes Andréasson Public Relations, but in a gallery loft instead of in their usual, somewhat crammed office settings. Participants are invited to act as translators in the Latourian sense, changing their understanding of what Andréasson Public Relations is: less strict business people and a little more like creative artists. Indeed, the company offer reaches beyond the actual event as it lingers in the memory of the participants (including current and potential clients), who may hope that Andréasson Public Relations can do for them what they did for themselves. The event thus potentially works its "magic" on both sides of the cleavage between reality and fiction: it immerses the participants, so as to change their perception of Andréasson Public Relations, and at the same time, it works as a showcase for the sort of re-representation that they can provide, in much the same manner as a theater production may be both an immersing experience and a showcase for the artistic craftsmanship of the company. This is an example of the neoreality the entrepreneur is able to create, which, in the case of Andréasson Public Relations the forms part of what they are and can do.

At the entrance of Liljevalchs, the company logo was prominently placed on an easel, which was appropriate for the venue. Warhol himself was, of course, no stranger to the advertising business, and, incidentally, he also constitutes an example of a "product" endowed with an aura (see Warhol, 1975). Warhol's presence was no coincidence, and the same venue would not have been selected had the exhibition been on eighteenth century French romanticism. There is symbolic importance in the fact that the chosen gallery featured Warhol rather than Watteau; furthermore, it is not difficult to relate the exhibition to ideas about Andréasson Public Relations. Since the exhibition was about Warhol's later work, which in this instance was celebrated as being on a par with anything else he did, there is a suggested connection with the host. In the PR and marketing industry, youth is the norm, but guests would assume that experience and vitality exist in a happy combination at Andréasson Public Relations. Another significant aspect of Andy Warhol's art is that he managed to please and interest the aficionados as well as the general public. A Warhol exhibition provides something for everyone, and neither connoisseur nor average Joe will feel bored. Furthermore, one of Warhol's hallmarks was his use of images from marketing, which he translated into the art domain. Warhol becomes a mirror image of Andréasson Public Relations, who, through this event, translate artistic artefacts into the business domain.

Both can, thus, be perceived as transgressors, enlarging the domains of art and business respectively.

Staging Andréasson Public Relations amongst of Warhol's art creates an experience open for interpretation. Andréasson's choice of Lil-jevalchs and its exhibition can be interpreted as using the objects of the environment as a sign of signs, much in accordance with Fisher-Lichte's semiotic definition of theatricality. Participating in the event entices the audience into a heightened semiotic sensitivity, similar to that of a theater audience who assumes that the setting has been chosen for a reason, and therefore seeks to interpret it. The works of art surrounding us become signs for notions like "experienced vitality" and "something for everyone" which, in turn, are signs for creative, yet, sensible campaigns appealing to a wide audience that Andréasson Public Relations seeks to provide. In this sense, the result of the event is theatrical, for, in order to realize its potential, it requires an act of recognition of the symbolism of the mis-en-scene on the part of the spectator (Féral, 2002). It is, however, not a limitless openness, and this is where theatrical craftsmanship comes into play. The experience should be a "carefully orchestrated experience," in Ritzer's words, not an open book for the spectator to interpret however they see fit. The skill lies in subtly directing the subjective experience, which entails knowing your audience and their probable frame of reference; purposefully choosing signs that give the participants the freedom of interpretation, while at the same time ensuring the intended experience. The audience should become aware that they are involved in a theatrical event, heightening their propensity to interpret, but not feel that they are being manipulated. In the following, we will delve further into how this Ritzerian cage is construed.

Audience and Performers

Before being allowed to enter into the main hall, we are ticked off of a guest list by the door, a procedure that establishes a sense of exclusivity. A photographer who is posted by the door takes our picture, creating another instance whereby we are being positioned as important guests. Having a photographer can be said to serve multiple purposes: Firstly, it creates the impression that this party has enough status and importance to be portrayed in the popular press. Secondly, it tells us that the guests will be so many, and so important, that it is only through careful documentation that the hosts will be able to grasp who was actually there. Thirdly, although mere doctoral students (in our case), we are as important and interesting as the famous people we see already mingling with the other guests. Although the purpose of the pictures was uncertain at the time, the connotations were more in terms of potential than peril. Certainly enough, the following week, photos from the occasion adorned the pages of *Resumé*, the leading magazine for the Swedish PR and advertising business. The photos, together with a feature about Andréasson Public Relations published in the same issue, also aided in securing the memorability of the event; thereby escaping the imminent disappearance that Fiebach argues threatens the theatrical after its consumption. Instead of vanishing, the event was translated from an action to an object, and through this act of transformation, its travels were facilitated (Czarniawska and Joerges, 1996). Thus, the event was able to reach people far beyond the number of guests originally attending.

In a sense, the guests, like the art discussed above, could be regarded as Fischer-Lichte's signs of signs. They are a sign that the company has a good reputation and a strong network, which in turn is a sign of the company's professional excellence and skills. This works on several levels simultaneously, depending on the participant, and what recognition and meaning they may ascribe to the other guests. The participants act as each others audience and performers (see Sevón, 2002), and depending on their set of references and codes, create different, but not necessarily unforeseen, meanings (cf. Féral, 2002). Outsiders, such as ourselves, could spot a few famous faces— an aging football star, a popular singer, and a prominent politician. Their attendance heightened the sense of the importance of the occasion, as well as tickling people's curiosity about celebrities. For the present or prospective employee, there were other faces to recognize— namely those of previous employees. These are many, since the company is one of the oldest in the business, and many have gone on to bigger and better things. Thus, to the current employees, seeing the former employees in attendance signified a double meaning: Firstly, that being at Andréasson Public Relations could be the beginning, or even the springboard to an illustrious career, and, secondly, that in a tough business where badmouthing is common practice, former employees feel positively enough inclined towards Petter and his company to attend this celebration. Finally, since the guests were a mixture of business acquaintances and personal friends of the protagonist, Petter, the participants also potentially provided a message to the customers: At Andréasson Public Relations, our clients and business contacts get the same treatment as our personal friends. No matter what relation you have, you will have the same importance to us.

Moving on at Liljevalchs, after having had our picture taken, we enter the main hall where a buffet and a bar were set up (at opposite ends to create maximum mingling). A DJ is playing music. Presents, elaborately decorated, lie on display on a table. People are helping themselves to the buffet and bar, or standing around in small groups talking to each other. About a week before the event, Andréasson Public Relations won a prize for best IT-company campaign. The prize is on display in the main hall. Of course, this mis-en-scene not only served to impress friends and potential clients: Being in the PR business, placing products and brand names in the right settings and with the right connotations is, of course, a primary service Andréasson Public Relations offers. Again, the theatrical craftsmanship became visible, with the current event as a showcase.

The desire to impress the guests (hence the photographer, the prize, and the venue) certainly seemed to be there. Altogether, the impression was one of style and success, both for the company, which were able to host such an elegant party, and for the guests, who are prominent enough to belong in such illustrious company. We are all important enough not to content ourselves with make-do parties, but instead to take part in this somewhat opulent scene. Indeed, the uninitiated may have deemed the setting as extravagant and superfluous, but for "us," being used to luxury, this was supposed to be a condition of everyday life. The correct behavior was obviously not to stand in gaping awe at Andréasson's displayed wealth, but rather to seemingly take it for granted, effortlessly gliding between guests. The occasion comes with a grammar, in Burns' (1972) sense, that the participants are expected to master, which calls for a composed behavior. However, this grammar, although helpful in ascertaining that no-one behaves out of order, also contains a potential peril. For if the grammar is too conspicuous, and the conventions too apparent, then the whole event is perceived as fake and theatrical. There may be a preconceived notion of style, which Sauter (2000) argues exists in the performing arts, but we do not want to become too aware of this preconception. If the participants deem the occasion as theatrical, perceiving it as inauthentic, excessive and contrived, then the enthrallment disappears. There is no wish for a *Verfremdungseffekt* (Brecht, 1939/1982), as this would enable the audience to take a step back and regard the proceedings at a certain distance, with a critical and rational eye. In that sense, the aim of the experience entrepreneur is the opposite of Brecht's—rather than distancing the audience, the event manager seeks to draw his audience even further into the experience, lulling their rational logos.

On the whole, however, the invited guests seemed to perform their parts well—most stayed in the front hall, had a glass of wine, and mingled in cocktail party fashion. They seemingly interpreted the Warhol exhibition as it was meant to be seen—as a decorative frame, but not as the purpose of the gathering. The celebrities among the guests added to the impression of being part of the "in" crowd, and that the circles where Andréasson Public Relations moves are the places to be. And it seemed to work: One of the authors was recognized by an acquaintance in the PR/event business, who was visibly impressed that we, too, were important enough to have been invited. Indeed, the set up invited the visitors to cast the others present into roles one thought appropriate: customers, employees, PR-people, media representatives. By identifying others present, one may position oneself accordingly.

The Protagonist

As was evident already from the invitation, the event had a named main character, Petter, cast in the part of successful entrepreneur and birthday boy. Yet, his appearance was notably inauspicious: casually, even a bit sloppily dressed in a rather ill-fitted brown corduroy suit, he did not assume any central position during the evening by collectively addressing the guests or claiming the limelight in any other way.

However, we would like to argue that more work went into the part than might be apparent at first glance. Petter started out as a journalist, and among his guests were a number of former journalist colleagues, who were dressed similarly. Thus, his clothing could be interpreted as signifying Petter's professional background, and that this was something still dear to his heart. Then there was the setting, and the juxtaposition with Andy Warhol on the invitation, which also bore personal connotations. Petter's parents are both established and successful artists, and growing up in Stockholm, he remembers going to the Museum of Modern Art and Liljevalchs as a child. Throughout his life, he has maintained an interest in modern art, visiting exhibitions when the opportunity arose. In fact, Petter saya, it was this genuine interest that enabled him to secure Liljevalchs as the setting for his birthday party, something both he and his employees take evident pride in. By celebrating his birthday together with Andy Warhol, so to speak, he highlighted his artistic side and his background, and, by extension, his company.

Thus, it could be argued that Petter played his part quite well: the role of a serious, experienced journalist with an artsy side, now having successfully turned to the PR business. This is no self-centered diva, but rather a humble man, comfortable in letting others into the spotlight, and allowing them (both employees and customers) to influence the proceedings. In so doing, he appeals, in Sauter's (2000) terms, the sensory and artistic levels of the interaction between performers and audience. However, we would argue that the symbolic level could not be reached, lest he be perceived as inauthentic. If we are to be suspended from reality as we understand it, we must never become aware of it. We can accept neo-reality, but not a fake. The protagonist has to become his performance, so to speak. We can accept that the actor portraying Hamlet is not really a skilled fencer, but when we hire an entrepreneur, we want him to really possess all the skills that he appears to have. In that sense, the portrayal may be a risky one, for if the participants are given the impression of the presence of Féral's second cleavage, the one between representation and perceived reality, then the whole process will fail; instead of the sympathetic image sketched above, Petter would then be perceived as a hypocrite, displaying a false image.

Plot

As the invitation stated, the event was organized in order to mark a "65th anniversary" with the combined age of the founder and his company. Anniversaries relate to identity construction: this is who we are, where we come from, and where we are heading. An anniversary is not merely a consequence of a certain number of years being completed; it is simultaneously part of constructing an ongoing story. The overall plot was that of the company and the founder having reached a certain age and a certain amount of success. The event-specific plot was to be found in the sequential design of it. Since the event in question was a drop-in occasion, there was no collective beginning or end (unless one counts the resolute closing of the bar when the set time was coming to an end). Neither was there an explicitly ordered design or story in between. The activities consisted of "free mingling" and an optional tour of the exhibition at one's convenience. Granted, the plot might seem somewhat lackluster. Apart from mingling, wine being drunk, and snacks being eaten, not much happened during the evening. However, as with the protagonist's performance, there may be more to it than first meets the eye.

The optional gallery tour proved to be of some interest—rather than being shown around by a guide, the guides stayed in their appointed rooms of the gallery, and guided anyone who came into that room. Thus, it was the audience's wishes rather than the guide's that designed the tour. Again, there was the hope that the guests would translate this into a business context: If I hire Andréasson Public Relations, then it is my wishes that decide where we are going, and it is me, rather than Petter, who will be put in the center.

Furthermore, it could be argued that the mis-en-scene in itself provides a plot, not complicated, but yet effective: the visitor enters and is shown what a high-class and impressive setting Andréasson Public Relations can offer. Indeed, there have already been telltale results of this capacity: the elaborate gifts, and not least the price for best PR-company. The prize is displayed at the opposite end of the room from the door, so as to make sure that the visitors will have taken in the setting before the results can be shown. And, as is implicitly pointed out, you too can be part of this, hence the invitation to future and present customers, who can thus be reassured in their choice or egged on to make one.

Having come this far in our analysis, the event might seem overtly choreographed and planned, with every detail serving a purpose and designed to elicit a certain response from the audience. However, in this, Petter is not dissimilar from a stage designer or director, who will put similar amounts of work into setting, actors and plot. If the subjective experience of the audience cannot be completely controlled, every care should at least have been taken so as to orchestrate it to the intended effect. Therein lies the craftsmanship of the event entrepreneur, and it is this skill that attracts his clients.

Furthermore, one could argue that there was a certain type of directed behavior to be achieved from a select audience: to "mingle" is an organized activity, which should be done according to certain rules. Again, it must not seem too contrived—the impression was supposed be of a collection of friends, not an impersonal, professional occasion. Again, there was the risk of the veil falling, and being openly perceived as theatrical in the negative sense. The trick, it would seem, is to employ theatrical logic to create an immersive atmosphere while not letting it be apparent, lest the whole event be perceived as inauthentic and excessive. In order for the experience to enthrall, the excess and opulence must seem necessary and natural.

While the birthday bash at Liljevalchs has given us an opportunity to study how theatricality is used to create a temporary experience, our second case is aimed towards longevity. The creation here is the space itself, which is given meaning through a series of events and experiences. How is the inherent imminence of the theatrical experience overcome?

So Stockholm – Meeting, Mixing, Mingling

The park *Kungsträdgården* (The King's Garden) in central Stockholm has been a place for meeting, strolling, and being entertained since its opening to the public in the late eighteenth century. There are restaurants and cafés, outdoor performances in the summer, and an ice skating rink in the winter. In the midst of it resides a low building with glass walls that open to the park. A small, rather inconspicuous sign by the entrance says So Stockholm. In late 2004, this former art gallery became "a platform for meetings" and the event space for a company called Heart of Stockholm. Heart of Stockholm was founded in 1998 by Maria, an entrepreneur with a background in media and PR:

And so I thought that [what I am starting is] a company around something that is about, well, warmth and love…! And then you have Stockholm and so I thought about Heart of Stockholm, because it could be anything, there is no mentioning of the word event in the name. It can be anything, it can be a magazine or something else and so we did all kinds of things.

Maria wanted to steer clear of mass communication, where you do not know who receives your message, but to focus instead on personal relationships. She took over the art gallery space together with a business partner, renaming it So Stockholm. The idea to take over the gallery arose from a perceived need for a space for "physical meetings" to facilitate the creation of business relationships. In a sense, she is the epitome of entrepreneurship, in that she has literally grasped and created a space where her ideas can be made to happen. Her business is a perennial search for the next "moment to use" (Steyaert and Hjorth, 2003:19). So Stockholm bears the same eclectic mysticism of "being anything" as Heart of Stockholm (see quote above). The visitor to the So Stockholm website[75] will find that "So Stockholm can be a party or a t-shirt, a livingroom (sic) or a ride to a different place." In other words, it seems So Stockholm can be what you want it to be.

What is needed in Stockholm, according to Maria, are more cross-cultural arenas that bring together different culture-related activities such as music, design, and fashion, and connect them to the business sphere:

---

[75] (http://www.sostockholm.com/about.htm).

> *There has to be depth as well as business opportunities, that is what I find interesting and that is also interesting for [So Stockholm]. You have culture, and at the same time the culture is the basis of doing business.*

For Maria, depth is represented by the cultural component, contrary to the accusations of the culture embellishment concerning the experience economy. So Stockholm, then, is to function as a space and showcase for this cross-fertilization. Maria also has a wider reaching vision concerning So Stockholm. It is to contribute to the identity of the city:

> *This can be part of us contributing to the creation of a new San Francisco or Barcelona, [places] that have creative talent and where creative people want to be. That demands places where people can meet and mingle across boundaries.*

Thus, the aura of the city is to be changed, with So Stockholm contributing to the city's identity, shaping the perceptions of the city for both inhabitants and outsiders. Maria acts as the translator, with culture and creativity—two well-known concepts of the experience economy discourse—as her guiding stars, and mixing and mingling as her tools. Drawing on these concepts, Maria is an entrepreneurial example of the aforementioned trend towards a culturalization of the economy (Löfgren and Willim, 2005).

The business logic of Heart of Stockholm is formulated as social capital transformed into structural capital; the transformation takes place by providing people with the means to meet so that relations that lead to business (structures) are formed. The event is to function as the transforming mechanism. It can be employed to bypass existing, traditional channels and structures. As an example, she mentions young artists and designers who can access the market by being introduced in the right contexts—in meetings. There is a need to "build bridges" and to get "politicians to talk to people in the culture sector, who then talk to business people." Her reasoning could be seen as an example of trying to show how an experience may be the solution to a rational business problem. The potential emptiness of a series of meetings in an empty gallery is presented as a necessity, not at all excessive, but a vital part of the management and production processes. Like all business ideas, the idea of the meeting can be refined and theatricalized to varying degrees. One of the events So Stockholm has offered is the power mingle, which served to maximize mingling potential. Each participant was to supply information beforehand regarding their line of work, what they were looking for, and what they could provide. The information was printed onto name tags. By reading each others' tags, participants could scan quickly for a match between supply and demand. However, by making the logic and purpose of the occasion so obvious, you also risk undermining the spontaneity of the event. The participants find themselves transformed into literal signposts, taking away any illusion of a friendly gathering. Possibly, the director has become too diligent in her orchestrations. As Sauter (2000) points out, theatrical experiences are the fruit of an interaction—thus, there must be some perceived freedom of interpretation for the participants.

Overcoming Transience

While the means of theatricality help us stir the emotions and experiences that we seek, the enthrallment has the inherent downside of transience. Once the event ends, there is the risk that it will leave no traces, the participants reverting to their old selves. Continuity counteracts this risk and can be created by organizing a string of events (Ristilammi, 2000), where each event serves as a reminder and a restaging. For example, following "The World's First Trend Gala" in late October 2004, coorganized by Heart of Stockholm for a trend monitoring company, a Trend Bar was held at So Stockholm in February of the following year. As in the original event, the overarching idea was trend monitoring, and the event thus became a theatricalized way of presenting a participating media monitoring company. There were drinks, snacks, and music. Film clips from the gala were shown on a large screen on one of the walls. The winning Trend Agent from the gala was present, sharing her experiences with the audience of some one hundred people, a mix of the media monitoring company's and Maria's network', that crowded into the fairly limited space of So Stockholm. The other trend-related presentation of the evening was about the power of blogs. In similar fashion to the gala and to all other events at So Stockholm, it ended with mingling. The Trend Bar served as a reminder of the Gala, while also contributing to the narration of the trend monitoring company in question.

Another event of cross-fertilization was organized together with the University College of Arts, Crafts and Design, when an exhibition of student art work was held at So Stockholm. The space was momentarily transformed into its previous incarnation as a gallery. On Maria's part, the presence of the College signalled a participation and interest in the arts, on the College's part, it provided an exhibition space in the city center, which it lacks since relocating to the outskirts of Stockholm. The cross-fertilization sought for, and which Maria talks about as one of the main aims of her company, could also be described as acts of translation. Or rather, invitations to translation; the presupposition being that if ideas are translated from one realm into another, from art to business, then they would take on new and interesting forms. In that respect, it is the enabling of translation that is Maria's business idea. Taken together, these seemingly disparate events are joined by their repeated conformation of So Stockholm as an event-space in the city center, intended as part of the city's identity creation.

The events at So Stockholm work according to a certain dramaturgy. It could be called the dramaturgy of improvisation—which is no easy matter to master. There is a certain confidence in the idea that once the components are brought together, something felicitous will happen. So Stockholm provides the space—which, to follow Pine and Gilmore, needs to be transformed into a distinctive place (1999:42) in order to gain significance. The events linger on beyond their actualization through memory and narration, and Maria's effort is to turn ephemeral events, or meetings, into tangible business structures. As the meeting is the business, if the meeting does not lead into something else, the business is to no avail. If So Stockholm is a plain space rather than a distinctive place—in a symbolic sense, not just physical—then it is not working to its full potential. Furthermore, this symbolic value is to be reached through a string of events, each leaving behind a memory, which will add to the symbolic charge of the space. If successful, So Stockholm will be a place where "reality is exceeded by its representation" (Postlewait and Davis, 2003:6). Returning again to Féral (2002), So Stockholm would then be made into a representation of what is new and happening in Stockholm. It would invite such an interpretation by the residents of Stockholm, who would then eagerly want to enter the space, becoming performers by presenting themselves in this arena.

Performances, in the theater as well as in a social context, succeed or fail depending on the degree of perceived authenticity. This authenticity is constructed according to certain expectations and conventions, corresponding to the context. It is of crucial importance that the perception of authenticity is upheld if the theatrical elements are to work to their advantage, immersing the audience. The entrepreneur's orchestrations must be effective, yet subtle, lest the audience leave with the bitter aftertaste of having been manipulated. Thus, the theatrical machinery must function without a hitch, for, otherwise, the participants will become aware of its creaking, and conclude that they are at the theater, and not in the real world. The cleavage between reality and fiction must not become apparent. In the case of So Stockholm, the everyday space of the old art gallery must cease to exist in favor of the representational So Stockholm. However, the old, worn-in reality is a fickle opponent to keep at bay. During the events described, such mundane occurrences as a malfunctioning microphone, an inexperienced speaker, or a dirty floor made the process difficult, thereby jeopardizing the credibility of the representation. If the symbolic charge of So Stockholm diminishes then the whole concept runs the risk of being perceived as inauthentic, and Maria's visions of cross-fertilization dissolve into thin air, forgotten as soon as you step out into the park.

Concluding Remarks: Orchestrating Experiences

Events such as those described in this chapter are neither uncommon nor especially spectacular; however, their ordinariness does not lessen their power as illuminating examples. We do not necessarily have to examine lavish mega events to reflect upon the workings of the event and the entrepreneurial practices that enable the intended experience. To experience is to become emotionally engaged and consequently to feel a desire—to act, or to consume—and creating engaging experiences is, thus, seen as a value adding activity in the experience economy. By sheer economic size, experience design has become a non-negligible business. The proposed immersing, emotionally engaging quality of the experience, we argue, can be achieved by imbuing the event with theatricality, heightening the spectators' semiotic sensitivity, and inviting them to certain interpretations. Thereby, the entrepreneur can appropriate and transform settled perceptions of identity through the immersing qualities of theatrical magic.

Theatricality, we argue, may be attributed to rather trivial incidents—the key factor being how the participants—performers and audience—construe the event they experience. The theatrical setting, making the participants aware that they are entering event time and space separate from everyday reality, entices interpretation. By employing people and objects as signs of signs in this setting, transforming them into simulacra, the director of the event can imbue the event with meaning. The experience should be carefully orchestrated, thereby steering the participants' experience towards the intended effect. However, the aspect of interaction is vital – the audience must be given the perceived freedom to interpret the signs, lest they feel manipulated, but ideally, this subjective interpretation should follow the designated paths of perception. As in the theater, it is in the moment of the encounter between performance and audience that the experience is created, hence the immediacy and transience of it. And therein lies the rub – for the event is expected to *do* something, and this transition into action can only happen if the event overleaps its inherent immediacy and becomes memorable. The meaning created by the event must linger after the event itself has ceased to be, transforming the participants' notion of the organization presented. As we have seen in the case of So Stockholm, the concept of the event allows for refinement; providing not the transformation itself, but a space in which the participants are invited and elicited to translate, with a minimum of direction. Here, the service on offer is not the event itself, but an event-space, rich with positive connotations.

The notion of theatricality further brings us to consider authenticity—a key concept of the experience economy. Experience entrepreneurs claim to provide authentic experiences, which is paradoxical in an economy where performance (in a theatrical sense) is the paradigm. However, the authentic experience can rarely be achieved without careful direction and choreography. Authenticity, we argue, is not a given condition, but constructed through interplay, as is theatricality. It is based on certain conventions and behavioral patterns, as interpreted by the onlooker. What is "actually" fake or genuine, real or simulated, is not of interest here, as authenticity and genuineness are locally constructed conditions. In relation to this, however, lies an inherent problem in the translation of theatricality into the business realm—for while we at the theater are comfortable with simultaneously knowing that we a watching an actor, and perceiving him as Hamlet, the same does not hold true for business. If we become aware of a cleavage between an actor and his part at an event, then we dismiss the whole show as inauthentic. Enjoyable though it may be, it is not something that will have repercussions into "real" business life after the event has ended. However, if the representation presented rings true, then the event will be successful, not as an excessive embellishment, but as an effective means of organizing.

What we see as being of interest is the idea of events as actual driving forces and vital parts of the business process, not as isolated recreational instances. As a result, the boundaries between event and everyday organizational reality become less clear cut than is commonly thought. In management terms, this means that events are seen to be part of "real" business instead of being extracurricular activities. The "magic" created is the result of skillful craftsmanship, which can be furnished by the event entrepreneur. Events are instances where the entrepreneur enters as an external director, changing our perception with the aid of the experience. The subtle craftsmanship of the entrepreneur lies in employing the tools of theatricality to the designated effect, while not letting these ministrations become overt.

CHAPTER 8

SPORTS AS ENTERTAINMENT
A CASE OF KITSCH IN THE EXPERIENCE ECONOMY

HANS LUNDBERG

Opening

October 3, 1951, at the New York Polo Grounds, the third and decid-
ing match between the Giants and the Dodgers was played out in base-
ball's World Series. This particular match forms both the basis of the
elaborate introduction to and the narrative structure of DeLillo's novel
on post-World War II conditions in the United States, *Underworld*
(1997). A ball flies out among the spectators and is caught by a young
black boy. The ball is passed into the hands of several other spectators.
By using the narrative voices of these spectators, DeLillo continues his
social story of the United States from the 1950s up until the 1990s. The
event that these different people specifically share—their experience of
a ball game—comes to be seen as something extraordinary. They were
there. Over time this reified *there* creates an *aura* that reshapes, multi-
plies, vanishes and reoccurs as the narrative net of human storytelling
is woven in a never-ending variety of ways:

> *The two men begin to walk across the outfield and Al points to the*
> *place in the left-field stands where the ball went in.*
> *"Mark the spot. Like where Lee surrendered to Grant or some*
> *such thing."*
> *Russ thinks this is another kind of history. He thinks they will*
> *carry something out of here that joins them all in a rare way, that*
> *binds them to a memory with protective power. People are climb-*
> *ing lampposts on Amsterdam Avenue, tooting car horns in Little*
> *Italy. Isn't it possible that this mid-century moment enters the skin*
> *more lastingly than the vast shaping strategies of eminent leaders,*
> *generals steely in their sunglasses—the mapped visions that*

pierce our dreams? Russ wants to believe a thing like this keeps us safe in some undetermined way. This is the thing that will pulse in his brain come old age and double vision and dizzy spells—the surge sensation, the leap of people already standing, that bolt of noise and joy when the ball went in. This is the people's history and it has flesh and breath that quicken to the force of this old safe game of ours. And fans at the Polo Grounds today will be able to tell their grandchildren—they'll be the gassy old man leaning into the next century and trying to convince anyone willing to listen, pressing in with medicine breath, that they were here when it happened. (DeLillo, 1997: 59-60)

DeLillo characterizes some of the central values toward which human-kind and society aspire to. Values that sports have the power to conjure. Gestalt and voice are thereby given to the sunny side of sports, the side that appears and speaks loudly to contemporary society:

Today's sports movement, with its professional elite sports practitioners as commercial mirrors, is one of the most global phenomena that can be found in modern times ... A large measure of the pervasive force of sports can be explained in terms of the fact that it is a relatively easily understood form of entertainment and it is 'a concentrated simplification of life'...which can be brought to the masses quite simply through the use of modern technology. (Lindfelt 1999: 9, my translation from Swedish)

The capacity of sports to create magical moments for hundreds of millions of people around the world is undisputed. It is so because for a fragmentary moment we can, through sports, understand each other, share something, enjoy ourselves, feel happy, sense some togetherness, and be comfortable. Sports activities are entertaining and relaxing. They encapsulate a force that exudes qualities like the ones given gestalt by DeLillo and conceptualized by Lindfelt; sport as it appears in its *experienced immediacy*. Organized more systematically, *immediated experiences*[76] of sports most often end up in normative

---

[76] Bourdieu (1992), among others, has observed the social construction of the Olympic Games on two levels. The games are produced twice, once at the level of participation, and a second time through the media coverage. I suggest to use the construct *im-mediated experiences*, by which Bourdieu's observation is brought into chapter context (sports within the experience economy) in order to highlight that in the case of sports, the *immediate live experience* of a sport event most often

statements with positive connotations, focusing and praising the contribution of sports to the good of the individual, and accordingly, the good of humankind. Discussions within that realm end up turning sports into something inherently good; a phenomenon good by nature; a foundational and objective dimension not to be further discussed. Such discussions on sports see any kind of external influences on sports as dangers and threats gnawing at the purported "original purity" of "traditional sports values," which is given its purest form in the Olympic manifesto. In a March 6, 1929 speech, Baron Pierre De Coubertin, founder of the modern Olympic committee, declared sports a religion. He articulated the emotional ecstasy related to sports experiences as a passionate movement of the spirit (Lindfelt, 2005: 1). Today, almost eighty years later, this kind of sports spirituality[77] is omnipresent in society. Empirical evidence for this *sports grand narrative* is delivered around the globe every day, around the year, in newspapers, magazines, Television channels, sport facilities, retail stores, and consumer practices.

This chapter is not about the sunny sides of sports but about the production of sports as sunshine. Or more stringently put, the concept of *kitsch* is used in order to analyze today's primary discursive manifestation of the sports grand narrative, *sports as entertainment*. The concept of kitsch allows us to analyze what "makes dead thought the object of fascination and desire and obscures its own dark side by hiding it in light" (Linstead, 2002: 667). The bombastic aspirations embedded in the sports grand narrative produces thoughts and ideas that are objects of fascination and desire in contemporary societies. These are increasingly presented as "unproblematic" and "self-evident" which is reason enough to undertake inquiry into the dark sides hidden in the light.

---

is *reified* by the *mass mediated experience* of the event and less often a critical inquiry into the event. This norm within sports journalism is an important reason why the sports grand narrative is able to reproduce and enlarge itself without major disturbances. This aspect is further commented upon in section two.

[77] Sports spirituality is just one aspect of a general pattern of individualization, now also of religious faith. For instance, in *Newsweek*, in a vast 18 paged special report on "Spirituality in America 2005", it is noted that a kind of religious patchwork is at hand where today's spirituality seekers pick and choose what feels nice from established religious creeds and skip the rest: 'People are looking for transformative experience, not just a new creed or dogma,' says Surya Das, a US-born Tibetan lama whose spiritual journey began in 1970" (Newsweek, Aug. 29/Sept. 5, 2005: 54).

Despite elaborated critiques from various academic disciplines on the idea of sports, on the societal use of sports, and on the level of practicing sports, it still has a "wild card," or self-proclaimed, freedom from serious societal and scholarly debate. I think one reason is the role business administration scholars have (not) played. They are generally absent and not part of the ongoing construction of a sports grand narrative as providers of economically related models for enhanced performance of some sports organizational aspect. In the Unites States management research context, Weick et al. (2005), highlights several reasons why sports is a relevant object for organization scholars, while Frisby (2005) especially emphasizes the need for more critically oriented analyses of sports. This chapter can, therefore, be read as a wish for more European business administration scholars to engage in critically oriented analyses of sports. The attempt undertaken here departs from my understanding of the theme of this book by distancing the concept of the experience economy from its roots in marketing management and brand management. *Sports as entertainment* and its "young" academic parallel, *sports management*, are two fields totally dominated by those experience economy roots. In fact, sports as entertainment has, at least since the 1980's, practiced what later became conceptualized by Pine and Gilmore (1999) as the experience economy:

Michael Jordan made watching basketball or eating Wheaties an experience. Experiences are events that engage individuals in personal ways. Such engagement is the objective, the raison d'être, of what Pine and Gilmore (1999) dubbed the 21st-century experience economy... When David Stern became commissioner of the NBA in 1984, he methodically set about improving the experience value of NBA basketball. Buoyed by great basketball and great stars, Stern added concert[s] like opening ceremonies to games. He speeded up game play, introduced flashier uniforms, improved halftime entertainment, and promoted giveaways for fans. He improved television coverage with more cameras, better angels, instant replay, zoom lenses, better announcers, and human interest segments. By adding showbiz and glamour to NBA Basketball, Stern increased its appeal. He made it more entertaining by making it more experiential. (Fielding & Pitts, 2003/1998: 72)

Purpose

The purpose of this chapter is, therefore, to do an analysis of the 'grand narrative' of sports as entertainment, where it can be seen as a proto industry of the experience economy. In such an analysis:

The ambition is to shatter grand narrative and to problematize any linear mono-voiced grand narrative of the past by replacing it with an open polysemous (many meanings) and multivocal (many-voiced) web of little stories. (Boje, 2001: 12)

Although, rather then rejection (shattering), Boje advocates resituation of grand narratives (2001: 41), which is a less radical approach relative to Lyotard (1993/1979). Such an approach holds that "grand narratives can be resituated to have both strengths and limitations" (Boje, 2001: 38) and also that local/smaller stories can be seen as "embedded in and sometimes resisting grand narratives" (Boje, 2001: 35). The analysis proceeds as follows: The concept of sports as entertainment is presented in section one. I comment upon the central role of mass media in relation to sports as entertainment in section two. Two concepts—"aura" and "nostalgia"—are proposed in section three as crucial for understanding and analyzing the use of immaterial resources which characterize sports as entertainment and as discursive and everyday practice (de Certeau, 1988/1984). Section four addresses the role of escalating production of aura founded in nostalgic storytelling and the memory re-activating everydayness of the world of sports. It is given gestalt by using two sports stars—Henrik Larsson and David Beckham. The consumption side of sports as entertainment is, thereby, in focus and analyzed through the concept of kitsch. In order to try to avoid doing what is criticized (substitute one grand narrative with another), section five shatters Boje's "nicer" approach (everything will "get better" if we have polysemous and multivocal webs of little stories). Boje's approach is problematic vis-à-vis how sports is organized in Sweden: Resistance from local/smaller stories appears to not be a solution, rather, the alternative web of stories is transformed into a local grand narrative that opposes the global one, but at the bottom line raises the same kind of bombastic claims its "opponent." The result is a kind of "grand narrative battle" between global grand narratives and local/smaller countergrand narratives that altogether shatters any alternative web of smaller stories of sports.

Sports as Entertainment

A sports grand narrative needs to be measured and sized, cherished and criticized, by the same standards of rigidity and thoroughness that are applied to art and religion. Why so? Bauman (1998), from a sociological perspective, and Lindfelt (2005), from a comparative theological perspective (partly discussing Bauman's view), note that the contemporary postmodern quest for peak experiences (Bauman), with sports as a specific example (Lindfelt), functions as "main supplier" of transcendental experiences for the masses; a kind of peak experience that once was the privilege of only a chosen aristocracy (Bauman, 1998: 238-240, Lindfelt, 2005: 10-13). Secular, postmodern peak experiences, with transcendental aspirations, demand dramaturgical talents and spectacular temples of equal dignity to those of religion. The main discursive face of sports today, sports as entertainment—a growth oriented "alliance" of nationalistic and regional interests, corporate and nationalistic capitalism, and global mass media—provides a solution for this demand. The role played by sports actors and advocates[78] in this "alliance" is twofold: First, to promote an understanding of sports grand narrative as the universalistic mission to bring mankind together in a global village. Due to such glorious aspirations, sport is "of course" entitled to constantly crave help and support without further questioning. Secondly, following their first role, they guard over the "unfortunate side-effects" accompanying such help, that is, the constant risk of sports to become romanticized, politicized, dumbed down, and financially exploited.

From a discourse analysis perspective, sports has exactly these "risks" to thank for its modern form, and also for its contemporary omnipresence. Sports has developed its tremendous social legitimization through its historically proven capacity to serve as a means to various ends. With changing ends, the need for various discursive legitimization has shifted over time. As a main trajectory for development and growth, sports has come to be proficient at serving different masters, both one at a time as well as several intertwined. From its modern emergence in Great Britain in the second half of the nineteenth century, sports spread throughout the industrializing Western nations for various reasons: Sports functioned as a new means for the upper-class/upward striving of the middle class it its efforts to "manage" and

---

[78] As one myself since a young age, I write from an insider's perspective, borrowing some methodological tools from social and cultural sciences in order to do something about my acquired blindness.

make sense of the emerging worker. I also served a middle-class societal invention, the idea of leisure time, which, in part, can be seen as a kind of spillover effect from the eras protoreformative relaxations of the harsh conditions ruling working time for those classes. This is a process of reciprocal production, which historian Eric Hobsbawm terms "the two forces of a capitalistic mode of production": the innovative capacity pushing the capitalistic system forward and the sociological effects holding it back (Hobsbawm, 2001: 126). After this first process of societal legitimization in the era of nationalistic capitalism,[79] sports has, especially post-World War II, gradually engaged with corporate capitalism as a second main master, although without waving goodbye to the first. Sports' capacity to engage with two masters who are intertwined is overwhelmingly manifested by its increased beyond-any-description presence in contemporary mass media; as exemplified by disagreements such as the fight between public and commercial channels for broadcasting rights of sports events, or agreements such as the corporate capitalization of nationalistic based competitions (with the Olympic Games as the most obvious example). Today sports have risen as a Master *Sui generis*:

The sociologist, Johan Asplund, claims that 'a more unambiguous goal for human endeavors than what is provided by today's sports competitions may have, perhaps, never existed.' (Lindfelt, 1999: 9, my translation from Swedish)

Put in numbers (figures from the Unites States sports industry alone):

In 1990 sport was a $63.1 billion-a-year business, ranking 22nd among 400 plus industries in the United States (Comte & Stagel 1990)... In 1999 Broughton, Lee, and Nethery estimated the Gross National Sport Product (GNSP) to be $213 billion. Regardless of the measurement used, one fact is crystal clear: Sport was a booming business in the 1990s! (Parks & Quarterman, 2003: 9)

---

[79] Sports hase been given similar functions in other modes of production as well. Sports as one of the main tools for communist regimes attempting to "prove" their after World War II/cold War is a most accentuated example. With its vast system of state employed instructors, systematic doping programs on a national scale, and talent factories separating sports talented children from home and parents at pre-school ages, the examples provided by those regimes are so far uncontested as the most systematic examples of contempt and perversion of the central values that humankind and society aspire to, values that sports has the power to conjure.

Lindfelt is one of few that has noted the need for conceptual nuances in line with this development and, therefore, proposes a distinction between traditional elite sports and sports as entertainment: "In those many cases, which directly reflect and express the divide between traditional elite sports and sports as entertainment, it is most often the case that economic aspects decide on how the sports culture is to develop" (Lindfelt, 1999: 59, my translation from Swedish). I agree with Lindfelt, but also note that after having identified economic aspects as decisive, he, in his central sports texts (1999, 2005, 2006), leaves those very same aspects rather unelaborated, which is why they are in focus here.

Sports as Mass-Communicated Entertainment

"Mass communication" is so central in relation to sports as entertainment that one might even equate them. Mass communication is such an all-encompassing concept that it is impossible to do it even the slightest justice in a short text like this.[80] Starting with some very basic reasoning, I put forward, instead, general questions regarding sports journalism in order to empirically underpin this discussion into the book theme and to contextualize im-mediated experiences as drawn from Bourdieu's notion of the role of media in society.

Critiques of sports journalism as cheerleading are as old as modern sports itself. Why? Some primitive logic might be enough to lead the way: If we hold it to be reasonable that out of the total range of all sporting activities performed in our world, a very small part of those activities—to a large extent elite activities—are caught up by the logic of mass communication and that, out of the total range of this already tiny part, mass media coverage of sports is completely dominated by those sports that "qualify" as mass mediated entertainment, some simple propositions can be made: A) People's everyday sports activities are minimally reflected in the media coverage of sports. This proposition should be contrasted with the fact that health issues, and citizens' rights to have equal access to sports activities and sports fostering capacities are held forward by Swedish authorities as the foundational reasons for society to support sports with tax payers' money. B) People's everyday consumption of elite sports does not generally qualify as entertainment in the mass media coverage of sports. C) There is a maximal reflection of people's everyday consumption of sports as en-

---

[80] See instead *Sport as Entertainment: The Role of Mass Communications* by John Goldlust (1987/2004) for introduction.

tertainment in the mass media coverage of sports. It may seem that what have just been written are truisms or platitudes.

Why, is sports journalism not subject to commonly accepted norms of publishing in professional journalism? Think on how societal sectors like culture, business, and politics are reported upon (even though publishers have been criticized for their lack of vigor at times), and compare this with how sports journalism is presented in various media.

Why, is serious sports journalism so hesitant to debate the a kind of sports "journalism" that has increased dramatically within sports as entertainment, where sports coverage takes less and less space? Focus is placed instead on the sports star's life outside his or her sporting activities; on the sports commentator's opinions of different sporting personalities; on the sports commentator's opinions of other sporting commentators' opinions; on the opinions of sport stars on any issue under the sun; on the appearance of sports stars as program leaders or panel "experts" on complex societal issues; on sports stars as participants of quiz shows on television; or, last but not least, the eternal "question" of how sports stars can make so much money and be so bad at what they do (when they are not our heroes, of course). When sectors such as culture, business, and politics are, to some extent, also are under the influence of this kind of paparazzi spell, this does not pass accompanied with sounds of silence. Serious journalists in these cases neither shut up, yell, nor scream, but calling it "critique," use their abilities to critically investigate.

Why then, is serious sports journalism in such a minority? I have been collecting articles from leading Swedish sports journalists for four or five years now. There seems to be an increasing amount of solid sports journalism showing all the capacity for in-depth investigation one might request. The problem seems to be that these journalists are still too few and that they still do not influence sports praxis to the same extent as journalists within the fields of business, politics, and culture. It can also be observed that sports increasingly receives serious coverage as a societal phenomenon on a broader scale. Besides the increasing coverage of in-depth investigative sports journalists, sports has become the subject of journalism in places other than the sports pages. More and more specialized journals are available where sports' central social roles are discussed at length. Increasingly research on sports is being produced where it is considered as something other than a physical activity. If all these aspects of sports journalism joined forces, then maybe their impact on sports praxis might increase.

To sum up: When all aspects of sports as entertainment are gaining as much attraction (and quite often more) as the sports activities themselves, is it not at a discursive level still more accurate to speak about sports journalism as a vertically integrated part of the sports industry, with a rather symbiotic relation to sports as well as the interests that feed on sports and sports-related consumption? It is not an "alliance" that feeds upon, and therefore nurtures, a one-to-one correlation between the *immediate live experience* of a sport event and the *mass mediated experience* of the very same event? Of course there have been improvements to the overwhelming role of cheerleader that sports journalism has historically had since sports' infancy. But have there been enough? If we have a development where fewer and fewer sports and athletes reap more and more media attention, both in relative and absolute terms, the media event becomes as important, or more important than, the sports event itself. This line of development is central to understanding media's fundamental role to the income side of sports as entertainment. It is notoriously difficult to place value on the industry's most overwhelmingly dominant and volatile immaterial resource, its sports stars (Smart, 2005, Andrews & Jackson, 2001). Valuing immaterial resources is difficult enough within more "traditional" business sectors where brands are built up more systematically and are mirrored as intangibles in the financial spreadsheets. Surly, nonhuman brands are also subject to rapid changes and trend shifts, but at least they do not get stoned, rape women, hit their wives, snort cocaine, and create sex scandals (Teitelbaum, 2005). Rather than artificial efforts to extend and apply the concept of a "brand" to star athletes, I propose that star athletes can be analyzed and interpreted in terms of Ivar Björkman's (1998) use of the concept of *aura.*

Immaterial Resources of Sports as Entertainment: Aura and Nostalgia

An ostensive definition holds that aura is "the distinctive atmosphere or quality that seems to be generated by someone or something" (Concise Oxford English Dictionary, 10th edition revised, 2002). I turn to the concept of aura in order to question the increasing use of branding in sports. Branding, when used in relation to the athletes themselves does not, in my estimation, adequately capture the dynamic by which sports superstars acquire signification. Mass media is a crucial socioeconomic and cultural factor explaining how aura becomes a key immaterial resource within experience economy driven practices but does not say it all. It does inform us about the last and decisive step in the production of aura, but there are structural determinants that set the scene. An example from American economics provides us with some clues to understand macroeconomic factors behind aura as an immaterial resource. Professional sports is an established field in American economics for at least one special reason:

> *The sports industry continues to be the focus of much research by professional economists. A few seminal contributions...have been followed by an explosion of research in the past fifteen years. The reason for this, in our view, is that the sports industry provides unusual opportunities for both theoretical and empirical research. A central issue addressed on the theoretical side of sports economics research is the duality of market cooperation and market competition that is unique to the sports industry... The industry is unique because the legitimate monopoly goals of the team owners must be balanced against their illegitimate monopoly objectives. The legitimate goal is the preservation of competitive balance on the playing field. Without this balance, fans lose interest in the game and the league is an economic failure. The illegitimate monopoly objectives of the owners are the exploitation of the fans and the players. Owners appear to use their monopoly power in the product market to restrict output by limiting the number of teams. In the past (and perhaps even to some extent in the present), they appear to have used their artificial monopsony power to capture monopoly rents from the players.* (Fizel et al. 1999: 3)

Monopsony "is that state of affairs that [is obtained] within a market when there exist[s] only one customer, which multiple sellers have to fight over."[81] As an example, there has only been one gold medal football team in Norway in the last thirteen years, Rosenborg FC (they have thirteen straight gold medals in Norway's highest league). In many other countries there appear to be more competitive teams, but in practice, we find the same limited number of teams competing for the gold medal year after year. This can be seen as a form of *artificial monopsony*. The point being that the proportion of people on the earth who can apply themselves in professional sports at the highest levels of the professional hierarchy are but a tiny fraction of an already very small group of people who can apply themselves in professional sports at all. Only an even smaller fraction of the highest elite can be consid-

---

[81] http://sv.wikipedia.org/wiki.Monosponi, 2005-02-12.

ered as the "right" elite: practitioners in teams aspiring to gold within sports that are considered to be economically viable (sports as entertainment). This microscopic number of athletes, responsible for but a nano fraction of the total production of sports, forms the fundamental base for mass consumption of sports and sports-related goods. This unique market situation informs us about how it is possible to reap considerable economic value based on very few aura athletes despite their enormous paychecks.

Besides *structural* (artificial monopsony market dynamics turn star athletes into postmodern gods) and *technical* (the volatility of those gods is not adequately reflected in the static term "brand") reasons why aura here is argued to be a more adequate concept relative to brand, the primary reason is *aesthetic*: The ideal for a brand is to become as pseudo-intimate as possible with whomever wants to and can pay. Aura vanishes when the intimacy become too intimate:

> *Some company recently was interested in buying my 'aura'. They didn't want my product. They kept saying, 'We want your aura'. I never figured out what they wanted. But they were willing to pay a lot for it. So then I thought that if somebody was willing to pay that much for it, I should try to figure out what it is.*
>
> *I think 'aura' is something that only somebody else can see, and they only see as much of it as they want to. It's all in the other person's eyes. You can only see an aura on people you don't know very well or don't know at all. I was having dinner the other night with everybody from my office. The kids at the office treat me like dirt, because they know me and they see me every day. But then there was this nice friend that somebody had brought along who had never met me, and this kid could hardly believe that he was having dinner with me! Everybody else was seeing me, but he was seeing my 'aura'.*
>
> *When you just see somebody on the street, they really can have an aura. But then when they open their mouth, there goes the aura. 'Aura' must be until you open your mouth* (Andy Warhol, 1975: 75, quoted in Björkman, 1998: 7).

Aura as a concept emanates from art aesthetics and encapsulates the *beautiful* as well as the *ugly*. Brand as a concept emanates from market aesthetics and only allows space for what's accepted as the beautiful. A branded athlete has to fulfill societal norms to perfection, otherwise sponsors leave immediately. This counts for the vast majority of elite athletes, but especially for aura athletes. In some sports (i.e., Mike Tyson in boxing, Roy Keane in football, Vinnie Jones in football, Eric Lindroos in ice hockey, Sir Charles and Shaq O'Neill from NBA basketball) "ugly" behavior of all kinds fuels the aura, with ingredients for new stories, stories that grow to mythological levels as time passes by. According to psychoanalyst, Stanley H. Teitelbaum (2005), who has worked extensively sports stars, the societal consequences of this "ugliness" are made unconscious by sports consumers because of our psychological need for *superman*:

We tend to anoint our sports heroes as gods because we need the feeling of specialness we get from affiliation with outstanding athletes. We need to perceive them as wonderful, through a tinted lens that enhances their grandeur. And we need for them not to disillusion us. Thus we often invent superman, though our heroes are frequently imperfect. Many come from dysfunctional or traumatic backgrounds, and they are not always equipped to handle the stress of stardom. Professional athletes may develop unrealistic views of themselves, and maladaptive behaviour often emerges off the field in conjunction with their distorted self-image. Many star athletes have been catered to for their special talent since early childhood, and they have been conditioned to think special treatment is their due. Hubris and an attitude of entitlement and grandiosity become central dimensions of their psyches. They may consider themselves above the rules of society and believe they will not be held accountable for their moral or legal transgressions...

In recent years unprecedented numbers of star athletes have fallen from grace as a result of self-destructive behaviour off the field. Drug-related crimes, alcohol abuse, and sexual transgressions have become everyday news. An attitude of omnipotence and invulnerability seems to underlie their poor judgement and impulsive acts. Their violence toward women is particularly alarming. Famous athletes are increasingly accused and convicted of domestic violence, assault, gang rape, and other forms of sexual abuse, and several high-profile athletes have been involved in murder cases (Teitelbaum, 2005: xi-xii).

In Umberto Eco's (1972) model of the superman formula, based on a semiotic analysis of the comic book hero, he concludes that Superman is based on a narrative paradox:

> *Superman then, must remain "inconsumable" and at the same time be "consumed" according to the ways of everyday life. He possesses the characteristics of timeless myth, but is accepted only because his activities take place in our human and everyday world of time. The narrative paradox that Superman's script writers must resolve somehow, even without being aware of it, demands a paradoxical solution with regard to time* (Eco, 1972: 16).

The paradoxical solution is the breakdown of a sphere of the concept of time:

> *In Superman it is the concept of time that breaks down. The very structure of time falls apart, not in the temporal sphere about which is told, but rather, in the time in which it is told.*
>
> *In Superman stories the time that breaks down is the time of the story, that is, the notion of time which ties one episode to another* (Eco, 1972: 17, emphasis in original).

Hence, when we consume sports centered on superheroes *also* in our human and everyday world of time, the very structure of this temporal sphere is forced towards breakdown. The experience economy, as conceptualized by Pine and Gilmore, seems to offer opportunities to capitalize on this breakdown through its exhaustive focus on escapist and entertainment realms of experience (1999: 30). With a focus on the "present" satisfaction of various desires, the "past" become a prepackaged ingredient in the production process of a theme (Pine and Gilmore 1999: 46-52); an ordered plot that allows consumers to escape the frightening "future" in the present and in an entertaining way. This breakdown of the notion of time that ties one episode to another is not done, though, without disturbance and resistance. Canadian sociologist Anouk Bélanger provides us with a case of how *nostalgia* does not allow itself to be disciplined just like that. She analyzes how the materialization of sports as entertainment in the human and everyday world is moving forward with the increase in significance of successful sports teams, sports events, and hypermodern sports and multifunctional venues for cities and regions that are attempting to build up their brand and, hence, position themselves as "entrepreneurial" (c.f. Ramírez-Pasillas, 2004, for her discussion of regional brands). She discusses this phenomenon as a *spectacularization of space*:

As global corporations scan the world for preferential locations, particular places are forced into a competitive race to attract inward investors. All of this is leading to increased global inter-urban competition around entertainment industries, where cities must reimage and reimagine themselves...as 'world-class'. Sport stadiums and other complexes have become increasingly important in this dynamic... In this context, urban centres worldwide have been swept along by a new phase of entertainment consumption indicating the integration of a new entertainment economy with a new urban economy. In its wake, this phase, which can be called the spectacularization of space, is creating a new urban landscape filled with casinos, megaplex cinemas, themed restaurants, simulation theatres, stadium and sport complexes. As cities around the world are being transformed into aggressive entrepreneurial cities through the industry of the spectacle, so too are identities and memories being reforged within these spaces (Bélanger, 2000: 378).*

Bélanger develops her arguments around an analysis of the case of the Molson Centre in Montreal where the Molson Brewery Corporation, a large beer manufacturer, lent its name to the new arena, which replaced the Montreal Forum, the legendary, but now former, home arena for the National Hockey League team Montreal Canadians. The symbolic significance of change a home arena is highlighted by the collective anger the replacement provoked:

the prospective closing of the Montreal Forum in favour of a new high-tech arena created an uproar of reaction in the city and launched an unprecedented wave of nostalgic sentiment... Not only had the Forum provided a home for legendary hockey games, but also for concerts and political rallies that were significant in the development of Quebec's pre- and post war popular cultures. As a much more self-consciously corporate space, the Molson Centre threatened to redefine that vital tie to the Quebec public by creating new exclusions and more distance from 'the people.' (Bélanger, 2000: 390-391)

As a consequence of this uproar, the Molson Brewery Corporation was forced to engage in a massive marketing campaign in order to convince the general public that it was, in fact, possible to move memories, legends, and traditions from the Montreal Forum to the Molson

Centre. The campaign opened with a remembrance match between contemporary legends (players) and legends from the Montreal Canadians' past, which was brought to an end with a formal ceremony out on the ice. Some days later, there was a large auction that the general public could attend for the price of five Canadian dollars. At the auction, bids were made on all of the Forum's historical artefacts. The campaign ended with a closing parade through Montreal. This case of collective ritual behavior manifests the *mourning* of the destruction of "the notion of time which ties one episode to another." By transforming the symbols underlying "the unprecedented wave of nostalgic sentiment" to neutralized and redirected aura commodities, the *praying* to and the *celebration* of those symbols may go on in the new temples of sports consumption:

> *The day before the opening game in the Molson Centre a parade was organized called `le Grand Déménagement' (The Great Move). The parade was designed to move the team, and the ghosts and the memories, from the old arena to the new arena—The Stanley Cup banners and some living legends. The theme of the parade was 'the pride and soul of the Montreal Canadians'. Even the Forum's Zamboni (the machine that cleans the ice during hockey games) was officially part of the parade; in fact, it led the parade! Plundering the vault of historical symbols, the parade's organizers also included an Olympic torch meant to reinforce the ideal of transferring the traditions and memories of the old building. Molson was clearly trying to bank on symbols in enacting tradition in the streets of the city and included strolling giant ghosts in the parade that 200,000 people came to see. The promotional discourse was clear: the ghosts of the Forum were moving into the Molson Centre and the parade invited people to come and see it with their own eyes. In addition, on the same day an 'open house' day was held for the public to get familiarized with their new space (150,000 people attended)... This open house event was connected in the campaign with the claim that the arena was an 'all-Quebecois' masterpiece – the people's masterpiece. The open house was to strengthen a sense of public ownership and public identification with the building. (Bélanger, 2000: 391-392)*

A Case of Kitsch in the Experience Economy

We might summarize the discursive pattern so far as the ongoing post-World War II *muzakification*[82] of sports, that is, the tendency for sports as entertainment to serve as make-up (Hjorth and Pelzer, 2003b) for the profit driven production of mass-customized experiences. The other main aspect of this pattern is that sports as entertainment is still able to appear as legitimate with reference to the spirituality of the Olympic manifesto, or versions thereof. This is the historical heritage of sports having served two masters since infancy and (beyond sports) just another example of the patterns of coopting behavior of managerial discourse in general (Hjorth, 2001, 2003a). As a "new" aspect of this discursive pattern, the *intensification* by which the superheroes of sport are brought to a stadium near you, or at least to your television sports channel every hour of the day, renders the sports superman *as real as* anything else where the distinction between "factual" and "fictional" broken down. The resulting "factional" spaces could have been opportunities for entrepreneurial endeavors aiming at resituating and renegotiating images of a sports superman but this space for play (Hjorth, 2005) is silenced by the script writers who creates the proper place when the sports superman is constructed as *the most real:*

> *I call a strategy the calculation (or manipulation) of power relationships that becomes possible as soon as a subject with will and power...can be isolated. It postulates a place that can be delimited as its own and serve as a base from which relations with an exteriority composed of targets and threats...can be managed... A Cartesian attitude if you wish[...]*
>
> *It is also the typical attitude of modern science, politics, and military strategy. The establishment of a break between a place*

---

[82] *Muzak* is a music genre that is used as background music for the benefit of other interests that are thus placed in the foreground. These interests are most often economic interests. "Taylorism" is considered to be a pioneer in this area, but the period of significant development of this genre was at the end of World War II: "By the late 1940s 'travel muzak' was broadcast on trains and passenger ships, and Muzak had become commonplace in workplaces; the idea to combat monotony and offset boredom at precisely those times in a work day when people are most subject to these onslaughts ... While this may have enhanced the quality of the working day, its primary objective was to maximise worker output" (Connell & Gibson 2003: 194). Today, in the age of singing mobile phones and oh-my-God-so-many gigabytes Mp3-players, the idea of "travel muzak" has extended dramatically, although, not any longer in order to maximize *worker output* but to maximize *consumer output.*

appropriated as one's own and its other is accompanied by im-
portant effects[...]

The "proper" is a triumph of place over time. It allows one to
capitalize acquired advantages, to prepare future expansions, and
thus to give oneself a certain independence with respect to the
variability of circumstances. It is a mastery of time through the
foundation of an autonomous place.

It is also a mastery of places through sight. The division of
space makes possible a panoptic practice proceeding from a place
whence the eye can transform foreign forces into objects that can
be observed and measured, and thus control and "include" them
within its scope of vision[...]

It would be legitimate to define the power of knowledge by this
ability to transform the uncertainties of history into readable
spaces. But it would be more correct to recognize in these
"strategies" a specific type of knowledge, one sustained and de-
termined by the power to provide oneself with one's own place.
(de Certeau, 1988/1984: 36, emphasis in original)

Sports as an uprising master *sui generis*, a master of its own kind and
in its own right, then has to solve its narrative paradox similarly to the
script writers of cartoon/cinematic Superman. The "proper" as a triumph of place over time (de Certeau): It is the analogous destruction
of the temporal sphere of everyday life and the temporal sphere of the
cartoon/cinematic life of Superman. Constructed as the most real, the
production of the sports superman by proper place script writers is
treated as one of the most serious activities on planet earth. The sports
superman feels himself to be accordingly important, a belief with consequences that are becoming increasingly apparent (Teitelbaum). Still,
not much is said about the consumption side of sports as entertainment.
I think this is where the concept of kitsch becomes useful. Relative to
makeup, kitsch is that which does not recognize itself as makeup but as
a serious intensification with a surface.[83] The concept of kitsch enables
us to calibrate the analysis of the intertwined production and consumption processes of sports as entertainment. Given that the analysis so far
shows that the production of sports as entertainment at large is a made-
up process, the focus from now on is the idea that the *consumption of*
make-up as the most real turns sports of entertainment to a case of

---

[83] My thanks to Daniel Hjorth for clearing out my misunderstandings of the differences between "kitsch" and "make-up."

kitsch into the experience economy. In order to provide a more in-depth interpretation, the concept of kitsch will be introduced, acknowledging the problems of applying the concept on an individual level, as "the discourse of depriving experience of beauty and surprise" (Kostera, 1997: 163). An example from Glasgow, Scotland, illustrates the spiritual importance of sports in an everyday context. It illustrates a dimension of sports as a source of comfort and as something that offers some relief in one of life's most difficult situations:

> *Two year old Andrew Morton passed away last Friday. He was killed from a shot in his head. He will be buried in a Celtic's shirt signed by Henrik Larsson.*
>
> *"Henrik Larsson was a hero of mine as well as Andrews," says Sharon McMillan, 34, the mother of Andrew, to Sunday Mail.*
>
> *The family's garden is crowded with flowers and football shirts brought there from mourning people. Glasgow Rangers shirts have also been given to the Celtic family.*
>
> *"It is so touching to see Celtic's and Rangers shirts side by side," says Sharon McMillan.* (Text TV news, Monday, March 07, 2005, page 307, 10.50 pm, my translation from Swedish)

The rivalry between the Glasgow football clubs Rangers FC and Celtic FC is not as old as the conflict it materializes, the one between Catholics and Protestants, but it is probably as passionate. To play *The Old Firm*, the derby match between the two teams, is, according to some who have done it, a larger than life experience.[84] In this environment, the Swedish national team's world-class striker, Henrik Larsson, was the big star for several years before signing with Barcelona FC. Larsson entered the divine level of the gods. When he was back in Glasgow, playing there for the first time with his new team, by scoring an important Champion's League game. Out of respect for the Celtic's fans, for the city and for the years he had their, he decided not to celebrate the goal he scored. As a new player in a club like Barcelona FC, that is a very risky decision. With 115,000 Barcelona FC annual members and an average spectator rate at Nou Camp of 75–80,000 per game, very few players take the risk of being accused of being disloyal, thereby giving several hundred thousands of passionate Catalans a reason to come knocking at your door. Henrik Larsson solved that

---

[84] Just as an indication: When Googling *The Old Firm*, approximately 53,700000, hits are given.

equation in a trustworthy way and became more respected in both camps. To stay reasonably ethically sane in contexts like these is truly an achievement. It is, of course, not possible to fully understand the family's decision in a situation like the one described in the quote above but to understand anything about this story one has to appreciate the mechanisms that make sports what it is in many people's lives. Sports is a societal force that on an individual level, exudes closeness, fellowship, and intimacy in our everyday lives has nothing to do with kitsch.

The concept of kitsch might to be useful at a discursive level when discussing the consumption aspects of sports as entertainment as a protoindustry of the experience economy. In her article, Kostera discusses kitsch as "not being equivalent to 'low' or 'popular' culture [but as] a degrading construct" (Kostera, 1997: 163). In one of the few business administration (organisation theory) articels following up on Kosteras' pioneering contribution, Linstead (2002) discusses kitsch in a similar way, or more specifically, as an "unthinking quality" that has four main conceptual dimensions: "its being based on the principle of return; its being human-centred or anthropocentric; its being a form of mass sentiment and its being a collective defense mechanism" (Linstead, 2002: 662). Dwelling somewhat on the two anthropocentric tendencies sets the scene for da discussion of the consumptive aspects of the sports superman: The tendency to let "human needs and desires predominate over all the world's other considerations" (Linstead, 2002: 667) and to see "human form [as] ... the world's highest form of development" (Linstead, 2002: 667), are worth noting when reading Pine and Gilmore (1999) systematically with the case of sports as entertainment in mind. Regarding the ultimate goal of the transformation economy (Pine and Gilmore, chapter 9 & 10)—*man is the product*—it is hard to find a more obvious representation for such a goal than the sports superman. As earthly creatures given divine qualities that we constantly strive in vain, to resemble, we have made sports gods in the image of our own functionality to which our sense of our own symbolic importance has blinded us, turning us into self-obsessed and self-idolatrous beings (Linstead, 2002: 668). However, as Kundera discusses, any idea of a naturalized relation between the physical and the metaphysical is necessarily problematic, which is signified by our customary objection to faeces: "The objection to shit is a metaphysical one" (Kundera, 1984: 249 in Linstead, 2002: 668). There are two propositions to be dealt with here:

...one, the question of perfectibility, the other the question of con-
trol. If God is perfect, then God does not change. But defecation is
the outcome of a process of transformation, growth and decay.
That which changes cannot be perfect. But, perhaps worse, it is a
process over which the body has no control. Shit happens. That
which lacks control over its own processes cannot therefore be
all-powerful...we have made God in the image of our own func-
tionality, to which our sense of our own symbolic importance has
blinded us. We have become not only self-obsessed but also self-
idolatrous beings. The kitsch response here, faced with the in-
compatibility of the two propositions, is denial of the least flatter-
ing, the one which we cannot accept without overturning our es-
tablished assumptions...Kundera is able to assert that the aes-
thetic result of anthropocentrism and anthropomorphism, [is] 'the
categorical agreement with being', [that] is 'a world in which shit
is denied and everyone acts as though it did not exist'. In fact,
kitsch could almost be defined as: ...the absolute denial of shit ...
(Kundera, 1984: 248 in Linstead, 2002: 668)

Treatment of new and old gods could be seen as evidence of what
Kundera terms the "absolute denial of shit"—the kitsch response. But
there might be reason to add nuance. Since Kundera's proposition was
written in 1984, postmodern consumerism has generally become pro-
foundly sophisticated; however this does not seem to count for sports
as entertainment as consumer practice. "Shit" represents imperfection
and lack of total control, which never enters sports as entertainment.
Sport-as-entertainment consumers believe in the story about its sport
as the most real and in this sense it is more like Kundera's "old fash-
ioned kitsch," where games and play are treated with spiritual serious-
ness while existential matters are made religious patchwork to play
around with. It is degrading construct that is highly successful. The
fact that elite institutions like the opera take sports into consideration
legitimates sports supermen because "increasing glitter and virtuosity
adds a sensual, even erotic, dimension to kitsch, suspended as it is in
tension between power and submission." Kitsch, thus, "makes dead
thought the object of fascination and desire and obscures its own dark
side by hiding it in light" (Linstead, 2002: 667):

The concept of sport is so central today. When the Prime Minister
orders a Cabinet reshuffle, he is "sending in his best players."
Sport has mythological qualities. Ordinary people perform in an

arena, and become gods for a moment. (Niklas Rådström, author with Sport och fritid [Sport and Leisure], recently performed at the Royal Opera House, Stockholm. Cited in Lundman, T. Svenska Dagbladet, 2004-12-13, my translation from Swedish)

These postmodern gods become public goods because of these mythological qualities. Sports stars and their associates can become gods for far more than a moment; they may, with some permanence, enter into God's kingdom. This process is not without resistance, though. Religious authorities thought the idea of choosing British football player and national team captain David Beckham and his wife Victoria as representatives for Joseph and the Virgin Mary at Madam Tussaud's Christmas gathering in 2004, as a sign of complete ignorance (*Svenska Dagbladet*, 2004-12-08). A brief reflection upon David Beckham's biography reveals why a football player may end up with such an odd proposition and why that gives us some clues to an aspect that appears to be specific for these sports supermen: Beckham *started* as a national icon by being a successful but harmless supertalent at a young age. After establishing himself, he was *degraded* to a national refugee forced to leave England after being shown the red card in a crucial game in the 1998 World Cup, which led to England losing to France, and thereby being forced out of the competition. After years of turmoil, he once again was *upgraded* to national icon after scoring 2-2 via an award winning "goal of the decade" free kick against Greece in the last minute of the last qualification game, taking England to the World Cup in 2002. After that, he was *degraded* once again when his divine aura collided with another one: that of Sir Alec Fergusson, coach of Manchester United. They performed the "Manchester is not big enough for the both of us." Once again, driven out of England, he was transferred to Real Madrid that thereby invested in the Asian market (souvenir sales, popularity of team via Beckham), allowing him to transcend national borders by *upgrading* him from national rollercoaster to global divinity, or a postmodern god.

Everyday people do not pray to those gods, hoping or asking for protection, avoidance of condemnation, blessings and so on; instead, they turn to them when they demand something material (shoes, clothes) or something immaterial (joy, rage, love, hate, nostalgia, hope, etc.). *Postmodern gods* are not to be feared and worshipped, but to be worshipped, consumed, and degraded, in that order, and then resurrected back up to be worshipped again. This worldview is, as Stephen Linstead puts it, endowed with the narcissistic properties of kitsch that

"underpin a cosmology which positions humanity at the centre of creation. Kitsch proposes that the world is, in fact, as we want it to be"
(Linstead, 2002: 664). Kitsch changes reality to fit the map. To have
convenient gods like this, gods that adore our worship during their fifteen minutes of fame and accept our degrading and denial of them
when they are put back into their eternal hours of forgotten seclusion,
is—to paraphrase Linstead—in fact, as we postmodern consumers
want it to be. Unlike Caesar, who had slaves whispering about his mortality, Teitelbaum (2005) shows what kind of gods we, as experience
economy consumers, create when we, as their volunteer slaves, scream
about their immortality as long as we have need for them. Accordingly, various degrees of hubris and egoism not only flourish but are
fundamental prerequisites for competition and "survived" at these
sports levels:

> *Unfortunately, sport, like so many other parts of our society, has
> partially abdicated its position as a role model... In the highly
> commercialized world of sports, there exist features of extreme
> egoism. It is about getting as much as you can at any cost, on the
> pitch as well as in life in generally. Consideration for your oppo-
> nent, a fellow human being, is often minimized. A sport ethics
> group would be kept very busy* (Sylvén, S. Svenska Dagbladet,
> 2005-02-13, my translation from Swedish).

Sylvén misses the role everyday consumers play in the construction of
sports egoism. The rulebased world of sports as entertainment very
much functions as "a suspension of the ordinary world" (Lindfelt,
1999) that is simultaneously autonomous from, and intimately related
to, everyday life. Sports as entertainment is guilty of a false inference,
though, if it considers its present day status as a sign that it represents
central human life values and social values, if but fragmentarily. The
relationship is most probably the reverse. It is the increase of competitive elements in terms of demands on performance (Corvellec, 1995),
fixation with the human body, dehumanization, escalating competition,
increasing egoism, and so on, in the "ordinary world" that is reflected
in the consumption of a concentrated simplification of life of different
types, to which sports as entertainment has shown itself to be a very attractive alternative. It is so attractive that match results in the right or
wrong direction defines existential meaning and meaninglessness for
millions of people around the world.

By the way, the Giants won, five to four (DeLillo, 1997: 46). *This sunny, good old October day back in the early 50's...*

A Discursively Denied Swedish Practice

Trying to avoid providing a grand narrative while shattering another, the Swedish sports model here is analyzed as a case of resistance from a local story in order to explore if such resistance open up cracks for entrepreneurial endeavors or if it contributes to further closing and silencing of webs of alternative stories about sports supermen.

One cannot assume that the degree of openness and willingness to debate and discuss is "automatically" higher within a model of sports founded on idealism (Swedish) than those founded on commercialism (sports as entertainment). Lindfelt, among others, holds that the sports culture in several countries, Sweden being one of them, is extremely closed. External criticism as well as internal self-criticism is seen as something unwelcome, unpleasant, and unnecessary—as something taboo (1999: 11-12). Problems within the world of sports are to be discussed within the sports family. If problems are too vast or too costly to solve within the sports family, the main strategy is to claim that the problem is an external societal one. The chairman of the Swedish Football Federation, Lars-Åke Lagrell, is uncrowned master of this language game in contemporary Swedish sports. Cultural patterns at the collective and individual levels are visible also at the discursive level, which the example of *Riksidrottsförbundet* (RF) illustrates.

The concept of sports as entertainment is not used by RF, which is the top organizing body of all Swedish sports. This denial reflects a question that has not been discussed at great length in Swedish sports, the large differences that are found *within* the elite levels of sport. Those differences are more and more apparent as certain elite sports make an explicit entrance on the stage of mass entertainment industries in Sweden. One might wonder why this question is avoided. One explanation is that the RF is an organization that historically has attempted to gain hegemony in its area (Sandahl and Sjöblom, 2004: 52-55) and this has led to a strong reluctance to accept change in Swedish sports:

> *If the argument...that the development found in Swedish sports has led to a split between a commercial sector and a volunteer sector, and because of this the sports movement has lost its guiding ideology to the benefit of a position in terms of general sports propaganda, why, then, is the organization still intact...?*

The reason behind this seemingly strong unity is the Riksidrottsförbundet position on this issue; it has been mandated to act *as if* it was a
governmental authority. The state funding that the specialized sports
foundations receives, via their parent organizations—without specific
demands on how these funds are to be used—finances these various
activities to a large extent. This situation has a preservative effect on
Swedish sports. Neither the commercial sector nor the volunteer sector
of the sports movement wishes to leave the sports federation for fear of
loosing their funding (Sandahl and Sjöblom 2004: 54, my translation
from Swedish, italics by me).

Whether correct or not, RF still holds perspective that the only valid
line of division of different forms of sports is the one between elite
sports and nonelite sports. However, acknowledging this does not
mean that RF sees this difference as so articulated that there is reason
to create separate authorities for different forms of sports:

> *The sports movement wishes to protect this solidarity. It is a point
> of strength that one and the same movement can organize every-
> thing from our youth sports activities and exercise sports activi-
> ties to the highest elite within different sports* (from RF's policy
> document Idrotten vill, quoted in Sandahl and Sjöblom, 2004: 53,
> my translation from Swedish).

This quote can be seen as a central expression of what Sandahl and
Sjöblom call RF's sports propaganda position. Propaganda for what?
The traditional social democratic policy in this case is widely known
and reproduced as common sense knowledge, and can be summarized
as "out of the masses the elite will come." The elite should show solidarity with the mass and function as role models. The overall problem
with this alleged connection between the masses and the elite is that it
has, in no way, been empirically shown to exist, neither in Sweden or
elsewhere. At the European Sport Management conference in Ghent,
Belgium, September 2004, the British professor, John Lyle, highlighted a number of faults in theoretical models where the connection
between nonelite sport (mass sport) and elite sport is taken for granted,
and consequently not questioned. He claimed that there are no connections between investments in sports for all and international excellence, or the other way around. Bob Stewart and Matthew Nicholson's
research from Victoria University, Australia, is in line with this claim
since their study showed that there is no connection between international sporting success and organized sporting activities at the local

level. This assumed connection has been the point of departure for several national investments in sport in Australia (Bååth, Hans in Bååth and Lundberg, 2004).

In the light of such findings, the analysis undertaken in this section suggests that the alleged connection implicit in "out of the masses the elite will come," exists as a cliché and a wish dream. When seen as a construct that is taken for granted and gradually reified along time, some support is provided for the proposed Sandahl and Sjöblom "propagandistic" explanation. Openly acknowledging that sports culture is foremost economic in nature is not compatible with the RF's official view on Swedish sports ideology. Sports as entertainment as a concept can not be allowed to be let loose into the discussion because the discrepancy between RF rhetoric and sports practices would then appear as obvious as it actually is.

Conclusions on Inclusions and Exclusions

The conclusion of this grand narrative analysis is that the sports grand narrative and local variants thereof produce the idea of sports as unproblematic enjoyment, which is a weapon of exclusion because of each narrative's strive for singularity based on strictly coded and conditioned polysemous (many meanings) and multivocal (many-voiced) webs of little stories respectively. This overall silencing capacity effectively hinders entrepreneurial activities because cracks and openings where such activities settle and grow are discursively guarded and, therefore, emerging entrepreneurial activities are tracked and incorporated into the legitimate grand narrative at hand. This characteristic of the proper place (de Certeau, 1988/1984) is a most modernist one and is, at least since Lyotard (1993/1979), seen by many as a dead thought, or as kitsch. Reading sports as entertainment as a proto-industry to what later became conceptualized as the experience economy might highlight aspects of the latter by reflecting upon the "dead thought character" of the former. The idea of a foundational narrative of sports is the root resource for production of sports as sunshine. How it has survived to this day is somewhat of a mystery. This foundation is grounded in ideas of original purity, inherent goodness and chivalric ideals, and it is manifest in contemporary societies in one of two opposing ways: First as *sports as entertainment*, where the sports superman on universalist do-gooderism tour craves freedom from questioning and critical inquiry, favoring the original purity of their ideals over and above those "unfortunate" financial activities necessary for "producing the tour." Second as *sports as idealism*, where the sports superman is the defender of the nonprofit flag in constant search of the holy grail to save 'innocent sport' tainted by the enter of evil economic actors that turns entertaining sports activities into entertainment commodities; a moral contamination as a concrete result of specified actions. These two fairytales of opposing saviors both claim to be providers of transcendental peak sports experiences in service of better understanding between the races, nations, sexes, and value systems through sports. The dominant fairytale, sports as entertainment, has in this chapter instead been rewritten as the story of a contemporary Master sui generis that still serves but also craves to be served. The intertwined production and consumption processes that characterize the experience economy are fertile ground for the master's discursive product, *sportonomic superman*, to operate in financially profitable ways beyond the production of sports as sunshine. The alternative fairytale, sports as idealism, provides a case of excessively frenetic resistance from a local story drifting to propagandistic denial of the dominant fairytale, turning it into a local grand narrative. The case of the Swedish sports model illustrates a sports culture situated in an unproductive dwelling inbetween local traditions (sports as idealism) and global developments (sports as entertainment) where the former shows few productive strategies to deal with the local appearance of the latter. This method of resistance seems to not have the resituating capacity proposed by Boje's less radical approach (2001); therefore, I evoke the Weick et al., (2005) and Frisby (2005) plea in order to encourage more entrepreneurial scholarly endeavors into the field of sports. More scholarship is not important for sports, as such, but for how the use of sports in society at large produces exclusion beyond the sunshine of apparent inclusion. The first "task" might be to continue the conceptual untying of the seductive field of sports as entertainment that has been, to a large extent, highjacked by marketing and brand management thinking. The second "task" might be to engage entrepreneurially in resituating various everyday practices by inquiring the societal uses of sports other than those dominating today.

CHAPTER 9

EXPERIENCING THE DAIRY: UNLOCKING THE VALUE OF PERIPHERAL TRADITIONS

FREDERIC BILL

Introduction

While deliberations on the rise of an experience or cultural economy are traditionally connected to the various service, entertainment, and education sectors of the economy (e.g. Pratt, 2004; Gay and Pryke, 2002; Pine and Gilmore, 1999). There are additional examples of manufacturers claiming to be experience industries. The Swedish automotive company SAAB is a fairly recent case in point. It is in these areas that examples of transformations from secondary and tertiary sector operations to quaternary[85] sector offerings tend to be gathered. These areas constitute, one might argue, the center of focus for inquiries into these topics. When this "bias" towards the core is overcome, it tends to because peripheral groups or areas—in line with some kind of more socially aware approach to research—are pointed out as having been largely overlooked and neglected without justification. Female entrepreneurs and SME-founders living in what are considered peripheral geographic areas are two examples. As far as the latter are concerned, they tend to be considered in one of two possible ways: Either they are seen as peripheral entrepreneurs, carving a more or less meager existence out of the scarce resources available to them, or they are perceived as examples of venture creators that have overcome the difficulties mounting before them—creating against all odds feasible and thriving economic endeavors despite the seemingly poor

---

[85] This term quaternary is used to signify activities that go beyond services. There have been attempts to position the difference between the tertiary and quaternary sectors along the line of technical sophistication. Much could, of course, be said of this, but that would be beside the point in this context.

conditions for growth. What I would like to call the "classical" research approach in business administration, focusing on the grand entrepreneur and his ability, is simply moved from the center to the periphery or the periphery and center are made to switch places by a more or less fictive turning (e.g. Bill, 2003; Johannisson, 1988; Barth, 1963).

Endeavors emanating from or being strongly connected to the primary sector are consequently much less treated in the literature on SMEs and entrepreneurship as well as in the various treatises on the shift towards an experience economy. This arguably, goes, especially for the agrarian part (e.g., Sundin, 2004; Anderson, 2000). Even Anderson (2000), despite looking specifically to the periphery in search of entrepreneurship, notes mainly tertiary sector endeavors. Attempting to upset the traditional core-periphery relation, he seeks out new endeavors outside urban areas, finding, though, essentially tertiary sector business ventures that draw on the shift from a technological to a cultural paradigm. For instance, regarding an entrepreneur who uses an old castle crypt to stage themed weddings, he states:

He took a latent value form of tradition, heritage and antiquity and transformed it into an appropriate form for harvesting benefit. He tapped into a reservoir of time, drew of value and sold this imagery of time. (Anderson, 2000:100)

He does not, however, consider the possibility of drawing more explicitly on traditional countryside operations. Anderson's guiding presumption is that the relation between the core and the periphery is changing, due primarily to the contemporary transcendence of communication—with regard to both information transfer and corporeal movement. The earlier situation, where the core functioned as a center of gravity, drawing resources to itself from the surroundings, is complemented by a movement to make the periphery of value in itself. The other case presented is of a fifty-year-old steamboat–The "Puffer"–that has been renovated and is now used for cruises. The business vendors, a well-educated couple, offer customers a sea journey, where those who so desire may partake in the maintenance of the ship; in essence, paying for the treat of shuffling coal. Anderson analyzes the case, stating:

At a superficial level this business may appear to be just another tourist treat. Certainly we can explain this as the commodification of heritage, the making available for sale (or is it sail?) of an old way of life; one which seems peaceful, pleasant and nostalgic. This perspective meshes into the idea of post-necessity consumption, a facet of the growth of post-modern consumption. (Anderson, 2000:99)

This is a position that Hjorth and Johannisson (2003—in dealing with localised economic development—elaborate by bridging the individual and collective levels. In essence, Anderson (2000) has demonstrated conceptually, and moreover, illustrated empirically, that rural "entrepreneurs," guided by what is sometimes termed economies of scope, are able to change the existing use value of local resources to a higher market value, thriving on the postmodern consumer's search for quality of life.

I believe that Anderson (2000) has made an important contribution by elevating the transformation of customer preferences and the, still fairly novel, attempts to consequently exploit the latent value of the periphery. The social dimension of place and space seems, however, to be more or less absent in his article. Even though the periphery as place has moved closer to us, the periphery as space has, in some ways, moved even further away from the core. Activities in the periphery—in agriculture, fishing, and the likes—have become strange, or even exotic, to an increasing number of people. In essence, the areas Anderson deal with have become more easily reachable, but simultaneously less accessible. At this point it becomes possible to state that Anderson (2000), in a way, still deals with the core rather than the periphery since he is still looking for the tertiary sector and the "traditional" forms of experience offerings, like themed parties and steam engine adventure rides. The "Puffer" gains value, of course, by being fuelled by tradition and legacy, but the steam boat ride offer is not, in itself, different from other adventure experiences. It is not by necessity that it takes place outside the core. The periphery is an important part of the scenery and staging, but it is not the core of the offering.

With the intention of expanding on this idea of the periphery, I look therefore for value additions and experience staging where they are not normally sought. This is in operations still closely connected to a primary sector venture: In a middle-sized agricultural company, to be more precise. In many, I would even say most, countries, farmers form the single largest group of business owners and their companies are often very small. Furthermore, the formal education among the managers of agrarian sector SMEs would, in all likelihood, tend to be rather basic. It is my assumption that people could not normally be expected to follow through on higher education before settling on small scale farming as their preferred way of making a living. Companies, mostly in the Swedish primary sector, have the supply function to different industries and, sometimes, if to a diminishing extent, directly to local retailers. As could be expected of the primary sector, they form the underpinning of various second and third sector endeavors. Not only farmers but also forest owners and mine operators fill this basic and unglamorous, but still very essential, role for the economy. The primary sector SMEs could, therefore, be said to share several traits or circumstances, such as being hampered by a generally low level of education and a marginalized position in the economic structure. Not being able to transcend their allotted position, they are caught in a subservient position relative to what is normally considered the more refined second and third sectors of economic life. Aided by inspiration from Andersons (2000) and also, to some extent, the conceptual framework of Pine and Gilmore (1999), I intend to explore paths to transcend this situation. This chapter explores the potential to hotwire the primary and quaternary sectors of the economy, using the hitherto undertheorized, but still continually emerging, concept of an experience economy—sometimes also referred to as the cultural or creative economy (e.g., Pine and Gilmore, 1999)—as an important tool. This chapter is intended as an explorative or, perhaps, rather inspiring attempt to deal with the idea of an emerging quaternary sector in the economy by digging into a more bottom-up approach to the notion of the experience economy. This experience phenomenon, which is often elevated and put forth in many contexts, holds, I argue, an interesting but often overlooked potential for business undertakings in the primary sector, since it might be a powerful tool of transformation. It carries in it the potential of instantaneously shifting "basic" primary sector endeavors to "advanced" quaternary sector endeavors, increasing and shifting the market value of the firm's offerings in a momentary as well as lasting way, without actually changing those same offerings in any tangible manner. In other words, this chapter touches upon the growing body of research in the area of agri-tourism, which deals with the spread of, and motivation for, incorporating tourism related components into farm operations (e.g. McGehee and Kim, 2004). Still, it differs from that body of research, since the focus of my treatise is to dig into the very notion, or idea, of the experience.

Method

In carrying out this study, I initially performed a "faux" case study, using information from one company (Wapnö Ltd) that was of interest with regard to the theoretical points of departure. I read their homepage on the World Wide Web and from this information created a case description was created. I then used this case description for input to the discussion and interpretation. Information gathered from the Internet must, of course, be regarded as a very specific view presented by the enterprisers or entrepreneurs (with or without the help of a marketing bureau) in order to put forth the interpretation they wish to promote. This could, from one perspective, be seen as a weakness, since researchers are restricted to the information they choose to put forth, and are barred from asking critical, as well as follow-up, questions. The methodology I chose avoids this problem. The aim of this study is not to-once-and-for-all explain and pinpoint the phenomena of "primary sector driven experiences," but rather to gain insight—and perhaps even hindsight—into how an ongoing process of transformation could be interpreted and understood. We get one side of the story only, and probably a well-rehearsed side of it at that. This might not, at first, seam so different from what would be acquired by elite interviews. In those cases when, senior management is questioned, a rehearsed story tend to be given to the interviewer. Since I do not aspire to give a true or factual story, this "getting-the-rehearsed-story-only-problem" poses, however, less of a predicament for the current undertaking. Intending, rather, to bring a theoretical model or preunderstanding to bear on a phenomenon, in order to deepen the interpretative depth, of the model. The phenomena I have set out to study will also, in my view, gain from being treated as a socially constructed relational phenomenon, rather than as fixed, with an essence of its own (c.f. Berger and Luckmann, 1966). The main weakness with the method would be, rather, that I am left bereft of the richness and flavor that emanates from exploring and meeting several different accounts of the same story. Instead of a rich plurality, I meet only a surface with little depth. The color and richness of the plurality emerging in the meeting between real individuals and conceptual phenomena eludes me, more or less, completely as a result of this method. The main advantages of the "faux" case study method are availability and that the information being used has been considered and organized by company representatives. It is, therefore, a very good source when it comes to showing how the company wishes to be perceived. Shortcomings of the method are, especially, the lack of personal interaction and the absence of improvisation and critical follow up. In the next phase I ventured out into the field and visited the company *in situ*. During my stay I conducted an interview with the CEO of Wapnö Ltd. The plurality of the account is thereby increased as other voices are included and given room, in my text as well as in my understanding. This follow-up method alleviates the aforementioned problems, increasing the plurality and depth of the interpretation which simultaneously benefits from the fact that I have already become acquainted with the company from its web page.

In conclusion I think that the method, in its totality, has proven very useful, since the two elements have reinforced and enriched one another. The interview increased my understanding of the website in its totality, while the preunderstanding that I brought with me to the interview situation made the conversation easier and more fruitful.

The Case and Anderson

Wapnö Ltd is a medium sized agricultural company that, from a production perspective, focuses primarily on husbandry, foresting, and dairy operations. When one manoeuvres into their homepage, the menu of the site provides an overview of their various operations. As a visitor, I am to chose between the following topics: location, history, Wapnö Castle, the barn, happening at Wapnö, consumer, animals, forestry, horticulture, Wapnö dairy and environmental policy. This is illustrated by picture one, taken from the index page of their website.

Figure 9.1 Introductory Picture from www.wapno.se

The text in picture one is in Swedish simply because the company does not present an English version of their homepage. Regional or local character can take many different forms, but this circumstance could readily be interpreted as signification of the societal embedment of the company. Wapnö Ltd is a primary and secondary sector operation that also operates on the tertiary and quaternary levels of the economy. This makes the company a well-chosen case for the endeavor to go beyond the spatial periphery of Anderson (2000) into the cultural or social margins. It is a good illustration of the growing discrepancy between the diminishing spatial and the increasing social and cultural distances.

Figure 9.2 Pictures from the Barn and the Castle from www.wapno.se

Following the links on the menu page, some fascinating, or at least unexpected, information revealed itself to us—if the anthropomorphism is excused. First of all, is the simple fact that visitors to the site are actually introduced to a short version of the estate's history: An historical exposition that stretches all the way back to the fourteenth century. Visitors can then move from there to a presentation of the Castle. On to the "The Castle of Wapnö" page, there is information about the possibility to of holding weddings in this traditional milieu as well as using it for throwing theme parties. There are different possibilities, since the lavish rooms of the Castle differ somewhat from the rustic environment in the refashioned old barn. (See picture two).

In this way, a feeling of genuineness is evoked, drawing on the Swedish rural, or even agricultural, tradition as well as on the more aristocratic traditions of lavishness. As Anderson (op. cit.) noticed with regard to the Castle crypt operator:

He took a latent value form of tradition, heritage and antiquity and transformed it into an appropriate form for harvesting benefit. (Anderson, 2000:100)

The difference being, of course, that Wapnö Ltd is not selling these latent values; instead, they add them to their existing product line, merging several sectors of the economy rather then just establishing a tertiary sector undertaking. When the CEO initiated the transformation of the company during the mid 1990s, he begun with the Christmas fair:

I normally say that the Christmas fair was the first official thing we did, and that has meant incredibly much for the spreading of the brand. Then, nine years ago, we still were a traditional mature company, an agricultural company. [86] (Bengtsson, 2005-03-04)

He met, however, with a rather limited understanding, since people tended to perceive the company as it was, rather then as what it could become (Bengtsson, 2005-03-04). The changing nature of the agricultural company—the transformation to an open company—seemingly had a solid impact on the perception of the business. It scarcely affected the day-to-day operations though; today approximately 98 % of the work hours in the company are still devoted to the primary and secondary sector undertakings. Accordingly, the CEO also stressed the importance and centrality of the dairy operation during the interview:

When it comes to the dairy operations that we have and which are the clock of the company, the market contact is of course important. The channel to the customer is very important. (Bengtsson, 2005-03-04)

The next topic, "happening at Wapnö", is even more fascinating, since visitors are presented with the full schedule for the year's activities at the farm. At this point the website visitors are also presented with a very strong initial greeting:

Kom när ni vill
Passa på en vacker dag att uppleva livet på landet. Ni är alltid välkomna till Wapnö för att titta runt på gården på egen hand. Här finns gårdskartor som ni kan använda på er rundvandring på Wapnö.
Titta in till korna och kalvarna genom de stora fönster som finns in i ladugårdarna. I mejeriet har ni möjlighet att se hela processen från att mjölken kommer i ledningar från ladugården till att de är färdiga och paketerade i sina förpackningar.

---

[86] Since the interview with Bengtsson was held in Swedish, all quotes are my own translations to English. He used the Swedish word 'mogen' several times and I have translated it to 'mature', since it implies that companies are founded, grow and then stagnate when reaching a state of maturity. At this point they need to be imbued with new energy if they are to continue evolving, which is what has been accomplished during Bengtsson's time at the company's helm.

Figure 9.3 Pictures of the Cows and the Castle from www.wapno.se

"Visit us when you like", it says in Swedish at the top. It continues: "Take the opportunity to experience life in the countryside, on a beautiful day. At Wapnö you are always welcome to experience the farm on your own. We have maps of the estate that you may use on your tour. Have a peak at the cows and calves through the large windows that you find in the walls of the barns. In the dairy you have the possibility to see the milk pouring from the pipes that transport it from the barn and follow it until it is packaged and ready".[87] As we continue the exploration of the website, we encounter information regarding Sunday dinner in the Castle, Sunday dinners are a Swedish tradition, and how to get a table at the Castle's restaurant. Furthermore, there are many "traditional" events, mainly focusing the topics of Swedish rural life and the area of gastronomy. We also find information about the annual event of letting the cows onto pasture on the second of May:

Betessläppning på Wapnö 2 maj
Årets Betessläppning blev en succé med rekord många besökare.
Solen gassade hela dagen och både kor och människor stormtrivdes. Drygt 3000 personer kom till Wapnö söndagen 2 maj när vi släppte ut korna på vårpremiär. Många roades av de skuttande och spralliga korna när de slängde sig ut i det gröna. Inslaget med försäljning av färsk mjölk och bulle uppskattades både av gammal som ung.

---

[87] My own translation from the Swedish.

217

Figure 9.4 Happy Cows Out to Pasture from www.wapno.se

Visitors are, in the Swedish text besides the picture, informed that 3000 people attended the event, and that representatives of Wapnö Ltd added to the experience by selling them fresh milk. To continue the quotation from Anderson (op. cit):

> *He tapped into a reservoir of time, drew of value and sold this imagery of time.* (Anderson, 2000:100)

In staging these kinds of events, Wapnö Ltd transcends the sectors of the economy where it previously operated, offering its consumers the pastoral and timeless experience of husbandry as an added value.

Skogsbruk i parken

Figure 9.5 Picture of Horse and Wagon from www.wapno.se

Also presented is the event when young school children visiting the farm to try traditional farm life chores, like milking and sitting in a tractor. Likewise visitors are told that there is a large fair on gardens from past and present. The customers can partake in small educational tests, which are presented on the milk packages (which is sort of a Swedish tradition) and then find the answers on the homepage. Last but not the least visitors can actually see presentations of the animals producing milk; there are several pictures with comments of cows seemingly enjoying themselves. The animals are also interacting with human caretakers, who are presented with names and pictures. The visitor gets the impression that these cows are well cared for and that someone, who visitors can meet through his or her picture, is actually caring for them. Visitors to the site are also told about the planned expansion and reconstructions on the farm. When the forest is described further ahead we are told that it is taken care of by Södra, one of Sweden's largest forest operators. On the web site there is a very curious view, though, of a horse pulling a timber wagon (Picture 5). We are told that this is "foresting in the park," in the explanatory text below the picture, so it is probably a real. At the same time, it is hardly representative of the way the production of lumber is handled by Södra—at Wapnö or elsewhere—which is obvious when one reads what is said on the homepage. The picture is, at the same time, both a repetition and a recreation. It shows us something as it was in a way that makes it an experience and thereby adds something to the repetition, making it a recreation. Furthermore, you can actually see pictures from the farm, including a large machine that gives the impression of efficiency (Picture 6). The texts commenting on these pictures say that this is how the food for the cows is produced, and that the visitor may then simply follow the links to some pictures of grain and vegetables growing. In a way, the happy cows in the pasture and the tranquil cow and human interaction gives us a somewhat romantic impression of genuine husbandry. This impression is, however, connected to modern efficiency, intending perhaps to merge traditionalism with modernism, showing an improved traditional setting. At least this is how I interpret my perception. This interpretation particularly suits the picture of what is called a "witch circle," and the accompanying rhetorical question: "Are there UFOs at Wapnö?". The traditional supernatural or superstitious understanding of the countryside is reinterpreted in modern form. The repetition has been enriched by a small difference and brought forth as a variation of the traditional supernatural way of perceiving ones surroundings.

Figure 9.6 Harvesting Machine from www.wapno.se

Mystifying

The impression of the farm transmitted trough the website was, at least to me, flavorful. I hope that I have transmitted some of that flavor by means of my short pictorial description above. I certainly felt nearness and genuineness when browsing the site and would be willing to admit that it is kind of a strong experience. There are a number of pictures of the animals and some named employees. Furthermore, the web site visitor can find phone numbers to the various administrators and managers of the company, including the CEO.

I would like to raise the question of what about the case of Wapnö could be understood with the aid of Anderson (2000) and what dimensions of this agricultural company transcend his study. I intend to answer this query with the aid of the case above, illuminated and elaborated by interview material from my visit to the farm. First of all, the company that seemed so ordered on the elevated level of the homepage is beginning to blur. When the question of how the company had evolved came up, the CEO focused, for instance, initially on the aspect of profitability:

> *Wapnö was a traditional and mature agricultural company, which we refocused to a market oriented company. We wished to have our products brought to the consumer and on that journey, in order to market ourselves; we also opened up the company. That is our business idea, to have an open company. The consumer can see from were the products emanate and during that journey we have seen opportunities to do things like Christmas and garden fairs, and among those things are the castle. As means in the marketing of Wapnö. Of course this is in order to earn money on the company.* (Bengtsson, 2005-03-04)

That is, the seemingly straightforward transformation, as perceived from the homepage, starts to break up into a number of different transformations of varying reach. The nice and ordered picture put forth by myself in the case description above is obviously not really the one held by the CEO. His perception of the process differs in several ways. I experienced the various activities of the company as an integrated offering, carefully staged and performed. It might be that the offering of the company is as integrated in his perception as it is in my own, but it is seemingly far less ordered and well thought through for him. Rather then a planned process of transformation from mature and traditional to young and customer oriented, we meet a winding path of trial and error: a journey driven by the, more or less, obvious need to abandon ones current position; a travel guided by the vision of opening up the company in order to bring the customer much closer:

Partly there were many slumbering possibilities that where not used and also it was a way of reshaping in order to manage the future. It is plain when one is stuck in the mature world and therefore has to find something else. But the basic thought was primarily to make use of the resources at hand. To get life in to it, because that in which there is no life should be torn down. (Bengtsson, 2005-03-04)

It becomes obvious that the company is constituted by a number of ideas that come together to form a unity or totality. At the same time, this totality is just one of many possible totalities brought about by gut feeling and practical testing, or looking at what is at hand and trying to utilize it as best as one can. In the case of Wapnö this very practical approach has lead to a conceptual creation centered around traditional farm operations and the lavishness of the aristocracy, since this is what was at hand on the premises of the estate. So even though some events are chosen and others are not, the physical space actually delimits the choices at hand; giving, more or less unconsciously, an overall general direction in the development of the companies integrated offering. From the array of possibilities within this overall trend, some are chosen and tried, while others are left dormant. The guiding star is practicality though, or rather profitability, and everything else becomes a means of achieving it. As the CEO puts it, when discussing the Castle:

In principal it is cold economic considerations. And we have seen that the Castle has not been really successful up to now. I am right now trying to remodel it again… We think that it is an added value in increasing the experience of coming to Wapnö. It is a value and should be economically feasible, which we shall manage in the end. (Bengtsson, 2005-03-04)

When prodding the surface, the wholeness I perceived when visiting the company, as well as on the Internet, is broken up into parts that together constitute that totality, which I first met.
At one level this is of course fairly similar to what Anderson (op. cit.) presents in his article, when stating with regard to the steamboat operations:

> *At a superficial level this business may appear to be just another*
> *tourist treat. Certainly we can explain this as the commodification*
> *of heritage, the making available for sale (or is it sail?) of an old*
> *way of life; one which seems peaceful, pleasant and nostalgic.*
> *This perspective meshes into the idea of post-necessity consump-*
> *tion, a facet of the growth of post-modern consumption.* (Ander-
> son, 2000:99)

Wapnö Ltd offers an experience that draws on heritage and nostalgia, elevating the values of the periphery. There are, however, important dissimilarities as well: First of all, Wapnö is not mainly attempting to attract tourists; instead, the consumers of its dairy products constitute the primary target group. The notion of "post-necessity consumption" is used as a catalyst in meshing together several sectors of the economy, Simultaneously operating all the way from the primary to the quaternary sector, causing the various undertakings to support one another. What is more, though, is that Anderson (2000) never addresses the question of what could be found behind the scene of these kinds of offerings. What does it actually mean to commodify heritage, as he puts it?

This is where I believe that we need to expand on the distinction between place and space that I hinted at above. The place of the periphery is, perhaps, moving closer to the core, but the peripheral space is moving away. The countryside is more easily accessible but it is nevertheless also more exotic since more and more people feel less and less familiar with it. Together with the change to a more postmodern consumption pattern, this pattern supports the essential foundation of the cases presented by Anderson (2000). The company, Wapnö Ltd, gathers strength from being perceived as a *traditional*, while still *modern*, primary sector company where you, as a customer, are invited to, and even into, the company:

> *We wished to have our products brought to the consumer and on*
> *that journey, in order to market ourselves; we also opened up the*
> *company. That is our business idea, to have an open company.*
> (Bengtsson, 2005-03-04)

The company is traditional and local, showing off the cows when they leave the barns after the winter, and focusing on the closeness between man and animal. In one picture on the site visitors can, for instance, view a male farm worker caringly patting one of the cows. This creates an atmosphere of old times and genuine farm live, aspiring, thereby, to be a reproduction of old practices. There are pictures of the workhorse pulling the timber cart, and visitors are introduced to the old-fashioned castle and the rustic barn. Taken together, this creates a feeling of traditional husbandry, and, in this case, the sought after reproduction stands in for closeness and nearness. The animals are brought close to us and, at the same time, we meet the persons who are close to the cows when taking care of them. Wapnö seems like a harmonious farm of old, where food production is something natural, and the animals and the humans are close together, cooperating intimately with each other. To this image one could easily add the idea of the company as an entity that has evolved beyond maturity; a young and modern company:

We do not wish to be an estate; we want to be a company...
(Bengtsson, 2005-03-04)

The tension in the case description above is also easily perceptible in the accounts of the CEO. On the one hand, he represents Wapnö as a traditional agricultural endeavor, if not an estate, and on the other as a modern company that uses available technology:

We are an agricultural company, but evolve more and more towards a processing company. (Bengtsson, 2005-03-04)

This tension is reflected in the company, since we can find examples of very modern and sometimes even state of the art technology on the company website. Technology is presented alongside more traditional pictures of man/animal interaction. Like, for instance, the large concrete carousel, under construction at the time, where the cows of Wapnö are to be mechanically milked in an extremely efficient way. Likewise, we meet the large combine harvester, which efficiently makes sure that the cows will have enough locally produced and healthy food during the long winter months spent in the barn.

The company draws upon both the idea of progress and the idea of pastoral heritage, creating a bond with the visitors and customers by capitalizing upon the values of modernity and efficiency; shared values between the core and the periphery create a bond between company and customer. To this is added, though, the pastoral and traditional; the space that is moving away and becoming exotic. The nearness to, and experience with, animals that is no longer commonplace. In order to elaborate further upon this, I intend to draw upon Deleuze (esp. 1968 and 1964) and his deliberations on difference and repetition. Take, for an example, the combine harvester (Picture 6) on the website. It openly illustrates the fact that Wapnö uses efficient techniques for its primary and secondary sector endeavors. The combine harvester, which, of course, is a contemporary rural sight, appears as a genuine artifact of industrial farming. The large machine acts as a double signifier, activating ideas of efficiency as well as notions of traditional agrarian practices; representing, in a way, the company as whole, since it merges the idea of efficiency with the value of heritage and pastoral tradition.

Horse and cart, combine harvester, cow/human interaction and a castle; traditional farm operation may obviously be seen as many things. It seems—to use pictorial language—more like a multiheaded hydra then a single and well-understood concept. We have the work-horse pulling its timber wagon; we have the closeness between man and animal manifested through the young man patting the—seemingly fairly pleased—cow; and we have the large combine harvester giving an impression of traditional large-scale horticulture. We also meet the themed milieu of the castle and the barn, simultaneously putting forth the traditional rustic life in the countryside and the more lavish castle dwelling traditions of the Swedish aristocracy.

Taken one step further, we could conclude that this is not simply a repetition of something from a special historical setting; instead, it is a *socially sensitive* reconstruction of the past. Another time is being re-constructed, aided by a number of repetitions. We see how several signifiers or components (depending on methodological stance), are re-peated or activated on the website; signifiers or components that could, furthermore, probably be seen as somewhat anachronistic. It is, for instance, very unlikely that a representative countryside dweller from the societal context being repeated would have recognized it as something from her or his own chronological setting, mainly due to the fact that what is repeated or reconstructed is not a specific historical setting, but rather a space that is becoming exotic; the space, that is, of the pastoral periphery. Wapnö is not trying to present the past as it was, if, indeed, this were even possible; instead, a simulacrum of shards and pieces is used to recreate the past in a new way, presenting an idealized past "as it should have been." The company presents a multilayered repetition, mixing the techniques of creation, repetition, reproduction and recrea-tion, in order to create an experience appearing inside the mind of the perceiver.

Demystifying

Imagine that difference is not something natural or spontaneous, but an artefact that it is made:

> *Difference is this state in which determination takes the form of unilateral distinction. We must therefore say that difference is made, or makes itself, as in the expression 'make a difference'.*
> (Deleuze, 1968:28)

What is the same and what is different, therefore, depends on who is perceiving the repetition. Difference is a claim made by someone; therefore: "Difference and repetition are only apparently in opposition" (Deleuze, 1964:49). The one cannot exist without the other. When arguing that the repetitions taking place at Wapnö produce something different from that being repeated, I therefore operate on a naïve a level. Repetition can either take the form of "reproduction" or the form of "recreation." The modern way of dealing with the problem of repetition is to introduce the idea of human error, viewing the repeater, or agent of repetition, as mainly a source of error, and accordingly attempting to minimize this source through standardizing and fool proofing different procedures. This approach basically attempts, in one way or another, to eliminate human shortcomings, even though the repeater himself cannot be removed: "For there is no repetition without a repeater, nothing repeated without a repetitious soul" (Deleuze, 1968:23). He or she can be subsumed during the process of repetition. The overall aim being, of course, to eliminate more or less entirely the influence of the repeater on the process of repetition.

To be somewhat more substantial, it could be argued in relation to Wapnö—the aforementioned primary sector SME—that the integration of offers from various sectors of the economy constitutes a shift in perception rather then a change in kind. A farmer attempting this shift would still be doing, what has always been done in farming. The farmer would be repeating and thereby also reproducing the concept, as embedded in praxis as it may be, of farming.

It is undeniable that there could be a difference introduced in the repetition, for instance that ploughing could be powered by a machine instead of an oxen. It would perhaps be regarded then as a re-creation of the concept of farming, where the farmer is seen, for instance, interpreting the umbrella concept of sowing:

> *The first repetition is repetition of the Same, explained by the identity of the concept or representation; the second includes difference, and includes itself in the alterity of the Idea, in the heterogeneity of an 'a-presentation'.* (Deleuze, 1968:24)

Note that this is only one possible interpretation, one intended principally as an illustration. The farm scene viewed by a bystander might very well still be understood in the same way, as an example of farming—even though it could just as well be seen as the creation of something new, for instance, as industrial agriculture performed by an agricultural worker. The character of the difference imposed on the process of ploughing is determined, as has been pointed out above, subjectively from the relative positions of reproduction, recreation, repetition, and even creation as perceived by different subjects or entities.

In shifting from the primary to the quaternary sector, the farmer above will therefore not necessarily be required to *do* a difference, even though he might be attempting to *make* a difference in what is being done. The Wapnö company spends only an insignificant amount of the staff's total working hours—about 2 % (Bengtsson, 2005-03-04)—on maintenance of the "public" areas. Still, this openness is a major part of understanding the company. This is shown, for instance, by the public visibility and the impressive amount of visitors when the calves are let out to pasture in early spring. If we were to venture back to the theoretical perspective, it could be said that the meeting between a repetition of the more or less reproducing kind and a subject perceiving a difference in this repetition is a possible way of invoking a re-creation, or even a creation, rather then a simple reproduction. The subject might meet something perceived as arcane or genuine and therefore have an experience regardless of the intentions of the repeater, but the repeater could also attempt evoking precisely this experience and, thereby, create a new concept in the course of the repetition. Alternatively, it could be a question of substituting one concept for another. An experience could be, but must not be, an intended or unintended shift in the subjective perception of the nature of a repetition. The way to stage an experience, then, might be to do it as it has always been done. The experience being produced in the mind of an individual meeting a repetition is interpreted or experienced as a recreation rather then a reproduction—or this is how it could be argued in this very special primary sector context, by someone meeting a recreation, or creation, that is perceived as a reproduction (c.f. Anderson, 2000). The experience offered by Wapnö Ltd is powered by staging the ideal picture of the expected, pastoral and orienting. In their context, this amounts to various agricultural endeavors, implying repetitions of genuine husbandry and farming—in ways that are seemingly reproductive but that taken together add up to something more,[88] forming between themselves a simulacrum of old times, interpreted in a socially or culturally conscious way. The Dadaist and Surrealist painters who used shock as a means of introducing disorientation into their representations would have likely considered the experiences in this Wapnö way the antithesis of their attempts; that is, the repetition was in their case, put forth as recreation that introduced something unexpected or abhorrent (Hjorth, 2004). At Wapnö, the repetition instead takes the form of a cosy and warm recreation.

In Conclusion

Primary sector vendors, cooperating with their customers and other bystanders, may cocreate experiences simply through utilizing repetitions. Shifting from the primary or secondary, to the tertiary or quaternary sector of the economy, therefore, is not only a question of staging parties, holidays, and such in the geographical periphery. It may also be accomplished by drawing on the increasing social or cultural distance between the core and the periphery. In making their company open and transparent, Wapnö Ltd has merged their "traditional" primary and secondary sector undertakings—husbandry and dairy operations—with elements from the tertiary and quaternary sectors of the economy, thereby creating an integrated offering that draws on all the sectors of the economy in order to generate value. This means that they are doing what they have always done, but doing it in a transparent way. Tapping into, as Anderson (2000) has argued, latent values of tradition and antiquity, they may in fact even draw value from repeating in a way that is regarded as traditional, while still incorporating the efficiency of modernity into the venture. What they present, however, is not an image of the a time when the world was more pastoral, but rather a simulacrum that simultaneously provides a bridge to the understanding of the customer through its components of efficiency and

---

[88] It could be argued that a reproduction in itself could be an experience, for instance, when someone uses an old or outdated technique to produce something. This individual is simply repeating and thereby reproducing what has been done before, in the same way as it was previously done. This is a faulty assumption, though, since the simple fact that someone now perceives the reproduction as being a re-creation is, in itself, introducing a difference into the repetition. Thereby, the reproduction is in fact made a re-creation.

modernity, and exposes the customer to the harmonious strangeness of a periphery that has moved away from them. This merges sectors of the economy and time into a simulacrum that draws upon the positive aspects of various eras. Wapnö Ltd both preserves and bridges the gap between core and periphery. This is possible since difference emanates from a change in perception, when perception meets a repeated concept, but not necessarily, from a change in what is actually being performed. The primary sector vendor could, though, take an active part in this perception affecting process, for instance, by staging an integrated setting around a number of repetitions—like a simulacrum of times. Companies operating in the geographical periphery may well, as noted by Anderson (2000), position themselves on the higher levels of value creation, powered by the quality of life of the postmodern consumer. This can, furthermore, be carried out by drawing on the increasing social or cultural distance between the activities of the core and those of the periphery. Other companies, however, might be able to make use of this through merging aspects from different sectors of the economy into their overall offering; in essence, grafting new aspects and dimensions onto their offerings, making it possible to invoke an offering that is integrated in such a way that spans several sectors of the economy. Through invoking an integrated setting or contextual frame for their operations, they could simultaneously repeat and re-create their offerings on several levels. Integrating forward might be part of an attempt to renew and revitalize ones primary sector company, but as the present case has shown, this integration could be seriously enhanced by innovative attempts to close the gap between producer and consumer. The repetition, in a Deleuzian sense, of the traditional as a simulacrum of times, constitutes one such attempt. In this way, this chapter has attempted to shed some light on how experiences could also be used in normally neglected areas of the economy. Furthermore, it constitutes an attempt to venture beyond the easily accessible metaphors of theater and staging in order to problematize and fragment the concept of experience. If differences are made by means of repetition, then experiencing the dairy actually makes a difference.

CHAPTER 10

PLACE BRANDING IN AN ENTREPRENEURSHIP EXPERIENCE ECONOMY
THE KINGDOM OF FURNITURE AND LONG BEFORE

MARCELA RAMÍREZ-PASILLAS

Introduction

The history of branding The Kingdom of Furniture goes back to 1994. Johan Sjoberg, the business owner of the furniture store Svenssons i Lammhult conceived the initial idea of branding Lammhult in 1994. Lammhult is a community with an active furniture industry located in the region of Smaland in southern Sweden. For eight years, Johan Sjoberg worked together with other local actors in a network in order to develop The Kingdom of Furniture. This network renewed the local tourism infrastructure and started orchestrating periodic events to attract potential consumers. In 2001, the network launched shopping excursions (i.e., Design Days) from Malmo, Gothenburg, and Stockholm to Lammhult during the weekends of Easter Day and All Saints' Day. During these excursions, firms held lectures featuring designers, architects, and decorators, and prepared special exhibitions accompanied with traditional Swedish refreshments (e.g. fika). The activities of the Design Days were co-ordinated to promote the circulation of customers from store to store and to local restaurants. In 2002, Johan Sjoberg together with the local trade association and the Wood Centre Nassjo Foundation created the firm The Kingdom of Furniture with the specific purpose of branding Lammhult. The Kingdom of Furniture became a trademark through which the networked firms paid a fee in order to finance their joint activities. The Kingdom of Furniture also established an annual planning meeting and held the first mega-event (i.e., Designer's Saturday). Since then, The Kingdom of Furniture has hosted events for potential consumers from all over Sweden.

In this chapter, I use the example of The Kingdom of Furniture as an illustration of place branding as an entrepreneurial process in an experience economy. I focus on the organization of people, resources, and actions prior to the conception of The Kingdom of Furniture as a new company. I consider such an organization as an example of the strong significance of entrepreneurship in place branding in an experience economy. The question of how branding is initiated and organized in a place is critically important. The history of organization, concern, commitment, and invention in a community helps us bring out the entrepreneurial entrepreneur to place branding in an experience economy. The experience economy proposes that companies must orchestrate memorable events for their customers when they purchase a good or service (Pine and Gilmore, 1999). These events shall produce a personal experience for every customer. Politicians, business owners, and consultants have adopted branding management practices to promote the renewal of places with experiences in order to attract tourists and residents. As a consequence, the production of experiences as a tool of place branding has become a real-world phenomenon (Van Ham, 2002), which has been accelerated in the present renewal of places.

Studies on place branding still lack an opening towards entrepreneurship in an experience economy. The existing literature follows a strict management approach across the fields of marketing (Kotler and Gertner, 2002), public administration (Bennett and Savani, 2003) and regional studies (Evans, 2003). Such an approach emphasizes the application of the traditional marketing mix, the strategic planning process (e.g., Asworth and Voogd 1990, 1994; Kotler et. al., 1993, 1999) and the communication of the image of places (Papadoupulos, 2004). In this chapter, I want to make a contribution to studies of place branding from the perspective of entrepreneurship in an experience economy. I conceptualized branding as an entrepreneurial process introducing a new order and translating this new order into new social practices in a place. With Johnstone and Lionais (2004) and Anderson (1990), I elaborate on an entrepreneurial process as the organization of people, resources and actions 'bottom–up' for further invention of new social practices in places. My aim here is to study how an entrepreneurial process (organization for invention) initiates place branding in an experience economy.

This chapter proceeds according to the following structure: In section two, I examine the dominant views of branding—corporate and place—and discuss them in relation to entrepreneurship in an experience economy. In section three, I present place branding as an entrepreneurial process in an experience economy and introduce a model of entrepreneurs in the branding of a place. Section four includes the method of my study, and in section five, the story of 'The Kingdom of Furniture' is illustrated. In section six, I analyze the story according to the discussed model, and in section seven, I present my contribution to place branding in an experience economy and implications for future research.

Place Branding

Antecedent

The origins of place branding in an experience economy are traced back to corporate branding. Corporate branding is a crucial field of expertise for management in which entrepreneurship has been reduced into a representation of managerial entrepreneurs. Literature and practice on corporate branding has evolved for the last 50 years, exploring ways to increase value to companies, products, and services and, consequently, building brand loyalty (for a review see Louro and Cuhna, 2001). In the 1950s, such literature encouraged managers to build "brands" or, in other words, a good image for products (Gardner and Levy, 1955). Managers gradually developed "mark of ownerships," which resulted in a means for product differentiation and preference (Knox and Bickerton, 2003). They started using names, logos, symbols, designs, or a combination therein to identify the goods or services of one seller, or a group of sellers, from those of their competitors (Kotler and Gertner, 2002). Management writing recognized later, though, that a brand was more than a name, term, or sign given to a product (Balmer and Gray, 2003); thus, such literature proposed different models as the latest solution to branding challenges. Such models provoked the emergence of managerial entrepreneurs (Hjorth, 2005) who offered the solution of innovation to brand companies. Such claims seemed rather important, as companies needed to sustain their consumers' loyalty. The corporate branding models required that managerial entrepreneurs administered either: a holistic identity system for the company and its products (e.g. Aaker, 1996; Balmer, 2002); the visual elements, logo, and product design (Bailey and Schechter, 1994; Grossman, 1994); the emotional components (Keller,

1999); or a combination of the above mentioned elements (de Cherna-tony and Dall'Olmo-Riley, 1997).

In the 1990s, academics also stressed the importance of the people and organization behind the brand. This emphasis changed the focus of branding from the construction of the necessary brand attributes to the management of the planning process (Low and Fullerton 1994). Mana-gerial entrepreneurs approached corporate branding with a formula for success: brand planning that incorporated identity, image, and commu-nication strategies (Balmer, 2002). Consequently, corporate branding increasingly emphasized the importance of maintaining managerial control over brands. While literature on corporate branding continued to develop, urban planning, regional studies, and public management literature "borrowed" the concepts from the traditional marketing ap-proach and applied them to places.

Management and Managerial Entrepreneurs in Place Branding

Inspired by the success of corporate branding, public managers applied marketing strategies to promote places—communities, towns, cities, regions, and countries (Van Ham, 2002). Public managers relied on marketing strategies as places competed for tourists, residents, inward investment, and increased exports (Kotler et al., 1993). Place branding, it was argued (Kavaratzis, 2004; Papadopoulos, 2004), was the appro-priate way to describe and implement place marketing and image communication for communities, towns, cities, regions and, countries in order to improve the quality of residents' lives.

The precursor to place branding was place marketing (e.g., Asworth and Voogd 1988, 1990, 1994; Kotler et al. 1993, 1999). Place market-ing has existed in the form of promotion since the nineteenth century (Ward, 1998). New York State's slogan 1977 "I ♥ New York" comes easily to our minds as an example of such attempts (Gold and Ward, 1994). Other, prior examples can be found in the activities of the Ro-man Catholic Church in its early days in its efforts to promote visiting places where relics were the main attraction. The existing literature on place branding has taken two roads: a truly rationalized management proposition, and a managerial representation of entrepreneurship. The writings adopting a rationalized management proposition correspond to the literature stressing a "top-down" decision making process. In this literature, place branding is a management technique preventing failures in employment, education, housing, health services, or recrea-tion facilities (Bennett and Savani, 2003). Public authorities, alone or with the support of a committee, are encouraged to include marketing-branding planning in their policy making (Caldwell and Freire, 2004). Places are commodified, or treated as a product or a set of products, which should be positioned according to their competitiveness (Kotler and Gerter, 2002). Similarly, the users of such a product must be viewed in terms of target markets (e.g., Matson, 1994; Finucan, 2002). Table one summarizes such road to place branding.

Road taken	Major actors partici- pating	Mode of govern- ance	Govern- ing structure	Goals	Outcomes
Ration- alized Manage ment	ˉ gov- ernment ˉ com- munity groups ˉ busi- ness repre- senta- tives	ˉ individ- ual ˉ collec- tive	ˉ gov- ernment ˉ commit- tee based	ˉ working for issues of global competi- tive ˉ ness, so- cial ine- quality, poverty and em- ployment	ˉ definition of target markets ˉ improvement/new in- frastructure ˉ improvement/new entertainment ˉ rejuvenation of older industries ˉ revitalization of civic consciousness and self-confidence ˉ new image ˉ redefining ur- ban/rural position
Mana- gerial repre- senta- tion of entre- preneur ship	ˉ gov- ernment ˉ com- munity groups ˉ busi- ness repre- senta- tives	ˉ collec- tive (but govern- ment man- aged)	ˉ net- works ˉ public- private partner- ships	ˉ supporting specific needs of industry and soci- ety ˉ produce experi- ences	ˉ new urban/rural spaces ˉ new methods for en- tertainment ˉ new methods for running places ˉ new markets for ur- ban/rural living (resi- dents) ˉ new sources of fi- nancing ˉ new image ˉ redefining ur- ban/rural position

Table 10.1 Managerial Approaches in Place Branding

The advent of the "entrepreneurial city" (Hubbard and Hall, 1996) triggered a managerial representation of entrepreneurship, first in place marketing and then in place branding. The entrepreneurial city pursued entrepreneurial strategies in an entrepreneurial discourse through the promotion of entrepreneurial images (Jessop and Sum in Hubbard and Hall, 1998). Public authorities began building networks partnerships that became the managerial entrepreneur, in other words, governing structure (Van den Berg and Braun, 1999) or organizational and administrative structure (Kavaratzis, 2004). Managerial entrepreneurs nurtured a common compromise and purpose, and in turn, accomplished coordinated action (Anholt, 1998, 2004). It is this managerial entrepreneur, who was responsible for introducing innovation in order to create opportunities for places (e.g., see outcomes, table one) (e.g., Hankinsson, 2001; Ramírez-Pasillas, 2002). The managerial entrepreneurs concentrated on supporting the specific needs of business and society, while producing experiences to attract tourists and residents (Foley and Fahy, 2004).

Experiences are a central component of this road to place branding. Experiences reinforced a consumer's identity and a brand's ability to represent consumers, and assure their loyalty to a place (Hankinsson, 2001, 2004; Mommaas, 2002). Managerial entrepreneurs focused on the preservation and creation of emotional power sites, products, and services within places (e.g., Neill, 2001; Evans, 2003); though, when one inquires into place branding as an entrepreneurial process in an experience economy, the emphasis is no longer on the production of a brand marketing program designed to renew a location. The emphasis is situated on the stories not told by existing literature: the silent transformation of the official management story in everyday practices (de Certeau, 1984). Place branding as an entrepreneurial process in an experience economy focuses on the silenced stories of people as consumers that effectuate decisions and activities to produce experiences in a place.

Place Branding as an Entrepreneurial Process in an Experience Economy
Positioning
Consumption is a central phenomenon within place branding in an experience economy. Consumption is surrounded by behaviors (experiences) that people undergo during the act of purchasing a good or a service (de Certeau, 1984). Experience in place branding has, though, been dominated by a management discourse that includes two sides of the same coin: *(1) the production of experience, and (2) the consumption experience.*

In places, *the production of experience* is focused on the creation of a consumption–production system (the maker's side) (c.f. also consumption zones Anderson, 2000). A consumption–production system includes all the necessary "ingredients" suggested by place branding literature. While the makers (i.e., entrepreneurs) plan how future consumers will experience the products of such a system, consumers coproduce the experiences when buying said products. Still, the system will not work if the entrepreneurs do not themselves experience what they are constructing for further consumption-production. Experience covers all terms for the various modes through which persons construct reality (Tuan, 1977). I agree with Tuan that experience is related to *acting and creating:* "It means acting on the given and creating out of the given. The given cannot be known in itself. What can be known is a reality that is a construct of experience, a creation of feeling and thought" (Tuan, 1977: 9). Entrepreneurs thus experience the construction of a consumption-production system through their acting and creating (i.e. organization of people, resources, and actions for further invention). Once the entrepreneurs create a new system in a place, they introduce an opening in which consumers coproduce a new social practice—a *consumption experience.*

As mentioned above, the consumption experience is associated with the act of buying (the shopper's side). The "pure" experience—what is bought is not a good or service—is the experience in and of itself (Hjorth, 2007, this book). The consumption experience is hidden because it does not manifest itself through the products or services, but rather through the ways consumers acquire and use products or services. Such ways of consumption is translated into new social practices in a place. Both the production of experience and the consumption experience comprise an opening for place branding as an entrepreneurial process in an experience economy, as they are both associated with the creation of an opportunity in a place. In this chapter, I focus on the entrepreneurial side of the production of experience. This does not imply that the consumption experience is less important for entrepreneurship in an experience economy, it just stresses the fact that the entrepreneur's production of experience—*the organization of people, resources, and actions bottom–up (whether social, economic, cultural, tourist, or infrastructure development)*—has been silenced in the writing on place branding.

Place branding as an entrepreneurial process in an experience economy proposes some answers to the question of how an opportunity offers a gap for introducing new social practices. The dominate literature in entrepreneurship suggests that opportunities are there to be recognized or discovered (Shane and Venkataraman, 2000). Opportunities present a chance for entrepreneurs to offer a new value to society by introducing novel products or services and by creating a new company (Lee and Venkataraman, 2006). In contrast, other literature suggests that opportunities are created over time. "...all opportunities have a genesis: the process of preparing, arranging, trying out and relating, which place you in a position where you can transform occasions into opportunities and opportunities into an actuality" (Hjorth, 2005: 388). In particular, when reality is considered as a social construct, the scope of place branding as an entrepreneurial process in an experience economy changes dramatically. Local history and culture serve as a basis for the creation of opportunities. What is real for the entrepreneurs is their interpretation of the possibilities for branding places. The vision and actions of entrepreneurs enable the enactment of a new version of reality (Anderson, 2000), which is the branding of a place yet to come.

Entrepreneurs in the Branding of a Place

Place branding as an entrepreneurial process in an experience economy—as I approach it—is related to the phenomenon of community business entrepreneurship (Johnstone and Lionais, 2004). Community business entrepreneurship is distinguished from social entrepreneurship by focusing on business rather than pure charity or social purpose commercial business (e.g., Dees, 1998; Dees & Anderson, 2003). Community business entrepreneurship, similarly to conventional entrepreneurship, concentrates on developing organizations that are embedded in, and use the market in novel ways. Community business entrepreneurship differs from conventional entrepreneurship in its acceptance of low rates of return on its projects, because individual profits are not an objective. Entrepreneurs, instead, seek benefits and economic feasibility for the community. In line with this, the entrepreneurial process in the branding of a place is carried out to pursue community goals and, thereby, to introduce a new, disorienting order—the branding for a place yet to come—that results in new practices and new consumption experiences.

When place branding is initiated, the initiative taking entrepreneur has different resources to call upon to achieve community goals. The entrepreneur's main resource are their own contacts who become volunteers to benefit the community. The volunteers (i.e. skilled technicians, professionals, business people, and politicians) collectively form the entrepreneur for branding purposes.

Support from both private and public sectors is needed for constructing a new "branding" order at the local level; thus, a network of actors collectively composes the entrepreneur. The entrepreneur (i.e., network) has the ability to mobilize resources that depend upon the trust, that others place in the network. Members of the community do not have to worry that these individuals will use them for personal gain. The trust invested in them by the community increases the value of their social capital, which they leverage to construct a new social, symbolic, economic, and material reality. An entrepreneurial process implies the organization of people and resources, but also of actions for achieving such a reality.

According to Anderson (2000), the entrepreneurial process is only possible with the enactment of the entrepreneur's version of reality (Weick, 1977). Weick proposes that an environment is constructed by human actions. The entrepreneur's purposeful enactment corresponds to the experience—acting and creating—of an environment. Such an environment is influenced by the features of places: culture, economy, geography, history, and local heritage (Ramírez-Pasillas, 2002). The entrepreneur combines vision, ideology, commitment, concern, and concrete action (Johannisson, 1983). It is this combination of interests, features, actions, and resources that is central for place branding. Place branding as an entrepreneurial process in an experience economy takes on a tactical nature: there is an emphasis on a myriad of almost invisible movements/actions, playing on the environment and constituting a place for all people (de Certeau, 1984). The emphasis of such a process is not only situated in the material and economic construction of a consumption-production system. The emphasis is also placed on the social, symbolic, economic, and material construction of a branded place of everyday organization. The organization of people, resources, and actions for branding purposes spurs a feeling of disorientation to the consumption experience, requiring a reorientation (Hjorth, 2007). This disorientation, *the experience of becoming a branded place,* fosters the introduction of a new order, and the subsequent need for inventing new social practices (i.e., new consumption experiences).

The entrepreneur is at the center of place branding as an entrepreneurial process in an experience economy; it is she who creates opportunities. She enacts a new version of reality (i.e., the experience of becoming a branded place), which as a result, activates the community. A new network is formed; a collective vision is constructed; objectives are established; resources are pulled up; and entrepreneurial action is taken in the community.

In the branding of a place, the entrepreneur makes use of a variety of organizational forms when creating a consumption-production system in a community. She can employ not-for-profit organizations in addition to for-profit organizations. In agreement with Johnstone and Lionais (2004) the entrepreneur, instead, concentrates on securing consumers who prefer to buy from a community-based organization over others. The members of a community and its visitors extend their loyalty to a business that they perceive as contributing to their community. As a result, community is not only the location but also the means—environment—for creating opportunities.

Method of Investigation

As an example of place branding as an entrepreneurial process in an experience economy, I present a case study that was conducted in Lammhult, Sweden. I selected a community that is representative of a type of places that has difficulties becoming visible as a shopping and leisure destination. Literature has also put major emphasis on inquiring cities and countries (except Phillips 2002; Caldwell and Freire, 2004). I combined the analysis of documents, websites, field observation, and interviews with key informants into a story. I prepared a semistructured interview guide for the investigation; during the interviews, I asked the informants follow-up questions. The interviewees included actors from:

- the furniture firms (Svenssons i Lammhult AB, Norrgavel AB, Lammhults Möbel AB),
- Lammhults Service & Turistcentrum (Lammhult tourism office),
- Lammhults Industriklubb (Lammhult trade association),
- ALMI Företagspartner AB (government development agency),
- the Växjö kommun (Vaxjo municipality) authorities,
- The managers of Möbelriket (The Kingdom of Furniture).

The initial project manager of The Kingdom of Furniture provided several brochures and magazines that were used together with information from the Web. This research builds on previous work on regional brands (Ramírez-Pasillas, 2002) and on networks (Johannisson et al., 2002a, 2002 b; Johannisson and Ramírez, 2001) that was conducted in Lammhult. I identified the initial key informants using a "snowball" technique to locate other relevant actors. Snowballing is a sampling technique in which key known informants are asked to recommend other persons involved, in this case, in the place branding. Previous research in Lammhult facilitated the cooperation of individuals and access to information.

The Story of Branding Lammhult as The Kingdom of Furniture

The Kingdom of Furniture is the brand name given to Lammhult. Lammhult is located in the region of Smaland in southern Sweden (see figure two). The history of the Lammhult furniture industry goes back about a hundred years. The industry emerged when sawmills were established in Lammhult around 1903–1905 and people began selling furniture to earn a basic living. Strong growth of the industry, however, started when some former carpentry shops specialized in furniture production from 1921 to 1925.

Figure 10.1 Situating Lammhult in the World.

The industry continued to grow unimpeded until the 1940s when the Second World War began. Since then, new firms have arisen, and buyouts and mergers have taken place. Lammhult now has 1,950 inhabitants and 110 firms with 700 employees (Kommunstyrelsens Beslut, 2000). Of these, there are 11 furniture firms with 293 employees, four furniture stores with 50 employees, and 14 tourism-related firms with 88 employees (Kommunstyrelsens Beslut, 2000). Some of the best and most internationally well-known Swedish furniture producers are located in Lammhult.

Latent Entrepreneurship

In the 1994, Johan Sjoberg, business owner of the furniture store Svenssons i Lammhult, noticed a report in the local newspaper, Smalandposten, about the success of The Kingdom of Crystal, a small section of Kronoberg and Kalmar counties in southern Sweden, containing the municipalities of Emmaboda, Nybro, Uppvidinge, and Lessebo

(Kingdom of Crystal, 2000). In these municipalities, fifteen local glassworks had been organized for collective branding purposes. The next day the same newspaper similarly referred to Lammhult as The Kingdom of Furniture due to the location of high quality and design oriented furniture stores.

Sjoberg realized that the newspaper had opened up an opportunity that he and his colleges could not afford to miss. He commented to us:

It was the newspaper that suggested that Lammhult was The Kingdom of Furniture. In the newspaper...an article suggested that Svenssons i Lammhult was located in The Kingdom of Furniture, so you could say that it was not something that I thought for my self. While I read the newspaper, I realized that we could make it happen...It will take us ten or twenty years to be The Kingdom of Furniture, if we only decide to do so. I presented the idea to others in Lammhult in order to build The Kingdom of Furniture. At first, some persons were skeptical to the idea of developing The Kingdom of Furniture; they considered that Lammhult had other industries besides the furniture industry. But they understood that this was an opportunity that we all could benefit from...and they decided to collaborate to build Lammhult as The Kingdom of Furniture. The idea of creating The Kingdom of Furniture represented a vision...all one needs is a vision if you want to build something in the future.

Forming a Network

Sjoberg, who had been affiliated to the Lammhult trade association for a number of years, discussed his idea with other members of the association. Bengt Lund, a manager of this association, became very attracted to the "kingdom" idea when he heard about it from Sjoberg. Lund had been involved in another furniture producing area, Tibro, and in their local trade association for several years. When he met Sjoberg at the local trade association, they commented on the different possibilities for establishing The Kingdom of Furniture. Lund got enthusiastic about the idea and decided to participate in the creation of a kingdom. He commented in an interview:

When I heard the idea of building The Kingdom of Furniture, I realized that we could create together a new Lammhult; we, of course, believed that we could change things if we agreed on such goals and decided to cooperate to achieve them... Cooperation

*was not easy, it was full of challenges... people needs to trust be-
tween them...sometimes it takes years to agree and take action between all the participants... I also brought my connections to this
project as we started contacting people and talking about different concrete actions.*

In 1994, the furniture firms and the trade association agreed to cooperate and contacted the other two furniture stores in Lammhult, Nilsson
and Norrgavel. They discussed their ideas and propositions with them.
They talked about The Kingdom of Crystal. They knew that the origi-
nators of that project had been working on it for fifteen years before
they became known in Sweden.

They identified three clear strengths for Lammhult: design oriented
furniture manufacturers that were well known nationally and internationally, specialized subcontractors who were living in Lammhult, and
high quality and design oriented furniture stores. Considering these
strengths, Sjoberg and Lund decided to form a small network together
with the two other leading furniture retailers. Nina Litgard, marketing
manager of Norrgavel in Lammhult, commented upon the initial meetings:

*Well, Johan and Bengt visited us and invited us to join a group in
Lammhult...We were quite new in Lammhult so we decided to try
it out... In the meetings, we were sitting with furniture firms that
sell to final customers...so we all sold to final consumers... It was
tough at the beginning to talk about your firm. Gradually, we
started discussing sales and providing general information about
our firms until we finally set a common agenda for The Kingdom
of Furniture...*

Taking the First Steps

In 1994, the members of the network financed and built a sculpture at
the entrance of Lammhult; it bore the inscription, *Möbelriket i
Lammhult* (The Kingdom of Furniture in Lammhult) (see photo one
below). At the same time, the network members held a local workshop
with around twenty firms to define the activities that firms and the local organizations could carry out to develop The Kingdom of Furniture. Sjoberg, the initiative taking entrepreneur stated:

*The first thing we did was to build a chair sculpture with the title
The Kingdom of Furniture so that people knew that something*

was happening in Lammhult... Yes, Lammhult is The Kingdom of Furniture... Everybody who drove through Lammhult received a clear message: there is a new kingdom.

Figure 10.2 The Chair Sculpture at the Entrance of the Kingdom of Furniture

In 1998, the members of the network approached Thomas Hedhammer, chief of the information in the municipality of Vaxjo. The network wanted to raise funds for developing The Kingdom of Furniture and hire a project coordinator. Vaxjo municipality agreed to contribute approximately 30% of the cost of these initial activities. The network coordinator and a designer started formulating a logo for The Kingdom of Furniture. In 1999, a local association, Idé Lammhult, joined in The Kingdom of Furniture and became responsible for opening the Lammhult tourism office in the same year. The tourism office gathered information of all events and exhibit products of the local firms. Hedhammer, the representative from Vaxjo municipality commented upon this:

Johan and Bengt contacted us. They had an interesting project to help developing [sic] Lammhult. The project was about promoting the town as The Kingdom of Furniture. They talked to me about creating Lammhult as a furniture leader. In Lammhult, there are many furniture manufacturing firms and their subcontractors, and they are very important for the locality so we decided to provide financial aid through the local trade association. The association hired a project leader for The Kingdom of Furniture and they used the money to pay for advertisement in a local and a national newspaper... They also started a tourism office, which had an exhibition room for the local products, services, and events. The project was difficult as we received heavy criticism for helping firms in Lammhult... But such a project means a lot for a small community.

Figure 10.3 The latest Advertisement for The Kingdom of Furniture in 2005 (Text: The Inspiring Kingdom of Furniture, The good life)

In 1998, the members of the network organized a press conference to announce Lammhult as The Kingdom of Furniture in Sweden. Public and private organizations, including universities, were keen about being associated with Lammhult and this created legitimacy on which to build further initiatives. Bo Gunnarsson, one of the consultants from ALMI, a government development agency in Vaxjo, remembered the following about the press conference:

They organized a press conference to introduce Lammhult, but I cannot remember the exact date... Yes, Lammhult as The Kingdom of Furniture... Everything was natural... Lammhult is a center of furniture so it was, quite evidently that they named it The

> *Kingdom of Furniture. The local firms saw the opportunity and this is the interesting part. It is not about the specific business, it is a reinforcement for the whole community.*

Parallel to the press conference and the installation of the sculpture, the members of the network bought 50 advertisement spaces in Smaland-posten in 1998. The advertisement of a shopping destination informed potential customers of the 13,000 square meters of furniture exhibition of high design and quality. The ad included a photo of the furniture firms and a map of their location.

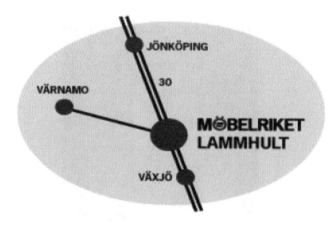

Figure 10.4 Situating 'The Kingdom of Furniture' in the Map

Self-Organization Followed

In 1998, the network, after lengthy discussions, agreed upon common hours of operation for the furniture stores in order to attract more customers to Lammhult. When the furniture businesses noticed that the common hours actually did benefit them, the network initiated monthly meetings and a more ambitious plan of activities. Litgard from Norrgavel mentioned:

> *The first activity for the furniture stores was to establish common opening hours...and it took quite some time to make an agreement among all the furniture stores. When we finally set the hours, we had a starting point. We began advertising in the newspaper as The Kingdom of Furniture and we saw the benefits of working to-*

gether. More costumers came to Lammhult and the results on sales were no longer the same...we sold more furniture.

In 2001, the furniture firms started organizing "design days" at Easter–and All Saints' Day in order to draw more customers to Lammhult. Around 1,000 people were expected to drive into The Kingdom of Furniture. Since more customers were expected to Lammhult, they would also need places to stay, so Vaxjo municipality leased to Jorgen and Maria Andersson an old farm, Asa Herrgard, a few miles away from Lammhult. Influenced by The Kingdom of Furniture proposition, this couple converted the farm into a resort hotel featuring design oriented decoration, good food, fishing, and bathing.

As a result, the network acquired a new member and improved the design days concept, expanding it into "design and gourmet trips." Such events required a more complete organization, including visits to furniture firms and local attractions, and even trips to neighboring areas such as The Kingdom of Crystal and the renowned furniture designers at Varnamo. Sjoberg commented on this:

Our objective was to organize events to attract as many people as possible to Lammhult. If the furniture firms were able to increase their number of visitors and their sales, their subcontractors and designers, as well as other local firms would benefit, too. We started organizing shopping days...but it was clear that it had to be more than shopping days...we are dealing with educated costumers, they are informed about fashion trends. For this reason, we created the design days... We started with a lecture with a designer, architect or decorator. We took them to the furniture factories and stores on the way. We stopped in the local café to have a 'fika,' and we had lunch at the local resort. Then, we complemented the experience with visits to The Kingdom of Crystal, the Bruno Mathsson Center and Collection Kallemo in Varnamo...and thus, we had a furniture gourmet experience. The experience at the end of the day was superior.

Launching The Kingdom of Furniture as a Company
In 2002, the network members closed down the Lammhult tourism office in order to redesign its activities. With the design days, The Kingdom of Furniture had already collaborated with other neighboring regions at Varnamo and The Kingdom of Crystal. Together, the furniture firms and Vaxjo municipality authorities began working on a project to

benefit the province of Smaland as a whole, and not only Lammhult. A joint development project was launched with the municipalities of Vaxjo, Alvesta, Savsjo, Nassjo, and Varnamo to create a new concept, The Kingdom of Wood and Furniture.

The project is still at an initial stage, but meetings are being held periodically. Sjoberg perceived this moment as an opportunity for action. He decided to launch a firm for enacting the branding of The Kingdom of Furniture, but extended the brand to include the whole province, Smaland. He discussed his idea with the members of the network, and opened up a firm that is owned by the local trade association and the Wood Centre Nassjo Foundation in 2002.

Figure 10.5 The Entrepreneur, Johan Sjoberg from Svenssons in Lammhult with the List of all the Firms Participating in The Kingdom of Furniture in 2005

Analysis of the Story

In this case, place branding as an entrepreneurial process in an experience economy was initiated when a business owner decided to make Lammhult known as the route taken to The Kingdom of Furniture. This initiative taking entrepreneur transformed an occasion, like reading a small report in a newspaper, into an opportunity. This opportunity contained the possibilities for community benefits, as well as for financial loss. This opportunity even included the possibility for failure if he was not able to find support for his idea in the local community. However, when he shared his idea with other local actors in the trade association and the local furniture firms, he inspired them to work together in a network in order to create The Kingdom of Furniture. Still, the organization of people, resources, and actions in a network for inventing such kingdom was not easy. The idea of creating a kingdom propelled a feeling of disorientation requiring reorientation as people in the network changed their way of relating to one another. People that had nothing to do with each other—and that were even competing for furniture customers—had to start collaborating in a network. Acting and creating for becoming The Kingdom of Furniture took years of discussion, attempts, and meetings to make it happen. Still, the entrepreneur, collectively composed of a network, gradually became a locomotive in the branding of the place.

The network members (re)constructed the original idea of the initiative taking entrepreneur into a joint version of a new reality for Lammhult. This joint version of a new reality corresponded to the creation of a collective vision of a consumption-production system. The collective vision of such a system constituted a driver for enacting The Kingdom of Furniture. Enacting The Kingdom of Furniture required entrepreneurial actions for gathering information, generating ideas, finding funding, and developing an imaginative creativity to reinvent the community. In the process, the network members built trust in one another and mobilized their own social capital and resources. As such, it was an ongoing process of social, symbolic, economic and material construction of the local environment (i.e., becoming a branded place). Within their enacted vision, the network members built in the expectation that the best for The Kingdom of Furniture is yet to come.

Place branding, as an entrepreneurial process in an experience economy, triggered the enactment of a new beginning associated with the community as a whole. Creating a consumption-production system meant inventing The Kingdom of Furniture as a shopping/leisure destination encompassing high quality design oriented furniture, crystal products, fishing, bathing, eating, and periodic mega-events to produce experiences. The experience of shopping at The Kingdom of Furniture provided a feeling of relaxation and peacefulness to the consumers in the countryside. The Kingdom of Furniture aimed at recovering the glamor given currently to well-known tourist destinations by means of unique experiences. Such experiences energized their customers and got them ready to return to their busy lives.

The members of the network used material and nonmaterial resources for creating a consumption-production system. They used material resources, new sources of financing, a tourism office, existing furniture shops, cafés, and restaurants for enacting The Kingdom of

Furniture; though, the nonmaterial aspects of those material resources were central for creating desires in consumers. The pleasure of being in The Kingdom of Furniture provided consumers an experience; consumers felt attracted to the local stores, and also imagined what they could do with the furniture. As they enjoyed their visit to The Kingdom of Furniture, the consumers felt that they were becoming special and transported to somewhere else better for a while. Thus, together, the material and the nonmaterial aspects of those resources influenced the process of social, symbolic, economic, and physical construction of The Kingdom of Furniture. It was this articulation of a new meaning related to The Kingdom of Furniture that made sense to the local community (and its consumers).

The members of the network created experiences in The Kingdom of Furniture having consumers co-producing them, and thereby, introduced new social practices (i.e. new ways for getting energized).

Culture, economy, geography, history, and local heritage in Lammhult colored the ongoing process of construction of the consumption-production system, which was a product of a bargaining between the realities of the current situation and the projected consequences of creating The Kingdom of Furniture. As such, it was just the nascent phase of branding a place in an experience economy. Branding The Kingdom of Furniture was just the beginning of the reorientation of the place: new practices changed the ways of living, the styles in use, and the interaction among local actors. For instance, visitors and residents now expect the annuals events to be held at The Kingdom of Furniture. People from neighboring towns repeatedly take a twenty-five minute drive to visit the furniture stores and get invigorated at The Kingdom of Furniture.

A Theory of Place Branding as an Entrepreneurial Process in an Experience Economy: the Nascent Phase

When inquiring into place branding as an entrepreneurial process in an experience economy, the organization of people, resources, and actions from bottom-up for further invention of new social practices could better be described as the nascent phase of an evolutionary trajectory. This statement implies that place branding in an experience economy develops in an evolutionary manner, following an a priori sequence of transitions. The entrepreneurship literature conceives of entrepreneurs as "change initiators" (Johannisson, 1983:12); it is only by analyzing the actions of the entrepreneurs that one can understand the nascent phase of place branding in an experience economy. During this phase, the often overlapping entrepreneurial actions undertaken to enact a new reality (i.e., becoming a branded place) consist of:

1. Creating a community business opportunity,
2. Setting a community entrepreneurial team,
3. Translating the community business opportunity into a collective vision for the enactment of a consumption-production system for a place, and
4. Tapping and (re)accommodating resources.

The nascent phase of place branding in an experience economy initiates with a community business opportunity. Kirzner (1979) calls it "opportunity recognition" and he asserts that during this phase, entrepreneurs need to be alert to opportunities. Though, this does not seem to be a sufficient condition for place branding as an entrepreneurial process in an experience economy. Hjorth (2005:388) suggests, instead, that opportunities "are rather created, in an ensemble of time.". This seems to be more appropriate, as the illustrated case in this chapter suggests, for place branding. The community business opportunities are created in order to reorientate places by introducing new orders into a more complex reality. Thus, an initiative taking entrepreneur is open to changing the existing order of things through new social practices. This opening constitutes a triggering event that is then transformed into a community business opportunity. The community business opportunity comprises a social, symbolic, economic, and material construction of a consumption-production system that will require the commitment and participation of the community. It also implies a new version of reality for obtaining community benefits.

In order to enact her version of a new reality, the initiative taking entrepreneur gathers a community entrepreneurial team. The community entrepreneurial team consists of the formation of a partnership or a network for branding purposes, which eventually results in a new organization—firm, or public office, department in an existing organization, or non-for-profit organization. The managerial approach to place branding has called such teams governing and administrative structures. Such structures plan, coordinate and control activities and resources. Yet, this does not seem to be appropriate for the nascent phase of place branding in an experience economy. Conventional entrepreneurial teams theory is significant here as such an approach refers to this phenomenon as a group of individuals that share interdependent tasks and outcomes, and who see themselves and others as a social unit (i.e., Eisenhardt and Schoonhoven, 1990; Cohen and Bailey, 1997).

Community entrepreneurial teams are similar to entrepreneurial teams in that they both have a common financial interest, and share altruistic service, compatibility, goals, responsibilities, and cohesiveness (i.e., Cooper and Daily, 1997; Kamm and Nurick, 1993). Though, community entrepreneurial teams create new methods for running places. They do not necessarily share in the new organization's ownership. They pay, instead, a fee for using the brand in order to create a financial base for their joint activities. They also do not share the direct economic gains of their new organization; the financial gains are reinvested in their branding activities. They receive the benefits of their branding activities through their own organizations' outcomes. Community entrepreneurial teams, as networks, glue together because of their complementary strengths, mutually compelling interests, reciprocity, and reputational concerns (Powell, 1990). They build trust over time as they share benefits and risks, and generate (other) new opportunities (Johanisson et al., 2002).

Next, the community entrepreneurial team transforms the original community business opportunity into a collective vision of a new reality (i.e., a consumption-production system). The consumption-production system incorporates a broad as possible range of affinities, projects, and future organizations in a place. This statement implies that the enactment of a new reality is a product of negotiation between the persons in the community, the entrepreneurial team, and their perceptions of the actual and future realities. The collective vision also aims to provide distinctiveness and prestige to a place. The community entrepreneurial team uses its creativity to envision a new reality that encompasses aesthetic and religious feelings in new urban/rural spaces, using new methods for entertainment, and by tapping into new markets for urban/rural living (residents). In order to become desired, the aesthetic and religious feelings are central for the (co)production of experiences in places. Such feelings are produced by creating a new meaning through place branding activities. The new meaning is associated with the material and nonmaterial aspects of the resources in use in order to socially construct a place that is visually artistic, different, or attractive.

Figure 10.6 introduces the nascent phase of place branding in an experience economy.

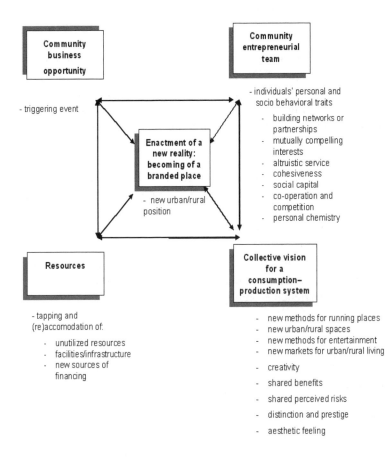

Figure 10.6 The Nascent Phase of Place Branding in an Entrepreneurship Economy

The community entrepreneurial team then taps into and (re)accommodates material and non-material aspects of the resources in order to build the consumption-production system and become a branded place. A new consumption-production system introduces new ways of amusing, new styles for use, and new ways of interacting among local actors. Shumpeter's (1934) theory of innovation seems relevant here, as place branding as an entrepreneurial process in an experience economy entails new combinations, although the combinations of place branding are different from the ones conceived by Shumpeter. The community entrepreneurial team mobilizes its social capital to gather new sources of financing; revitalize restaurants, cafés, public spaces and, cultural industries; and build a new image for a place.

There is, thus, a process of trying out, arranging, and combining resources in order to transform a community business opportunity into a collective vision, and a collective vision into an enacted reality. As such, it is an ongoing process of construction, always evolving, and its actions will change the existing reality, the vision of a new reality, and the enacted reality.

When place branding in an entrepreneurship experience economy is approached in the nascent phase, change in the organization of people, resources, and actions is continuous. Creativity helps put "old things into new combinations and new things into old combinations" (Weick 1979:252). If this occurs in place branding, it means that evolution has ensued. Evolution triggers subtle changes in the direction of a new order. Changes in the direction of increasing a new "orderliness" will be related to the introduction of management practices in the branding of a place in an experience economy.

Conclusions

Place branding as an entrepreneurial process in an experience economy is the nascent phase of an evolutionary trajectory. During this phase, success is associated with the ability to organize people, resources and actions in relation to the local features of a place. Only with the organization of people, resources, and actions, can the branding of a place be successful. Such an organization is carried out from bottom-up in order to create community business opportunities out of the transformation of the existing order of life and the invention of new social practices. In the case discussed here, individuals who were firmly engaged within their community created the means for branding a place. They doggedly enacted an environment to construct a new social, symbolic, economic, and material reality. For The Kingdom of Furniture place branding as an entrepreneurial process in an experience economy included:

1. creating a community business opportunity,
2. building a community entrepreneurial team with local actors in the private and public sectors,
3. constructing a collective vision for the place,
4. developing trust among the community entrepreneurial team members,

5. fusing a unique collective creativity for (re)inventing a community,
6. creating new sources of financing,
7. associating and creating the consumption experiences according to the particularities of a place,
8. ensuring community benefits over personal gain.

When place branding is seen as an entrepreneurial process in an experience economy, there is an important theoretical implication. Place branding evolves from an entrepreneurial process to a managerial one over time. The organization of actors in a network or partnership (i.e., a community entrepreneurial team) develops gradually into a new organization—firm, public office, or department in an existing organization, or non-for-profit organization. The new organization brings people and resources together to keep up with the success of the brand (e.g., building/improving rural/urban spaces, performing mega-events, designing and communicating an image). Such development is of course not always the case in all places, but this corresponds to the evolutionary nature of place branding in an experience economy.

Figure 10.7 introduces my image of the evolution of place branding in an experience economy, which could be better described as constituted by *three phases*. The first is *the nascent phase* of place branding that has been discussed extensively above and which The Kingdom of Furniture is an illustrative example. This is the phase where the characteristics of the branding of place emerge out of the organization of people, resources, actions, and history that coevolves to support them.

The second phase is dominated by the creation of a new organization in charge of the branding of a place. At this stage, there is a hired staff responsible for planning and executing the branding strategy. There can be a fee for the use of the trademark, which constitutes the financial foundation of the organization's autonomy. The new organization holds mega-events (e.g., conferences, workshops, exhibitions, concerts, and festivals) periodically to produce experiences in the place. Such events are a core strategy to attract consumers to the place. The residents are well aware of the brand. They develop a sense of belonging and a self-image related to the place. They also become proud of their place.

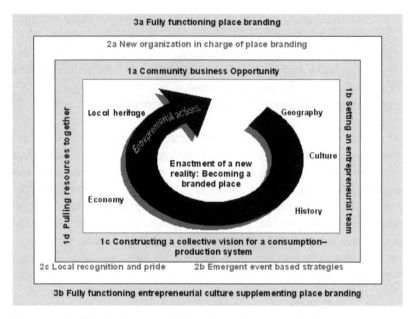

Figure 10.7 The Evolution of Place Branding in an Experience Economy

The third phase is the mature phase of place branding in an experience economy where the organization has achieved a fully functioning branding for a place; there is a well-established marketing/branding planning process that provides straightforward goals for the place and there is also an established identity and image for the place. The organization has descriptors for the city (e.g., LA: The City of Angels) and comprehends the tourists' feeling when visiting a place (i.e., excited, fascinated, peaceful, vibrant, etc.). The profile of the potential consumers is fully identified (e.g., age, income, interest, and values). At this stage, unknown places have been transformed into shopping and leisure destinations, where consumption experiences are the core attraction. Places appeal to more consumers while residents charge more for their products and services. There is also a fully functioning entrepreneurial culture supplementing place branding. The successful branding attracts other entrepreneurs to do business in the place. Public and private organizations are keen to be associated with the branding as it provides the image of an entrepreneurially enacted environment (e.g., the entrepreneurial city as described by Hubbard and Hall, 1998).

Finally, there are many implications for future research. The question of how branding is initiated and carried out is still critically important; thus, there is a need for case studies of entrepreneurial entrepreneurs in place branding in an experience economy. Furthermore, place branding is a nonlinear process that evolves over time. An evolutionary approach to place branding will help create an accurate picture of the myriad changes in the organization. There is little known about the organization of people, resources, and actions behind place branding in an experience economy. There is an increasing need for research that compares the organizations of people, resources, and actions where branding occurs. We also lack case studies of failed attempts at place branding. The question of why branding happens in certain places and not in others could be also be answered with an entrepreneurship approach. Hopefully, other researchers will be inspired by this chapter to take a closer look into this global phenomenon of place branding as an entrepreneurial process in an experience economy.

CHAPTER 11

THE EVENT OF DISORIENTATION AS A SPACE FOR INVENTING NEW PRACTICES

DANIEL HJORTH

To live in this pluralistic world means to experience freedom as a continual oscillation between belonging and disorientation
(Vattimo, 1992)

It is the event-dimension of potential—not the system of language and the operations of reflection it enables—that is the effective dimension of the interrelating of elements, of their belonging to each other. [...] In becoming is belonging. (Massumi, 2002: 76)

This chapter inquires into one entrepreneurial side of the so-called experience economy. In order to do so I develop the concept of experience as related to the act of trying, participating, and having been affected by taking part. Experiences, conceptualized in this way, are seen as constituting an event. Entrepreneurship in the experience economy is, therefore, discussed as the process of creating a social event, introducing a new order in the opening of the event's disruptive impact, and "translating" this new order via organization creation into new social practices. My inspiration is taken from Vattimo and Massumi, as cited above, suggesting that the experience I here set out to study is one from which postmodern citizens draw pleasure and joy: it is the event that holds together the two sides of bringing life beyond its present limits and the belonging that characterizes processes of becoming. It is the curious event of the consumer-becoming-producer that lies at the heart of the experience economy.

The empirical cases used are concentrated to stories where companies or projects (also cultural) are involved in making a business out of organizing the production of aesthetic events/products/services. The cases include Volkswagen's luxury car project—Phaeton; Alessi as a "high-end" kitchenware producer; and, Thomas Kinkade, "the painter of light." These are all used as examples of experience-economy-entrepreneurship (E^3) that accomplishes the organization of the event of the consumer-becoming-producer. E^3 actualizes the event dimension of potential (Massumi, 2002) established in that particular relationality of the experience economy that holds the virtual consumer-becoming-producer.

Introduction

Alluding to Spinosa et al. (1997), I believe it is fruitful to describe an entrepreneurial event as one that changes the style of relating to objects and people, and which results in a new order, requiring new forms of organization of everyday practices. To qualify as an event, an experience has to be set off from the "ongoingness" of the everyday. There is thus as element of what Kirkeby (2005) describes by the Greek *epiphaneia*—something taking place in the "now" that takes the "now" with it, thereby transforming it. I make use of Heidegger's and Deleuze and Guattari's descriptions of the aesthetic experience as one centered on disorientation and the creation of affects, and say that this particular aesthetic quality of the experience is decisive for it to be related to as event in the experience economy. I suggest that an understanding of the experience economy from an entrepreneurial perspective would benefit from this emphasis on event and on the event as an aesthetic experience.

An event, having created a rupture or disorientation, makes space for introducing the transformative insinuation, the supplementary order that changes the way we organize our everyday life. Entrepreneurship is the creative force that introduces such a new order in this space. Such new orders, in the context of social practices, need to be "translated" into new forms of organization. This is entrepreneurship in the experience economy as I approach it in this chapter: "making use" of people wanting to get "disoriented," and enjoying the subsequent organization into new social practices—the qualitatively new belonging that comes with this process of becoming. A prime tool in these processes is, of course, new media technologies. The concept of "virtual reality" is not restricted to a "cyberspace" context. Every idea that can be actualized through differentiation and creation is virtual (Deleuze

1988). Entrepreneurship in the experience economy, as discussed in this chapter, is only operating with a heightened sensitivity (sensation not dominated by perception) before these actualization processes; before the passages, the potentials, the transformative qualities of experience. Their possibility resides in the relationality of interactions:

> *Relationality is the potential for singular effects of qualitative change to occur in excess over or as a supplement to objective interactions. Relationality per tains to the openness of the interaction, rather than to the interaction per se or to its discrete ingredients.* (Massumi, 2000: 191)

Relying on the works of Michel de Certeau (1984; 1997), Massumi (2000; 2002), and Spinosa et al. (1997), this chapter tries to make a contribution to the way we conceptualize (and perhaps sense) the experience economy from an entrepreneurial perspective. The chapter proceeds according to the following structure: First, I discuss 'experience' and 'event' in order to position this paper vis-à-vis dominant essentialist uses of the concept of experience. Secondly, I develop the "aesthetic experience" as characterized by opening and disorientation. This leads us to the need to reflect upon the driving forces in seeking experiences (in the context of an experience economy), wherefore, I discuss the pleasure of an experience economy in section three. Fourthly, the entrepreneurial process of creating events in the experience economy is discussed in relation to three illustrative cases: Alessi, Volkswagen's Phaeton, and Kinkade. In the fifth section I read these examples through previous discussions (the development of an entrepreneurship perspective from previous publications) and developments in this text. This reading, finally, creates possibilities for clarifying this form of "experience-economy-entrepreneurship" which is a contribution to the broader, and predominantly managerialist, discussion of the experience economy.

Experience and Event

I seek to focus this discussion of experience on three things: 1) the experimental aspect, the act of trying, 2) the social aspect of participating, and 3) the affective aspect of being moved by participation. The possibility of describing, studying, and analyzing experiences in relation to entrepreneurship depends, in my reading, generatively upon these three. They are all taken from the descriptions of the meanings of the latin *experientia*. One could point out that a differentiation has already been attempted, where the entrepreneurial experience, as approached here, is tied to the *creation* of an experience, whereas the Pine and Gilmore (1999) version of experience prioritizes an economic logic consistent with *producing* experiences. This, in turn, might be objected to as a classicist reading—leaning on the Schumpeterian distinction between adaptive and creative response. What is emphazised in this text, though, is rather the desire to create (novelty) that sets entrepreneurship apart from a managerial focus on utilizing resources efficiently. In addition, it is the sensation side of experience that is in focus because "[S]ensation is the mode in which potential is present in the perceiving body" (Massumi, 2002: 75), and, in addition as the event-dimension of potential is central to my descriptions of E^3.

The problem with experience from a poststructuralist approach—to which I commit myself—is that the concept is firmly embedded in subjectivist epistemology; that is, a more or less Cartesian understanding of the relationship between subject and object shapes the way scholars have approached experience, from which analyses of experiences via the self-grounded experiencing subject follows. This Cartesian subject represents a misdirecting start on our way to describing and analysing experience. This image of the subject suggests an extra-discursive point of reference; a touchstone for anchoring knowing; a foundationalist epistemology; such a thing that thinks—a mental substance, a *res cogitans* (distinguished from the *res extensa,* the body extended in objectified space)—is an image of the self-identity of the "who of discourse." We would, instead, emphasize Descartes' invention as discursive in the sense of being simultaneously both an event and a system. When uttering, "Je pense donc je suis" / *Cogito ergo sum,* Descartes is creating and repeating. He speaks and is spoken (by language). Language is not only what comes from us as speaking subjects, but we also speak *from* language, in which we are also spoken. It follows that what we say changes who is speaking and that this "who" is called into being in the context of a discursive event. Furthermore, narrative operates as the form of everyday speaking and knowing, which in turn "provides the ongoing context in which the figures of discourse are embedded and achieve their determinations of sense and reference." (Schrag, 1997: 19). Let us clarify further:

...the who that is announced on the level of discourse is already a participant in and a respondent to the narratives that have shaped the tradition and those that envision future developments of self and society. It is in this sense that narrativity provides the wider

horizon for the constitution of discursive meaning (Ibid., p. 21–22).

In the following passage, René Descartes, struggling with the challenges of British empiricism, describes himself as meditating over the problem of knowing. The narrative contexts that come together in this story relate the philosophical problems formulated by the empiricists to the situation in which Descartes develops his method of doubt, but also to the personal story of Descartes' journey and, the situation that provided (by bad weather) him with time to think:

> *At the time I was in Germany, where I had been called by the wars that are not yet ended there. While I was returning to the army from the coronation of the Emperor, the onset of winter detained me in quarters where, finding no conversation to divert me an fortunately having no cares or passion to trouble me, I stayed all day shut up alone in a stove-heated room, where I was completely free to converse with myself about my own thoughts.* (Descartes, [1637] 1988: 25)

No wonder he arrived at the "Je pense donc je suis." What we can learn here is that this travel narrative, together with a "conversation" with Francis Bacon and Thomas Hobbes on "what could be known," form the context of the discursive event, "Je pense donc je suis." For this event to happen, the discourses of empiricism and of personal letters are crucial. Descartes utterance makes necessary a thing that thinks—a thing beyond the changing nature of the body (to which the empiricists' much appreciated senses[89] belong)—while at the same time locating this "insight" to the lived body of Descartes-on-travel/in-motion. The subject of speech/speaking—the philosopher/scholar Descartes—blend with the spoken subject of empiricist/rationalist philosophical language to form the discourses that—in the context of the spe-

---

[89] Sense is here the analytical-philosophical concept of sense. This is a passive sensory input through which *sensation = sense datum* is received. Such sense-datum, furthermore, is, in analytic philosophy, taken as a discrete stimulus, the elementary unit of experience. With Massumi (2002), the perspective used in this chapter sees continuity as elementary as discreteness, and relation as primordial as individuation. "There is also, in every experience at whatever level, a dimension of activity (if only by virtue of the coming-together of continuity and discreteness - think quantum). This disqualifies any fundamental reliance on stimulus-response of input-output models, as well as any simple active-passive framework." (Massumi, 2002: 259).

cific travel narrative—produce the meanings our reading of Descartes construct. Descartes' utterance becomes a discursive event through making a philosophical point (in the context of narrating the philosophical debates) and through being convincing (in the context of a personal/confessional travel narrative). We might call this the effect of a "conceptual persona" (Deleuze and Guattari, 1994), which in this case is the solitary and doubting Descartes. This persona is a product, it is presupposed by the concept *cogito* (I think). For Descartes this would not be so. According to him, he is correct because his language mirrors a divine order that finally is anchored in *res cogitans*, which his method of doubt has uncovered and demonstrated.

What is the point of working with the subject as situated, as emergent in discourse and action, as a "subject" (the term looses its value as a starting point) resulting from a self-narrative—simultaneously stretching into a future and responding to a past—shaping the context for this discourse-action amalgam? How does this "subject" change the way we can discuss "experience"? What would experience be for this "subject"? Derrida has emphasized that speaking within a structure (a language, grammar, syntax, or discourse) "is to repeat the decision of the structure" and so one may not be the author of that structure (Colebrook, 1999: 108). We cannot, therefore, speak of the autonomy of the subject. There is no self-grounded entity that can *possess* experience. There are, however, multiple subject positions becoming and perishing in discourses operating in the wider context of narrative. These subject positions, this "subject", can be related to as temporary effects or (more properly) gifts of discourse that are like surpluses or excesses of the system. Here we turn to Foucault for clarification. We can summarize his use of discourse as Colebrook (1999) does: "Discourse is positive. It marks differences, produces empiricities, effects relations and constitutes decisive limits." (p. 173). To conceptualize this productivity of discourse—what produces the subject as an excess, as a gift—that results in various subject positions to which interests and experiences could be attached, Foucault (like Deleuze) emphasizes the need to use the concepts "incorporeal" (event) and "immanence." We can understand this need when we have given up the Cartesian subject as an intending decision maker from whom action and results come. The productivity of discourse establishes meaning and effects bodies/actions/materials as an event. The force of language is conceived in a philosophy of immanence where language is not a doubling, or representation, of an outside/transcendence. We conclude this discussion by elaborating on these concepts.

Foucault finds a theory of meaning in Deleuze's *The Logic of Sense* that liberates us from representational thought (which goes back all the way to Plato). Platonic essentialism gives rise to thinking in series: the copy (a material chair; written language; knowledge) is grounded in the original (the eternal idea of a chair; spoken language; the self-present subject). Deleuze's concept of event, instead, stresses that thinking and meaning are positive and differential: "not the replications of some presence but forms of force and difference in themselves." (Colebrook, 1999: 174). Foucault/Deleuze point us to the event which is the passage from corporeal to incorporeal: the passage from the sounding of a word (the corporeal, physical, and material sound unit) to the becoming of a meaningful sign that "makes sense." It is this passage that is the event, the positive and differential force of sense. The event, Colebrook notes, "is the way the actual or 'what is' affirms itself differentially, and each time as different." (Ibid., p. 174); so, the "who" of discourse should be sought in the event where positions and selves are effected. In an experience economy there is a discourse of "experiencing." This incorporeal force does effect certain self-relations (which are corporeal, material) that constitute the experience seeking person who is ready to experiment; think of the thousands of applicants to the television show *Big Brother*.

How is this possible, we might object? How could people choose such activities, seek such experiences? These questions repeat the mistake of buying into a Cartesian point of view. Conventionally, we speak in this inherited language: subjects have preferences, they make choices/decisions, and they have knowledge. A philosophy of immanence invites us to rethink the concepts of experience and subject. A philosophy of immanence thinks experience as that which forms experiencing subjects. There is experience as there is, say, perception, and from this the experiencing subject or perceiving subject is formed:

We do not begin as subjects who then have to know a world; there is experience and from this experience we form an image of ourselves as distinct subjects. Before 'the' subject of mind, there are what Deleuze refers to as 'larvar subjects': a multiplicity of perceptions and contemplations not yet organised into a self. The notion of an outside or *transcendent' world is produced from this immanence, not produced by a subject, but effected passively (Colebrook, 2002: 74, emphasis in original).

Deleuze relies on Spinoza (who lived from 1632 to 1677; note Descartes lived from 1596 to 1650) for this philosophy of immanence (Scruton, 2002; Montag and Stolze, 1997) and on his radicalization of Hume's (who lived from 1711 to 1776) empiricism. This version of empiricism states that: Life is creativity and a continuous flow of experiences; experiences give rise to expectations based on the repetitious creativity of life; such ideas or imaginations also extend experiences beyond life; and, so, one should be committed to the unique, singular experience. The "who" of discourse is a collection (assemblage) of experiences and stories relating those experiences, a collection or event of creative life. This does not mean that we can also avoid inventing concepts that enslave us, and ideas that blind us to the creative becoming of life. As an example, we could desire the materialization of a business idea; to connect with other bodies (physical but also bodies of thought) to create extended ideas/images that increase our productive capacity; to form a "social machine" that can organize our investments in these images; and end up in an institution such as a limited company that, in turn, put constraints on our initial desire to create. The experience economy—as I approach this in this study—could be read as a reaction against this tendency. Instead of investing into institutions—political, business, cultural, or religious—young people (in particular) seek the singular experience. They are drawn towards shorter engagements, an event that can channel their desire in various ways but which keeps them free from an institution that—for historical-cultural reasons—is bound to "enslave them."

The Aesthetic Experience: Opening and Disorientation

The point of discussing how the aesthetic experience is part of entrepreneurship in the "experience economy" lies in the way aesthetics affects us. The aesthetic element of the experience is crucial for the emergence of a space for creating new social practices. I am not targeting the experience of art in the traditional sense of visiting a gallery or walking around a museum. Even if this distinction of certain places for art is both obsolete *and* relevant, it is rather aesthetic experiences occurring in everyday life (in relation to art or not) that interests me here. There is a rather obvious "aesthetization" going on in today's businesses (cf., Björkman, 1998; Stenström, 2000) that is visible in how leaders are held accountable to demands for "good performances" at press conferences and general shareholders' meetings; in the way commercials address customers and potential customers via "lifestyle" micro series; and in the pressing awareness of the importance of design for the success of products/services on the market. This book is focused on a rather recent continuation of this development that falls into two parts: First, the emergence of an additional demand of customers, in other words, that every decision making process (regarding a product or service) should, to some degree, also include an experience—the event surrounding the act of buying. Secondly, how does the market of experience-as-product, transform what is sold/bought into, not so much a core product/service, as an experience in itself.

These experiences, these events of consumption, form the subject of the experience economy. What this subject desires, I argue, is the aesthetic element of such experiences. At the same time, it is the aesthetic element in the "experience economy experience" that forms the desiring subject. Seeking to describe what differentiates the aesthetic experience, I turn to Deleuze and Guattari, and Heidegger. I will move through these thinkers rather quickly starting with Heidegger, from whom I borrow a way to distinguish what is different about the aesthetic experience. Heidegger is, however, problematic on several accounts, and a short criticism will lead me into Deleuze and Guattari's view, where the function of art is distinguished from that of science and philosophy (Deleuze and Guattari, 1994). The question is: How does the event of the experience in the context of the experience economy work? I suggest to work with a conception of experience well described by Massumi (2000: 197, emphasis in original), who has stated that: "Every experience, as it happens, carries a 'fringe' of active indetermination. Experience under way is a constitutionally vague *something doing*' in the world." This emphasizes what traditionally would be described as the aesthetic quality of experience, but which is characteristic of experience as such. It is this indeterminacy that I find interesting and central for an understanding of experience in an experience economy.

Heidegger is critical of the subjectification of traditional aesthetics; instead, the aesthetic experience is discussed as the experience of an event, not reducible to, or controllable by, a subject. The event is characterized by participation and disorientation. A subject position is, rather, the possible effect of such an event and not the condition for its appearance. In his famous essay "The Origin of the Work of Art" (1971) Heidegger states that the aesthetic experience is characterized by participating in a clearing of openness where truth happens. People that become part of such an experience are "standing within" this truth as it happens in the work (of art). Such participation is further characterised as "taking us beyond ourselves and our subjective standpoint"

(Scheibler, 2001). Participating in the event means a discontinuity from the everyday ongoingness of life. We find this emphazised also in Vattimo's (1992) and in Benjamin's (1999) discussions of the aesthetic experience, where the blow, the (German) stoss, or shock, mark this discontinuity that leaves us in a state of disorientation.

From a poststructuralist perspective we would still have problems with the "pure experience" of Heidegger's phenomenology for the same reasons we have problems with the structuralists' attempt to base knowledge on the structures that make experience possible (concepts, language, and signs). As poststructuralists, we need to ask—with Derrida—what the structuring force of the structure is; what the structuration of structure comes from in order to make structures possible. We, then, affirm the impossibility of founding or grounding knowledge either on phenomenological "pure experience" (without subject) or on the structuralists' signs and chains of concepts (in language), noting as well that relativism is equally impossible. To make sense at all is always already to make use of concepts that make us understood. Deleuze regards this as an opportunity and asks us to grasp this (entrepreneurially, we would add) as a challenge to transform life, to create in this in-between (in the impossible necessity, as Derrida called it). We discussed the problem with experience in the previous section, and the problem with basing knowledge on structures is that one has to pretend to be outside of said structures in order to explain them. Deleuze, instead, refers us to difference and becoming. These are concepts of the in-between, and of movement, and deny us the possibility of thinking in terms of ground and closure. What does this mean for the (aesthetic) experience; the event of disorientation? We can also see Deleuze as radicalizing Heideggerian phenomenology in the sense that he rejects a focus on phenomena (appearances) as these always point us to the world of which they are a part. Deleuze instead uses the concept of simulacra, which are not *of* some world but, rather, all there is, without origin behind them. The (aesthetic) experience is, therefore, not an experience *of* something (deep, underlying), but a positive force of creation that produces affects that move us.

The experience would work in the following way: through producing affects (something intensified by aesthetic experiences), we are taken back from composites of experience that we have imagined and invested in, to the affects whence those composites have emerged. "Affect, as presented in art, disrupts the everyday and opinionated links we make between words and experience" (Colebrook, 2002: 23). "Affections are what happens to us (disgust, or the recoil of the nostrils at the smell of cheese); perceptions are what we receive (odour, or the smell itself). Affects and percepts, in art, free these forces from the particular observers or bodies who experience them. [...] Affects are sensible experiences in their *singularity*, liberated from organising systems of representation." (Ibid., p. 21–2, emphasis in original). Skillfully staged events in the experience economy play with the sensation—as much as the perception side of experience.[90] It is of course in our "organised systems of representation" that we feel comfortable and oriented. "Destroying" this sense of homeliness, the aesthetic experience re-locates into a space of becoming—of becoming reoriented. This gives us pleasure; to "make sense" of our experience; to allow us to enjoy a moment of "being lost." Such disorientation is, one could argue, a relief from a surplus of well-organized systems of representation that bombard postmodern citizens everyday. As such, this pleasure of the disoriented moment and the process of reorienting, might be the pleasure of a childhood memory, of becoming-child: restoring a sense of wonder before the world.

Allow me to summarize: The event, the experience of the "experience economy," when intensifying the aesthetic quality (present in every experience), plays more with the sensation—rather than perception—side of experience, and is a disorientation requiring a reorientation. It is this openness, the "event-dimension of potential, the experience of *becoming*, that allows for the introduction of new order(s) and the subsequent need for new organization of this order. I describe this as the distinctly entrepreneurial process in an "experience economy." Before continuing, I should extend my argument that there is a pleasure in the event of disorientation that drives the "experience economy." How does this work? Why do people desire these experiences?

The Pleasure of an Experience Economy

Our initial description of experience as related to "the act of trying," "participating," and "having been affected by taking part," can now be redescribed in light of the discussions above. Such a new description would emphasize "the act of trying" as the playful side of experience; "participating" as this belonging that is in becoming; and "having been affected..." as the sensation side of experience that is intensified by the

---

[90] "...'perception is used to refer to object-oriented experience, and "sensation" for "the perception of perception," or self-referential experience. Perception pertains to the stoppage- and stasis-tending dimension of reality [...] Sensation pertains to the dimension of passage, or the continuity of immediate experience (and thus to a direct registering of potential) (Massumi, 2002: 258-9).

aesthetic of experiences. The pleasure of the "act of trying" is the pleasure of playfulness. The desire for this pleasure might come from memories of childhood or it might come from having drawn pleasure from connecting with others in the aesthetic experience. Disorientation provides a relief from closed systems of representation and we can enjoy becoming-oriented as the experience of openness of such sense-making systems. The pleasure from belonging is the pleasure of power—the increased productive capacity that resides in relating desires. The pleasure of sensation, finally, is the pleasure of immediacy, of staying in the moment, of experiencing the joy of "…what is not myself and in so doing expand who I am and what I might become" (Colebrook, 2002: 132).

Based on previous experiences we form images and anticipate, or invest, in the future pleasure from such experiences. We become desiring. Such desire is productive—it creates new connections from which this pleasure can be drawn. That is, the event of openness and disorientation in the aesthetic experience of "the experience economy" forms subject-positions that desire new connections with this event, thus producing it through anticipation. "It is the capacity for imagination to expect, anticipate or extend experience that produces formations that seem to govern human life but which are actually outgrowths or 'fictions' produced from life" (Colebrook, 2002: 82). Such a productive power of desire, such creative functions of imagination are, however, often subject to social formations. The desire to create—to connect with others to enhance life—has traditionally been coded or organized into specific forms of desire. It is ordered into "art" or "industriousness," making a local desire into a social interest. Scholarly as well as lay analyses of human beings often start with this generalized interest and assume we are born with desires for specific ends. From this, one concludes that the *homo oeconomicus* model of human action contains explanatory power. What we have missed, then, is the process of forming interests from local desires.

Desire is the power to become, to imagine, to produce images, that also enslaves us. Power is not negative (as we learnt from Foucault), but productive. It produces us. What we are—as actual subjects in various discourses and narrative contexts—are only temporary effects of the virtual force of becoming. The process of actualizing the virtual is one characterized by difference and creation; so, to the extent that we can also be *homo ludens* (playing humans) we desire this event of becoming-other, or variation, differentiation, and creation. Such processes are, then, also open to generalised interests operating in the opening of the disorienting event. One might, therefore, enter into a *Big Brother* contest desiring this process of becoming, an openness of which one knows very little, and still become produced only through a limited range of possibilities. This is, we would conclude, not a creation process but a realization process. The real rests in the image of the possible that is realized. It is all prepared and fixed. To compensate for this false creation, one manipulates the context using mass media and projects a public image of the spectacle as "an open game." Entrepreneurial processes, we have to admit, are often processes of *realization* rather than *creation*. Desire is directed in certain directions; the openness of the disorientation experienced is an occasion (event from *eventus/evenire*—a social occasion or activity) used as an opportunity—an opportunity to introduce a certain order that demands certain forms of organization.

As consumers in the experience economy we pay to become subjected to simulations—images of what we could become—but enter processes of realization of specific interests. We can buy this anyway because the experience of being disoriented is an experience of openness and of virtuality (what could become), and this is what the playful in us desires. We pay to become co-producers of a second order, belonging to the interest that directs the set-up of the experience. Entrepreneurship—which centers on how something can be brought into existence—brings the shock element of art, the openness of the aesthetic experience, and the practices of management (efficient direction of order) together. We can study and conceptualize this, as I have tried to show here, in the language of aesthetics. How does this form of entrepreneurship work, then? I continue this chapter by describing this process.

Entrepreneurship and the Creation of Events in the Context of an Experience Economy

I want to exemplify how the previous conceptualization of this new possibility for entrepreneurship in the so-called new economy works. I will do this by drawing from three examples where this form of entrepreneurship, to various degrees and in shifting ways, is at work. We can describe E^3 as covering the creation of an event of sensation, one that effects an opening and a disorientation, which, in turn, can be used as a space for inventing new practices, practices that change our ways of living, the styles used to order how we relate to people and things (de Certeau, 1984; Spinosa et al, 1997). In addition, it might be useful to make a further distinction between disorientation and reorientation, since they are both parts of this entrepreneurial process. We might describe the latter part of initiating a new order—in the wake of disorientation—and the subsequent creation of a new organization, or new social practices, in the style of a novel business as reorientation.

Alessi – "Family Follows Fiction!"

Alessi (founded in 1921) has changed from being a:

> *"Workshop for the working of brass and nickel silver plates, with foundry" (so read the sign over our stand at the first Milan Trade Fairs in the twenties) into one of the "factories of Italian design."* (cf., www.alessi.com)

The change from a metallurgical and mechanical industry into a workshop actively researching the field of applied arts has been a gradual one over several decades. "Officially", Alberto Alessi, the present C.E.O. says:

> *"my career at Alessi began in July 1970, the day after I graduated in law. My dad immediately set me to work on new projects. I threw myself into the job. With a strongly utopian view of 'multiplied art,' I developed my cultural-theoretic manifesto championing a new commercial civilization offering the consuming masses veritable artistic items at low prices."* (Alessi, 2000: 19)

The "form follows function," typical of Scandinavian design of the 1950s, has almost become a truism in the way industrial design is framed and taught at design schools. Well aware of this "truth" Alessi states with characteristic playfulness: "Family follows fiction!" Almost avant-garde in its posture, Alessi is, in this way, located at the edge. But the dictum reveals more than what is first acknowledged when confronted with it. For the message also comes from a conscious strategy to challenge the way we think about consumer products and peoples' relationship to "things." Traditionally focused on metal and, specifically, stainless steal products for the kitchen, Alessi gathered designers in a workshop to explore the ideas of Donald Winnicott, a British child psychologist and learning theorist, who developed a way to conceptualize the role of playing in learning reality (1971). For Winnicott, the conceptual pairing of boundary and space is central and he explores how the child's relation to a safe other—primarily the mother—constitutes the sphere of security. The child makes use of transitional objects (e.g., the teddy bear) to experiment and traverse the space of reality, and breach the boundaries of the primarily safe. The Alessi workshop was focused on the role of transitional objects and asked: if you let children into a room full of things, which ones do they touch first. These things would be "transitional objects" in one sense, or in other words, the objects that led the child to break the fear of a new room, an unexplored place, and make it into a space-for-play. The desire to touch and play—affected by the aesthetics of the objects—transforms the place into a space for play.

Using our previous discussion of the aesthetic experience, we might see this moment when the transitional object enables a reorientation as a time of becoming. In this event the child is led by the desire for touching an object, by the desire to play that the object-as-play-potential represents. The desire to grab the object is the force that sets the child on a creative course: she sees the play that resides as potential in the relations between objects and context, the event-dimension of potential pulls her into the play. Alessi thought that this desire for the thing in itself should be translated into the world of "useful objects." The workshop initiated the new era of colorful plastic materials currently central in Alessi's style. These objects have a magnetic attraction for the hand. The hand desires to touch it—for its color and form—and we are drawn into imagining what use we can make of it. We start to play with this object, but in a direction ordered by Alessi: we reorient our kitchen practices so as to include Allessi's "playful tool."

Volkswagen's Phaeton – the Experience of Luxury

"On the road of life, there are passengers and there are drivers."

they tell us in the Volkswagen Phaeton movie (www.vw.com/phaeton/). And then we read:

"Drivers wanted!"

Volkswagen has constructed and launched a car designed to compete against the BMW 7-series and Mercedes 500 S-class, and this from a company born as producers of "the people's car." To make this possible, Volkswagen saw it as necessary to draw on art/literature to properly set the stage for their car. Phaeton, in Greek mythology, is the son of the sun god Helios. Helios drives the sun chariot over the firmament. When bullied by his school mates at a young age, challenging him as to whether he was really a son of a god, Phaeton was advised by his mother to "go and ask" his father in person. To prove to Phaeton that he indeed was his father, Helios promised to fullfil his every wish. Phaeton, of course, wished that he could drive the sun chariot. Although he was warned by his father that the horses might sense the inexperienced driver at the reins, Phaeton refused his advice and entered the chariot (a desire for play, the sensation of the event-dimension of potential). Of course, the horses ran for their freedom and good old Zeus eventually had to stop the emerging catastrophe with a classic thunder bolt. By then the earth was already burnt (the creation of deserts). Phaeton's sisters mourned their brother and their tears explain the presence of amber today.

Volkswagen uses this story obviously to focus on the car/chariot and the "first race in history'. There is an immediate question here, and the editor (Buchholz) of motor magazine (mm) also asks it:

Buchholz: Warum hat VW für sein neues Modell eigentlich ausgerechnet den Namen des populärsten Unfallopfers in der griechischen Mythologie gewählt?
Why did VW, of all names, actually choose the name of the most popular casualty in Greek mythology for its new model?

Bobsien: Der Wagen des Gottes Helios hat die wilde Fahrt unbeschadet überstanden. Er hat nach der Sage jedenfalls weiterhin die Sonne am Himmel entlanggezogen. Der Fahrer, Phaeton, wurde herausgeschleudert...
The carriage of the god Helios has survived the wild journey undamaged. According to the saga it continued to pull the sun along the sky. The driver, Phaeton, was flung out of the vehicle....

Buchholz: ...und starb.
....and died.

Bobsien: Zeus hatte bestimmt, daß der Fahrer nicht überleben sollte.
Zeus had decided that the driver shouldn't survive.
(Interview with VW speaker Jens Bobsien by the editor of motormagazin Christain Buchholz)

Clearly the sense of drama is well established. The Phaeton is further contextualized by the *Transparent Factory* (glass construction) built only for the purpose of assembling the Phaeton cars at Dresden (a baroque city). The *Transparent Factory* stages production in a totally new way and makes this also into a drama. One can watch workers in white overalls moving around on parquet wooden floors with gigantic robot arms bringing the hanging cars to the workers, and not the other way around. This is on display since, again, the factory has glass walls. The idea is to communicate a new era in car manufacturing, an era that indeed thrives on the manufacturing tradition (handicraft) of Dresden, an old porcelain center.

The staging is already a way to snatch people out of the everyday and convince them that they are part of something bigger, mythological, literary, or artistic. Having the opportunity to sit down in one of those god-like creations (you have to spend some €70-80,000 to buy one) is a culmination of this staging process and exemplifies, par excellence, the aesthetic experience. Emphasis, however, is placed on seduction via extreme customization. Luxury dazzles you as part of the staging event. If you are to pick up a car you have bought, a specially designed train transports you from Dresden's central station out to the factory. While there, a gourmet dinner and an "event area" awaits you and will entertain you to make sure your appetite for "the best" is satisfied. Soon enough this moves into a reorientation when the idea of "what this car could do for you" is in focus. Producing and selling Phaeton is a theatrical event, a staging where I as a customer become part of a tightly directed play. My part is the main character and this intoxicates me—on the center stage—to the extent that buying this time becomes an experience of some magnitude. The car becomes the remaining prop in relation to which I will always be able to construct myself as the central character.

Thomas Kinkade – "The Painter of Light"

We believe that the walls of the home are the new frontiers for branding. (Thomas Kinkade, Artist, Writer, CEO, Real Estate Developer)

One in 20 American homes proudly displays a Kinkade art-based product; his sales reached $131 million in 2001 (Miller 2002). The Thomas Kinkade Lifestyle Brand—that's the official word from his holding company Media Arts, Inc.—also encompasses a *highly developed product portfolio, including a chain of 350 Signature Galleries, limited edition prints, Master Highlighter Events, portfolio building workshops, crews of artistic assistants, a listing on the New York Stock Exchange, books, and real estate (Media Arts Group 2003a, b).* (Schroeder, 2004)

Each product, artwork of Thomas Kinkade, the "Painter of Light®" is filled with the spirit of hope, joy and love. Drawing from an extensive library of available artwork, images are developed into a broad variety of products for distribution through our unprecedented network of galleries and dealers. Products are stratified to reach a complete range of consumers, providing quality products at all levels. (www.mediaarts.com, 2005–03–04).

Thomas Kinkade and his Media Arts Group have accomplished something that must thrill Pine and Gilmore (authors of the most widely read book on the experience economy). He has taken his lesson from both Marcel Duchamp and Andy Warhol, and made use of this with his own special twist through which people's homes are rethought as walls for his branding "products."

Note:	Duchamp destroyed the autonomy of the art object through showing how its status was an effect of the productivity of the museum institution. For him, context was all. A porcelain "fountain" made to collect urine in public toilets is only that in the context of the toilet. Duchamp dragged it into the art museum and, voila, it became art. Warhol, the father of Pop Art, commercialized art in the full sense, thus destroying a previously established principle characteristic of art objects—that they were not available for circulation as commercial objects. "Andy Warhol's *Dollar Signs* are brazen, perhaps even insolent reminders that pictures by brand-name artists are metaphors for money, a situation that never troubled him" (Bourdon 1989, p. 384). Until Warhol, the art object primarily constructed perceivers or spectators. After Warhol they were more like consumers. "Warhol appropriated his subjects from mass-produced printed sources and composed them in a serial manner, accentuating their banality and underscoring his own detachment from the subject" (Prather, 1998). Through his work and framing of it, Warhol relativized the aura of the artist as did Duchamp relativised the aura of the art object.

Indeed, Kinkade has extended this beyond the accomplishments of Duchamp and Warhol. Kinkade creates originals and sells the copies as mass products distributed through a logistically efficient chain of authorized galleries. What he paints is nostalgia and belonging; typically, small cottage houses on the countryside with light coming from the kitchen window, and smoke from the chimney. The image communicates a sense of origin and homeliness. Buying one becomes an act of participation in a grand becoming: in 2002 over ten million people (the vast majority being United States citizens) had bought his work. In this becoming is belonging, a certain belonging to the object and the "global spirit" it bears witness to:

No matter what you might think of Kinkade's artistic merits, his celebrity suggests that he's tapped into a collective longing among Americans for real community. (Brown 2002)

Why is this working? One answer is just to point out the effectiveness of management knowledge when applied in new markets with little or no competition. As Kinkade himself points out: "I created a system of marketing compatible with American art" (in Orlean 2001, p. 128). To this we could apply our previous discussion of the aesthetic experience in the context of the "experience economy." We would then stress that what is bought is, indeed, not an object but a sense of community and belonging communicated in the picture. Kinkade's images are precision tools. They open a wound—the loss of belonging that is retrospectively attributed to a traditional society that no longer exists—and offer a remedy in the form of a comforting image.

Kinkade's paintings are made to comfort the spectator, to convey that there is a community where your true self is located, and the promise that this community- to-come is somewhere to be found. There is a reference in these paintings to a communicative praxis in which the self is implied. "Community is constitutive of selfhood. It fleshes out the portrait of the self by engendering a shift in focus from the self as present to itself to the self as present *to, for,* and *with* the other" (Schrag, 1997: 78, emphasis in quoted text). Kinkade's images are, in this sense, productive of a certain subjectivity, as certain self in community. We need to stress here that the communalized self is *in* rather than *of* history. We must not mistake context conditioned for context determined. To the extent that Kinkade's images are considered to reveal a "true" state of humanity or a "truth" about our lives, his buyers would rather be determined as characters *in* his paintings, which, if considered to describe a true condition of "our life', makes us selves *of* Kinkade's stories and thus of "true life."

This desire to connect or to "be" someone in a community operates with varying force depending on the culture. American culture might, in this respect, stand out. As Greenblatt (1980) has pointed out, a self is a "sense of personal order, a characteristic mode of address to the world, a structure of bounded desires." Self-fashioning would then be said to occur "...at the point of encounter between an authority and an alien, [and] that what is produced in this encounter partakes of both the authority and the alien that is marked for attack, and hence that any achieved identity always contains within itself the signs of its own subversion or loss" (Ibid., p. 9). Reminding ourselves of Deleuze's philosophy of immanence and becoming, we can clarify that every social whole (culture, society, community), is produced by desire and reproduces this desire. This desire to connect and enhance life—positively and productively—also produce social wholes that code and order local desire into general social interests. Kinkade's paintings—again, most, typically, without any people in them, showing a lonely house on the countryside with light coming from inside and smoke from the chimney—play skillfully on this desire to connect and enhance life. The paintings portray an emptiness, a place to be filled, and offer the spectator an opportunity to become the missing character in the image, to fullfil a purpose, to find meaning, to become the event of the painting, or that which actualizes the event-dimension of its potential. This has proven to be a highly successful way of selling an experience. The physical painting is more a prop in this play.

The "Experience-Economy-Entrepreneurship" of Alessi, Volkswagen and Kinkade

My examples are picked to illustrate what I find to be one central characteristic of E^3, which answers to my reading of the experience economy and my understanding of entrepreneurial processes. Entrepreneurship in the experience economy is a particular form of entrepreneurship that produces the experience economy, as well as being produced by it. There are, however, some central characteristics of this form of entrepreneurship that resonate not only with the cases described above, but also with elements of my previous conceptualization of entrepreneurial processes (Hjorth, 2004; 2005). These are:

1. Entrepreneurship is practiced as a form of social creativity that operates in the organization of reigning orders.
2. Dominant among such orders is presently a managerial order directed by emphasis on economic efficiency and control.

3. Entrepreneurship, therefore, needs to create new orders, which in turn demand new forms of organization.

4. Operating always on a playground ruled by the strategic impacts of managerial discourse, entrepreneurship has to operate via tactics, that "...produce a *difference* or unpredictable event which can corrupt or pervert the strategy's system" (Colebrook, 1997, p.125).

5. Such transformative "insinuation" of an anomalous supplementary element into a prescribed order (described by Ahearne, 1995: 163) can be generatively described in spatial terms as the creation of "space for play."

If we make this conversant with the image of entrepreneurship to which I committed this chapter in the opening we are provided with new possibilities to imagine and describe such forms of experience economy entrepreneurship.

From Alessi we learned that product design can make us experience the sensible, not as subjected to the conventional flow of everyday concepts, but as a singularity. As such, it is an event representing an opening in the system of representation. Such an opening is at once a moment of power, the power of life becoming, and a vulnerable time when the introduction of new orders easily translates this singularity into new organizations of concepts/representations/practices. Alessi's playful design creates a disorientation, albeit of a modest kind, when disrupting the conventional order of what a thing is and how it could be used. Experiencing the sensible is also to take part in this opening event. Buying the object represents the decision which allows the consumer to enter a space for play and imaginative use. The objects function as transitional objects, (in Winnicott's sense, 1971), establishing the buyer as a playful self. Buying and owning Alessi products includes this experience of "becoming-playful." The experience of an Alessi product shifts the balance between perception and sensation (in experience) towards the latter.

Volkswagen's Phaeton is, to some readers, perhaps easily classified in the genre of luxury cars. Same old story. What I (Hjorth and Pelzer, 2007) find intriguing, though, is the new kind of thinking that goes into staging the car primarily as a fruit of aesthetic considerations. The Phaeton is not only designed to change your sense of driving. Most cars are said to do that. Phaeton, however, is presented literally on its own stage, in the theater of Phaeton and with all the scenes and props needed for the performance of a drama that disrupts the continuation of a conventional car buying praxis. Alluding to Greek mythology, inventing car assembly as a performance in search for its audience (the *Transparent Factory*), and re-inventing the factory worker as a visible prompter (in white shiny overalls, moving around on polished wooded parquet) all contribute to the force of the event of buying Phaeton. Such an opening is a space for play in which the buying decision literally holds the key to future life in the golden seat of a Phaeton. Car manufacturing is pulled onto the stage and adds a disorienting force to it. It looks like no other car assembling. "Car making" is deterritorialized, uprooted from its belonging in the social and economic context of its historical development, and re-territorialized as, literally, a piece of theater. This bewilderment creates the opening; the new order demanding new organization: The buyer has to reposition herself to make sense of the event.

Kinkade, finally, appears to me—apart from whether we like his "art," as such—as an almost perfect example of an experience economy entrepreneur. He brought ways of thinking into the reigning cultural order of "good art" that could not have been generated in this context (cf., Spinosa et al.'s [1997] describes such acts in terms of cross-appropriation). Taking his lessons from Warhol and Duchamp, he seems to have thrived upon the subversive elements built into art as a transformative force. Kinkade tactically made use of the crisis of art in society. Operating on two planes he thus introduced a new order into this opening and commercialized art in the fullest sense. On the second plane, his motifs play on the central desire for community and belonging, which appears to be especially strong in American culture. His images produce an aesthetic experience that disrupts the fragmenting everyday practices of the spectator being confronted with this picture into which she could insert herself as the last missing piece. Kinkade's images tactically makes use of the crisis of art scorned by "the everyday woman" for being incomprehensible and esoteric, and offers something completely comprehensible in this opening. Doing so, he also makes it possible for everyday men and women to become buyers of art, inventors of the art buying practice that they had always reserved for others, and to feel as if they are joining self-selected communities of "good taste." The Kinkade buyer becomes special and part of a greater whole. In becoming-owner is also the answer to the call of the picture, asking us to "come home," to give in to our belonging to the picture.

The experience economy experience centers on this tension between becoming-special and belonging. The experience, of opening and disorientation, is an event and, as such, incorporeal. The event of being cut with a knife can exemplify the play of statement and action in the event:

> *Thus the knife opening up a wound in a flesh is an attribute of the interpenetration of bodies, but the event of "being cut" is what is expressed by the statement "he was cut with a knife." The fact of being cut is a property of neither the flesh nor the knife; it is an incorporeal attribute of the flesh.* (Patton, 1997: XX)

Experience economy entrepreneurship operates in this openness of the event (intensified by the aesthetic sensation side of experience) and makes use of the disorientation that belongs to the action that is not yet placed into a context of a greater whole. Today you cannot simply buy a car or a mobile phone—there must be a story relating certain concepts that stage the experience of becoming an owner of this or that car/phone. The aesthetic experience (if only provided through the image of the product and the story communicating this image), we learned from Heidegger, becomes an event through participation and disorientation. The aesthetic experience disrupts the ongoingness of the everyday and creates an opening: we are taken back to affects and percepts, whence opinions ordering relations between concepts and objects emerge. We start to think "car" or "mobile phone" in a way that allows new concepts to order our relationship to such objects. We experience desire, the force connecting us with other desires—a greater whole—through which our productive capacities increase. The object is made into a transitional object in the experience of becoming unique and belonging.

PART V

MAKING SENSE OF EXPERIENCE ECONOMY

CHAPTER 12

KRONOS AND EROS
MAKING SENSE OF ORGANIZING IN THE EXPERIENCE ECONOMY

MONIKA KOSTERA

In this concluding chapter, I would like to address the methods that the authors of the chapters in this book used to make sense of experience economy organizations. The students of experience economy organizations whose work we have presented here adopted qualitative methods overall, inspired by grounded theory and ethnography with some additional discourse analysis, and have, in many cases, a somewhat more intensive engagement and presence in the field than is usual. They often react more directly to what they study than typical traditional ethnographers, and many of them had and still have personal ties to the field that transgress the relationship between the researcher and the researched. This approach, which I would like to call impressionist, serves, in my opinion, the study of organizations in the experience economy quite well. It is natural for students as well as for participants of such organizations to become involved and impressed by them. The images underpinning the experience economy organizations are different from those sustaining traditional organizations and presume an intense involvement and strong impression. To explain how this adds up, I will first briefly present the idea of sensemaking in organizations, then introduce the key image I use to make sense of the organizational type that is described in this book, and finally, I will try to depict the main attributes of the method suitable for addressing this organizational type.

Organizing and Sensemaking
Social contructivists do not believe in fixed, solid phenomena called organizations, but following Karl Weick (1969/1979), they instead like to think in terms of processes of organizing, or bringing together "on-

going interdependent actions into sensible sequences i.e., generat[ing] sensible outcomes" (Weick 1969/1979: 3). The results of organizing are cycles linked together as loops (and not chains of causes and effects). Weick described the three stages of a cycle of organizing. The first stage is enactment, which means that people bracket out a segment of their environment and make it real through their actions. The second is selection, where people try to reduce ambiguity by framing their actions with the help of their cognitive schemes. Finally, the stage of retention implies keeping the effects within their cognitive schemes. Seen this way, organizing is about active and continuous sensemaking, as much as it is about the practice of making the processes real or enacted (Weick, 1995). Communication is of key importance because of its role in the sensemaking processes people use. Sensemaking is an attempt to reduce multiple meanings and deal with multifaceted information. It is a task of incredible difficulty and complexity: the process lacks a given end or clear patterns to follow. Barbara Czarniawska (1998) proposes that sensemaking is to interpretation what uncertainty is to probability (Czarniawska, 1998). When we interpret, we choose from possible frames, whereas when we make sense we create them from scratch. It is an ongoing activity, which can be more or less entrepreneurial and more or less innovative. Some instances of sensemaking can be based on pure prejudice, while some give birth to completely new ideas and insights. The creativity of sensemaking processes does not guarantee creative results but it makes them possible.

Sensemaking consists of a frame, a cue, and a connection (Weick, 1995). The frames are cultural assumptions and basic images pertaining to the object of sensemaking. There are two kinds of sensemaking: belief-driven and action-driven. Beliefs define what people see and can shape expectations about the future and argumentation. Action-driven sensemaking creates commitment or manipulates reality. People either dedicate their efforts to making sense as a concrete result of their actions (driven by actions) or they go out and change reality to experience sense (driven by beliefs). These modes of sensemaking are connected, and every organizational belief, if it is strong enough, may be an important frame used for choices of action (see e.g., Hatch, Kostera and Kozminski, 2005).

The paradox of sensemaking processes in organizations is that successful results are stored (retained), extending the cognitive schemes, but at the same time limiting the possibilities of change: it is a process of ordering and directing. It can be more or less obsessive, more or less precise (Law, 1994). The way it is done is a strategy, what John Law calls the mode of ordering, not necessarily conscious but definitely based on a kind of internalized knowledge available within the organization. An organization's actual mode of ordering is typically quite regular and repetitive, giving the impression of being something solid, a thing—the organization.

The pattern according to which this is done depends on the cognitive schemes of the organization, and in particular, on the leading idea—the vision, which is conscious, and an underlying image, the archetype, which provides the actors with motivation and imaginative power. Organizations in the experience economy have a common leading idea, which, as the chapters in this book show, converge around the idea of experience as both something produced and consumed by actors. Often the production and consumption processes are simultaneous, or parallel, which makes this kind of organizing activity especially dependent on communication. Sensemaking in such organizations is based on the translation of individual experience into collective action. The motives for translation depicted in this book are: uniqueness, mediation, and massification (see Introduction).

The image underpinning organizations in the experience economy, or their key archetype, provides actors with space[91] (de Certeau, 1984) for their sensemaking activities, but is not necessarily conscious. Following the Carl Gustav Jung's (1968) ideas about the collective unconscious, I would claim that it is very rarely made conscious, even though it is realized in action every day. Archetypes are distinctive forms of understanding, attracting images of all human motivations and inspirations. They are concealed in the collective unconscious domain of reality and shared by all humans. Myths and symbols are constructed from archetypes. They can be seen as the foundation of culture and society, since they can turn individuals into groups.

According to Jung (1968), archetypes express themselves through images that inspire all human ideas. They offer models for human motivation, passions, and figures of imagination. They are universal and unvarying, but they inspire incessant interpretation and reinterpretation. Jung saw archetypes as a riverbed, from which inspiration can be taken to be used through the narration of myths.

---

[91] "A *space* exists when one takes into consideration vectors of direction, velocities, and time variables. Thus space is composed of intersections of mobile moments. It is in a sense actuated by the ensemble of movements deployed within it. Space occurs as the effect produced by the operations that orient it, situate it, temporalize it, and make it function in a polyvalent unity of conflictual programs or contractual proximities" (de Certeau, 1984, p. 37).

The study of archetypes in organizations can be useful for an under-standing of how myths and symbols work in the construction of culture. Archetypal images form ideas that influence leadership (Hatch, Kostera and Kozminski, 2005); provide female managers with imaginative space for the construction of their social roles (Gherardi, 1995); and offer employees fundamental ideas of participation (Sievers, 1994). The oldest mythology in Western culture—Greek myth—is often used to frame readings of archetypal ideas (Hatch, Kostera and Kozminski, 2005; Gherardi, 1995; Sievers, 1994; Bowles, 1989; 1993).

In the study of experience economy organizations, understanding archetypes can offer insights regarding the hidden images directing sensemaking. Archetypes support the belief-driven sensemaking processes in the two organization types and infuse them with different kinds of desire. Desire, understood in the Deleuzian sense, not as a lack that has to be filled but as a process. It a field of immanence, a Zen-like quality in that it can only be reached when the subject ceases to reach for it. Desire is already there but in order to become conscious it has to be constructed. It is will to power, grace, original energy (Deleuze and Guattari, 1972/1984). Desire, in the sense I use it here, is similar to de Certeau's notion of space—both are actualized by movements and exist as a potential field of possibility and power.

Kronos versus Eros

The archetypes that underpin organizing in the two economies, the managerialist and the experience economy, inspire different kinds of desire—the former a desire for power, and the latter, a desire for experience. I will describe the types of desire characteristic of them by referring two archetypes taken from Greek mythology: Kronos and Eros.

Kronos was one of the Titans, son of Uranus and Gaia, brother and husband of Rheia. He was a frightful god, violently passionate about power. His father, Uranus, was the supreme ruler and a terrible despot. Even his wife, Gaia, was concerned about the extent of her husband's relish of power. Kronos envied his father fiercely, and often fretted about not being as potent as him. When Gaia asked who among all her children would assist her in an attempt to weakening the power of her husband, Kronos was the only one who agreed. One night he surprised Uranus while he was in bed with Gaia and fatally castrated him. He then took over as the supreme ruler. A fear for revenge never left him, he was terrified of the prospect of his children killing him in turn when they grew up. To prevent it, he swallowed them whole as soon as they were born. After giving birth to the sixth child, Zeus, Rheia gave her husband a stone wrapped in baby clothes instead of the baby. Kronos swallowed the stone, thinking that it was the newborn Zeus. In the meantime, little Zeus was sent away to Crete, where he lived in a cave on Mount Dicte, suckled by the goat Amaltheia. When he grew up he returned to Rheia and Kronos, and with his mother's help tricked his father to regurgitate all the swallowed children, now completely grown up. Led by Zeus, the siblings together conquered and overthrew their father. Zeus proved to be somewhat less cruel than Kronos: he did not castrate or kill his father, but banished him, and later even let him join the demi-gods and heroes at the end of the world. The name Kronos may be derived from the verb *kreno*, which means to govern (Stewart, 2005). Kronos is often confused with the god of time, Chronos, a wise man with a long beard.

Kronos can be seen as the archetype of desire characteristic of the managerialist economy. Often mistaken for time management, this kind of desire is, in fact, all about power. When Taylorism took over as the ruling rationality of organizing in the economy, it was a formidable revolt against the old order, based on the patriarchal cultures of crafts and traditional farms (see Shenhav, 1999; Braverman, 1974). Scientific management was not the kind of revolution that overthrows and kills the old system, like the Bolshevik or Maoist revolutions. Instead, it was a castrating revolt, it rendered the old order impotent by taking away its resources: human, monetary, and intellectual. It undermined the potential of traditional artisanal shops and long-established family businesses to enter and develop in the new markets. Managerialism thrived on power and accumulated more and more of it, first by taking it away from workers and office employees, and then by reaching out to higher administrative levels (Braverman, 1974, Jacques, 1996). Even managers were subjected to routines of rationalization, speciali-zation, and standardization of their work. Factories were turned into giant machines, following Ford's example, where the workers were seen as mere fallible additions to the conveyor belt. Offices soon fol-lowed on the same path, turning into monstrous administrative mecha-nisms. Some companies equipped their offices with conveyor belts, most streamlined them functionally and aesthetically, so that they both looked and functioned independently of the employees' skill or indi-viduality. In fact, individuality was forbidden on workshop floors, as in offices. Workers had to be perfectly uniform, and no personal thing should be visible anywhere in the factory. Workers who did not conform, or perhaps just smiled, were fired.[92] Administrative personnel were not allowed to put photos or mascots anywhere in their workplace (Forty, 1986). Managers were instructed how to keep their desks tidy. Everything and everyone should be deprived of power and control so that the managerialist system's power would grow further. Enterprises began to grow on an unprecedented scale, in market share, physical measures, and income. Of the world's hundred biggest economies, more than half today are business organizations. General Motors' sales are slightly higher than the Gross Domestic Product of Denmark and twice the size of Ireland's. Still, the managerialist economy seems to be constantly fearful of possible pretenders to the throne. It has been swallowing its children: the potentially refreshing novelties in management originating from the Human Relations movement were immediately incorporated in the managerialist logic (Braverman, 1974), as were numerous other schools of thought, such as Total Quality Management (TQM). TQM, in practice, ends up becoming embedded in power relations within organizations and not anywhere as revolutionary as it promises (Knights and McCabe, 1999). Whether managerialism has managed to give birth to its own Zeus, still remains to be seen: it is still in its golden age.

Eros is older than the Titans. He or she (or rather; he and she) was one of the primordial gods, the three old ones who were there at the beginning (the two others being Chaos and Earth). Eros came between the immobile Chaos, the infinite void, and Earth, the mother of creation, and made it possible for them to see each other and break their solitude and silence. Eros is an androgyne, the most beautiful among immortals, the ultimate attraction, the power drawing together divinities and persons. S/he draws other's together but lacks a partner her/himself. S/he calls others to give birth to children, but has no offspring of her/his own. Eros is a mysterious god, beyond the grasp of humans and gods, but constantly present among them all. S/he is love but not necessarily a peaceful or benevolent deity. The primordial attraction is stronger than reason, life, and death, and in its pure form it

---

[92] "The implementation of this work ethic can be seen at the Ford Motor Company in the 1930s and 1940s where managers viewed laughter as a disciplinary offence (Beynon, 1980). They prohibited workers at the River Rouge plant from talking with colleagues, even during lunch breaks, and treated humming, whistling and even smiling on the job as evidence of soldiering or insubordination. In 1940 John Gallo was sacked because he was "caught in the act of "smiling", after having committed an earlier breach of "laughing with the other fellows" and slowing down the line for "maybe a half a minute" (Sward, 1948, pp. 312–13)" (Collinson, 2002, p. 276).

cannot be grasped by humans or gods: it is madness. Eros is often said to be equipped with two sets of arrows: golden ones, which inspire attraction and love, and lead arrows that cause aversion. Both love and hate are strong and absolute, they turn into the driving force and even obsession of the individual struck by the arrow, and no god or human is immune to them. Perhaps it is so because the substance that the arrow is infused with melts together with our blood, becoming ours, becoming-individual and unique. Eros is passionate and ecstatic. In this way s/he is similar to Dionysus, the wine god. They even share the same nickname, Bromios, meaning the Thunderer. S/he is often confused with a quite different deity: Aphrodite's son of the same name, the frivolous patron of infatuation.

Eros represents the typical organizing desire in the experience economy, where frivolous infatuation is often mistaken with consumption, but there is a difference between these superficial service organizations and organizations in an experience economy. The former are just another masque for managerialist organizations, while the latter are a powerful new phenomenon. As the chapters show, organizations in the experience economy are qualitatively different from managerialist ones: they are entrepreneurial, unabashedly eclectic, nonlinear and sometimes blatantly illogical. They are enacted via immediacy, subjectivity, playfulness, and performativity. They attract and seduce people to join and to consume, using images, sensations, and associations. Sometimes they lure people into lustful consumption, as in the case of places branding; sometimes they inspire passion and dedication, as with some sports events. The experience economy may involve any activity but typically includes what are seen as hobbies: festivals, film, sports, art, and so forth. The experience economy can successfully be performed only when it pertains to subjectivity: in the act of its consumption as well as production. This is its substantial difference from traditional services. There is no experience economy without a subject, no depersonalized or Macdonaldized act, it has to involve the subject in ways that touch the inner sphere of the individual. Even consuming dairy becomes a unique experience when it is incorporated into the experience economy. Its value becomes elevated and it grows to be a provider of exotic value for consumers in a world of postnecessity consumption.

Eros is a compelling ruler, and the desire that the archetype generates is beyond anyone's control. Organizations in the experience economy do not strive for managerialist domination, instead they are entrepreneurial, as many of the authors in the book claim. In other words, they evade control and ride the waves of uncertainty. But the motivation for people to engage in such organizations is very personal. The participants of the Sarajevo film festivals are not just any consumers of film; neither are they a demanding audience. They are passionately united with the festival. It has become part of their lives. The experience economy presumes an intrusive way of organizing, for good and for worse. In this book we have seen mainly positive examples, where the individuals act out of interest and dedication, but there are other possibilities as well, of organizations using manipulation and possession as their modus operandi. Some traces of this are present in the Phaeton story and in the case of the sports events. As the experience economy grows, examples of this kind of abuse will probably proliferate.

Today's experience economy organizations, as depicted in this book, have outgrown the way the experience economy was originally defined by authors, such as Pine and Gilmore (1999). The original definitions saw a world of relatively tame organizations, lighthearted and frivolous, as represented by Eros, the son of Aphrodite; however, the organizations we have presented in this volume are by no means lighthearted, even if they freely use kitsch or mundane symbolism. They run on a deeper and darker desire, the one derived from the primordial Eros. Triviality has no place in the experience economy. And even if it appears, it is related to something more severe and deep, like in Phaeton's fateful story. Love is stronger than death, goes the popular platitude, but if we reflect on the saying we can realize what it really means: that love is a power that is unstoppable, even at the usual ultimate human frontier, that is death; its meaning reveals some of the magnitude of the desire invoked by this archetype. Management in the experience economy loses control and moves into the domain of the carnivalesque. This is clearly shown in the case of Thomas Kinkade and his Media Arts Group that constructs feelings of real community through the mass production and distribution of paintings invoking nostalgia and belonging, or in the story of Andréasson PR arranging an authentic event that is highly choreographed and directed.

Studying the Experience Economy

The desire of Eros is not one that lends itself to abstract or rational depictions, or it loses its most vital characteristics in the process. It needs an approach based on empathy rather than intellectual abstraction. The qualities of experience economy based organizing processes—immediacy, subjectivity, playfulness, and performativity—make them particularly useful to study by means of narrative approaches (Czarniawska, 2005).

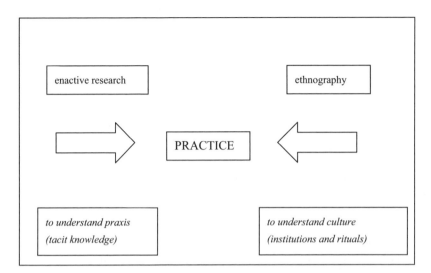

Figure 12.1 Methods for Studying Experience Economy Organizations

There are two main aspects of organizational practices in the field of the experience economy: the researcher can focus on trying to understand the praxis and to acquire tacit knowledge, or consider and problematize its cultural contexts and, thus, map institutions and rituals. The first aim is best achieved through the use of enactive research (Johannisson, forthcoming), and the second through ethnographic studies of organizations (Czarniawska, 2004).

Ethnography enables the study of phenomena in their real context. It aims at an understanding and interpretation of phenomena, sometimes also at extrapolation of the results to other, similar situations. The task of the researcher is to interpret the phenomena and to show how they came about. It is achieved through immersion in culture (Agar, 1986). It is a way of doing field research that presumes direct experience of the researcher. She is present in the field for prolonged periods of time, observing, making interviews, and taking field notes. Ethnographic studies aim at a presentation of how organizations are constructed and what nets of action they consist of (Czarniawska, 1992).

According to Bengt Johannission (forthcoming), enactive research is similar to ethnography, except that here the researcher her- or himself initiates an event and, through hers or his participation in the creation gains an insight combined with authorship. Self-knowledge is necessary as a starting point. The researcher is strongly present throughout the process but should not dominate it. The event is a creative act and all faculties of the researcher are engaged in the process, not just the intellectual but also the social, imaginative, reflective, emotional and so on. The creation process is a collaborative construction of a new reality. The aim is to produce something new, to transcend existing institutions. It is a method that merges the perspectives of the actors and the perspective of the researcher. Enactive research is based on experience that presupposes the direct creation of the experience by the researcher him- or herself.

These two approaches are not exclusive and there should be ways of, if not uniting them, bringing them together in a kind of mixed methodology. I wish to call this mix the impressionist method, because its aim is to capture impressions, as well as to impress.

Inspiration for establishing new approaches in social sciences often comes from art (Czarniawska, 1997, 1999; Kociatkiewicz and Kostera, 2001) and so it is not too farfetched to use impressionism in the arts to characterize the impressionist method. Impressionism was a nineteenth century movement. French artists, dissatisfied with traditional cannons of painting, began to exhibit their works in the 1860s. Short brush strokes are typical for the impressionist movement, with the aspiration being to depict light and produce an impression of the momentary view, the direct visual experience. The images suggested change and subjective view, rejecting ideals of beauty and static perspectives. They enjoyed painting outdoors, concentrating on beauty to be found in everyday life.

The impressionist method reminds one of impressionist art in that it is aimed at the depiction of real life, in its momentary, fleeting aspects. Its end result may be an impressionist tale—an ethnography whose aim is, according to John Van Maanen (1988), to engage the reader in the experience from the perspective of the researcher. The researcher seeks to understand the field but he or she immerses her or himself in it much more than in standard ethnographic practice. In some cases she or he might participate in its comings and goings, but it is not unthinkable to go as far as initiating certain activities with the purpose of studying them. To understand an experience economy means to experience it and this involves more than detached observation can offer. The researcher needs a stronger empathy with or, perhaps even as much as, a thrill from the field to be able to depict it.

Using impressionist methods and writing impressionist tales is in harmony with the type of desire that the experience economy is based on. Eros cannot be grasped or analyzed, s/he cannot be described through laws of statistics but s/he certainly can impress. Consumers and producers in the experience economy and its researchers alike can concentrate on experiencing the economy. While the former do so in order to immerse themselves in the experience, the researchers have an additional intention: to describe and to understand, although not necessarily on an intellectual level. The kind of understanding that is sought here is close to Michael Polanyi's (1958/1974) idea of tacit knowledge, or a kind of personal, action oriented knowledge, involving the personality of the knower. It is difficult to verbalize and it is often embodied. If a person knows how to ride the bicycle, the knowledge is his or hers, it is personal and becomes activated every time that person rides the bike. It would be very difficult to explain in rational terms what that skill exactly involves or learn it through reading a textbook. It is a "knowing of how to do things," a skill, or an "expertise." To depict it, one can try to share the experience by practical demonstration or telling a story. The impressionist method aims for storytelling to be as close to demonstration as possible. The reader should be able to intellectually grasp the scientific merits of the study described, but he or she should also be moved. Eros is not an archetype allowing for coldness or insensitivity. A method under the rule of Eros is not a purely rational method—it should be more like yoga: a means of reaching embodied insight.

WORKS CITED

Aaker, D. A. 1996. *Building strong brands*. New York: Free Press.

Agar, M. 1996. *The professional stranger: An informal introduction to ethnography*. 2d ed. New York: Academic Press.

Ahearne, J. 1995. *Michel de Certeau: Interpretation and its other*. London: Polity Press.

Alessi, A. 2000. *The Dream Factory: Alessi since 1921*. Milan: Electa/Alessi.

AMS. 2001. *Arbete för nöjes skull: Var finns jobben inom upplevelsenäringen?* Ura 3. Stockholm: Arbetsmarknadsstyrelsen.

Anderson, A. R. 2000. Paradox in the periphery: An entrepreneurial reconstruction? *Entrepreneurship & Regional Development* 12(2):91–109.

Andersson, L.G. 1999. Decamerone: Europeisk konstfilm; auteurer, och adaptationer. In *Film Analysis*, edited by L. G. Andersson, and E. Hedling. Lund, Swed.: Studentlitteratur.

Andersson, P. 2005. Memfis, Stockholm. *Made in Sweden: The Magazine about Swedish Film* 6:8–9.

Andrews, D. L., and S. J. Jackson, eds. 2001. *Sports stars: The cultural politics of sporting celebrity*. London: Routledge.

Anholt, S. 1998. Nation-brands of the twenty first century. *Journal of Brand Management* 5: 395–406.

———. 2004. Editor's foreword to *Place Branding* 1:4–11.

Armstrong, P. 2001. Science, enterprise and profit: Ideology in the knowledge driven economy. *Economy and Society* 30:524–52.

Arnason, H. H., M. F. Prather, and D. Wheeler. 1998. *History of modern Art: Painting, sculpture, architecture, photography*. 4d ed. New York: Harry N. Abrams.

Ashworth, G. J., and H. Voogd. 1988. Marketing the city: Concepts, processes and Dutch Applications. *Town Planning Review* 59:65–79.

———. 1990. *Selling the city: Marketing approaches in public sector urban planning*. London: Belhaven Press.

———. 1994. Marketing and place promotion. In *Place promotion: The use of publicity and marketing to sell towns and regions,* edited by J. R. Gold, and S. V. Ward. Chichester, U.K.: John Wiley and Sons.

Asimov, Isaac. 1991. The Lord's apprentice. In *The ultimate Frankenstein,* edited by B. Preiss. New York: Dell.

Bahto, S. 2002. Entrepreneurship and war: Some reflections in the context of 1992–2002 Bosnia and Herzegovina. Paper presented at the 16th Annual Conference on Research in Entrepreneurship, November, in Barcelona, Spain.

Bailey II, I. W., and A. H. Schechter. 1994. The corporation as a brand: An identity dilemma. *Chief Executive* 98:42–45.

Bakhtin, M. 1965. *Rabelais and his world*. Bloomington: Indiana University Press.

Balmer, J. M. T. 2002. Corporate identity, corporate branding and corporate marketing:
Seeing through the fog. *European Journal of Marketing* 35:248–291.

Balmer, J. M. T., and E. R. Gray. 2003. Corporate brands: What are they? What of them? *Journal of Marketing* 37:972–997.

Barish, J. 1981. *The antitheatrical prejudice*. Berkeley: University of California Press.

Barlow, P. 2000. Fear and loathing of the academic, or just what is it that makes the avant-garde so different, so appealing? In *Academic Identities*, edited by R. C. Denis, and C. Trodd. New Brunswick, N.J.: Rutgers University Press.

Barry, D., and S. Meisiek. 2004. NyX innovation alliances evaluation report. Research report from Forum for Kultur og Erhverv, Tranbjerg, Danmark, www.lld.dk.

Barth, F., ed. 1963. *The role of the entrepreneur in social change in northern Norway*. Oslo: Universitetsforlaget.

Barthes, R. 1978. *A lover's discourse: Fragments*. Montreal: Harper Collins.

Bataille, G. 1985. *The accursed share: An essay in general economy*. Vol. 1, *Consumption*. New York: Zone Books.

Baudrillard, J. [1970]1998. *The consumer society: Myths and structures*. Translated by C. Turner. London: Sage Publications.

———. 1982. *Der symbolische tausch und der tod*. München: Matthes and Seitz.

Bauman, Z. 1988. Sociology after the Holocaust. *The British Journal of Sociology* 39(4):469–497.

———. 1992. Survival as a social construct. *Theory, Culture & Society* 9:1–36.

———. 1995. Philosophie der Fitness. *TAZ* 25:19–21.

———. 1998. *Vi vantrivs i det postmoderna*. Uddevalla, Swed.: Bokförlaget Daidalos.

———. 2001. *Liquid modernity*. Cambridge, U.K.: Polity Press.

Beck, U. 1986. *Risikogesellschaft. Auf dem weg in eine andere moderne*. Frankfurt am Main: Suhrkamp.

Becker, H. 1982. *Art Worlds*. Berkeley: University of California Press.

Behar, R. 1993. *Translated woman: Crossing the border with Esperanza's story*. Boston: Beacon Press.

Bélanger, A. 2000. Sport venues and the spectacularization of urban spaces in North America. The case of Molson Centre in Montreal. *International Review for the Sociology of Sport* 35(3):378–397.

Benhabib, S. 1992. *Situating the self: Gender, community and postmodernism in contemporary ethics*. New York: Routledge.

Benjamin, W. 1999. The work of art in the age of mechanical reproduction. In *Illuminations*, edited and with an introduction by H. Arendt. Translated by H. Zorn. London: Pimlico.

Bennett, R., and S. Savani. 2003. The rebranding of city places: An international comparative investigation. *The International Journal of Public Sector Management* 4:70–87.

Berg, P. O. 2003. Magic in action: Strategic management in a new economy. In *The northern lights: Organization theory in Scandinavia*. Edited by B. Czarniawska and G. Sevón. Malmö, Swed.: Liber.

Berg, P. O., A. Linde-Laursen, and O. Löfgren, eds. 2002. *Öresundsbron på uppmärksamhetens marknad: Regionbyggare i evenemangsbranschen*. Lund, Swed.: Studentlitteratur.

Berger, P., and T. Luckman. 1987. Reprint. *The social construction of reality*. London: Penguin Books. Original edition, New York: Anchor Books, 1966.

Bishop, C. 2005. *Installation art: A critical history*. London: Tate Publishing.

Björkegren, D. 1994. *Filmens företag*. Stockholm: Nerenius and Santerus AB.

———. 1996. *The culture business: Management strategies for the arts-related business*. London: Routledge.

Björkman, I. 1998. Sven Duchamp: Expert på aura production. Ph.D. dissertation, Stockholms Universitet

———. 2002. Aura: Aesthetic business creativity. *Consumption, Markets and Culture* 5(1): 69–78.

Bocklehurst, M. 2001. Power, identity and new technology homework: Implications for 'new forms' of organizing. *Organization Studies* 22:445–446.

Bocock, R. 1993. *Consumption*. London: Routledge.

Boje, D. M. 2001. *Narrative methods for organizational and communication research*. London: Sage Publications.

Boltanski, L., and E. Chiapello. 2003. *Der neue geist des kapitalismus*. Konstanz: UVK Verlagsgesellschaft.

Bolter, D. J. 1984. *The Turing's Man: Western culture in the computer age*. Chapel Hill: University of North Carolina Press

Bordwell, D., and K. Thompson. 1997. *Film art: An introduction*. New York: McGraw-Hill.

Bourdieu, P. 1992. De olympiska spelen. Ett analysprogram. *Res Publica* 64:84–87.

———. 1993. *The field of cultural production*. New York: Columbia University Press.

Bourdon, D. 1989. *Andy Warhol*. New York: Harry Abrams.

Bowdin, G., I. McDonnell, J. Allen, and W. O'Toole, eds. 2002. *Events Management*. Oxford: Butterworth Heinemann.

Bowles, M. L. 1989. Myth, meaning and work organization. *Organization Studies* 10(3):405–421.

———. 1993. The gods and goddesses: Personifying social life in the age of organization. *Organization Studies* 14(3):395–418.

Brecht, B. [1939] 1982. *Über experimentelles theater*. Frankfurt am Main: Suhrkamp Verlag.

Brewis, J., and S. Linstead. 2000. *Sex, work and sex work: Eroticizing organization*. London: Routledge.

Bridge, S., K. O'Neill, and S. Cromie. 2003. *Understanding enterprise: Entrepreneurship and small business*. Basingstoke: Palgrave Macmillan.

Bröckling, U. 2003. Das demokratisierte panopticon. Subjektivierung und kontrolle im 360 grad-feedback. In *Michel Foucault. Zwischenbilanz einer rezeption. Frankfurter Foucault-konferenz 2001*, edited by A. Honneth and M. Saar. Frankfurt am Main: Suhrkamp.

Brown, J. 2002. Ticky-tacky houses from 'The Painter of Light.' *Salon*, March 18, http://archive.salon.com/mwt/style/2002/03/18/kinkade_village/

Burns, E. 1972. *Theatricality: A study of convention in the theatre and in social life*. New York: Harper and Row.

Burke, K. 1969. Reprint. *A grammar of motives*. Berkeley: University of California Press. Original edition, New York: Prentice-Hall, 1945.

Butler, J. 1997. *The psychic life of power: Theories in subjection*. Palo Alto, Calif.: Stanford University Press.

Bååth, H. and H. Lundberg. 2004. Report from European Academy of Sport Management, 22–25 September, in Ghent, Belgien. Växjö, SE: Växjö Universitet.

CALC (Casqueiro Atlantico Laboratorio Cultural). 2004. L.A.–Las Aceñas, from ex-industrial village to playful respons-ibility. Paper presented at the First International Workshop on Methods–research projects on art society relations, 2–3 October, Cittadellarte, Fondazione Pistoletto, Biella, Italy, www.calcaxy.com.

Caldwell, N., and J. R. Freire. 2004. The differences between branding a country, a region and a city: Applying the brand box model. *Journal of Brand Management* 12:50–61.

Callon, M. 1991. Techno-economic networks and irreversibility. In *Sociology of monsters: Essays on power, technology, and domination*, edited by J. Law. London: Routledge.

Cantillon, R. [1755] 1999. *Essai sur la nature du commerce en générale* (Essay on the nature of commerce in general). New Brunswick, N.J.: Transaction Publishers.

Cardoso, R., D. Trodd, and C. Trodd, eds. 2000. *Art and the academy in the nineteenth century*. New Brunswick, N.J.: Rutgers University Press.

Carlson, M. 2002. The resistance to theatricality. *SubStance* 31(2/3):238–250.

Carter, P., and N. Jackson. 2000. An-aesthetics. In *The aesthetics of organization*, edited by S. Linstead, and H. Höpfl. London: Sage Publications.

Castel, R. 1991. From dangerousness to risk. In *The Foucault effect: Studies in governmentality*, edited by G. Burchell, C. Gordan and P. Miller. Hemel Hempstead, U.K.: Harvester Wheatsheaf.

Caves, R. 2000. *Creative industries: Contracts between art and commerce*. Cambridge, Mass.: Harvard University Press.

Chang, R. 2001. *The passion plan at work: Building a passion-driven organization*. San Francisco: Jossey-Bass.

Chell, E., J. Haworth, and S. Brearly. 1991. *The entrepreneurial personality: Concepts, cases and categories*. London: Routledge.

Chia, R. 1996. The problem of reflexivity in organizational research: Towards a postmodern science of organization. *Organization* 3:31–59.

———. 1997. Thirty years on: From organizational structures to the organization of thought. *Organization Studies* 18(4):685–707.

———. 2000. Discourse analysis as organizational analysis. *Organization* 7:513–518.

Cohen, S. G., and D. E. Bailey. 1997. What makes teams work: Group effectiveness from the shop floor to the executive suit. *Journal of Management* 23:239–290.

Colebrook, C. 1997. *New literary histories: New historicism and contemporary criticism*. Manchester: Manchester University Press.

———. 1999. *Ethics and representation–from Kant to post-structuralism*. Edinburgh: Edinburgh University Press

———. 2002. *Deleuze*. London: Routledge.

Collinson, D. L. 2002. Managing humour. *Journal of Management Studies* 39(3):269–288.

Connell, J., and C. Gibson. 2003. *Sound tracks: Popular music, identity and place*. London: Routledge.

Cooper, A. C., and C. M. Daily. 1997. Entrepreneurial teams. In *Entrepreneurship 2000*, edited by D. L. Sexton, and R. W. Smilor. Chicago:Upstart Publishing.

Cooper, R. 1976. The open field. *Human Relations* 29:999–1017.

———. 1990. Organization/Disorganization. In *The theory and philosophy of organizations: Critical issues and new perspectives*, edited by J. Hassard, and M. Parker. London: Routledge.

Cornelissen, J. P. 2004. What are we playing at? Theatre, organization, and the use of metaphor. *Organization Studies* 25(5):705–726.

Corvellec, H. 1995. Stories of achievements: Narrative features of organizational performances. Ph.D. diss., Lund University.

Crary, J. 1999. *Suspensions of perception: Attention, spectacle, and modern culture*. Cambridge, Mass: MIT Press.

Czarniawska, J. B., and R. Wolff. 1991. Leaders, managers, entrepreneurs on and off the organizational stage. *Organization Studies* 12(4):529–546.

Czarniawska, B. 1992. Doing interpretive studies of organizations. Working paper, Lund University.

———. 1993. *The three-dimensional organization: A constructionist's view*. Lund, Swed.: Studentlitteratur.

———. 1997a. Symbolism and organization studies. In *Theorien der organisation: Die rückkehr der gesellschaft*, edited by G. Ortmann, J. Sydow, and K. Türk. Opladen: Westdeutschen Verlag.

———. 1997b. *Narrating the organization: Dramas of institutional identities*. Chicago: University of Chicago Press.

Czarniawska, B. 1998. Weick, Karl E. *The handbook of management thinking*. London: International Thomson Publishing.

———. 1999. *Writing management*. Oxford: Oxford University Press.

Czarniawska, B., and B. Joerges. 1996. Travels of ideas. In *Translating organizational change*, edited by B. Czarniawska, and G. Sevón. Berlin: Walter de Gruyter.

Dachler, H. P., and D. M. Hosking. 1995. The primacy of relations in socially constructing organizational realities. In *Management and organization: Relational alternatives to individualism*, edited by D. M. Hosking, H. P. Dachler, and K. J. Gergen. Aldershot, U.K.: Avebury

Day, R. 1998. Diagrammatic bodies. In *Organized worlds: Explorations in technology and organization with Robert Cooper*, edited by R. Chia. London: Routledge.

DCMS (U.K. Department for Culture, Media, and Sport). 1999. Creative industries: The regional dimension. Report from the Regional Issues Working Group. London: DCMS.

Debord, G. 1995. Reprint. *The Society of the spectacle*. Translated by D. Nicholson-Smith. New York: Zone Books. Original edition, Paris: Editions Buchet-Chastel, 1967.

de Certeau, M. 1984. *The practice of everyday life*. Berkeley: University of California Press

———. 1997a. *Heterologies: Discourse on the Other*. Minneapolis: University of Minnesota Press.

———. 1997b. *Culture in the plural*. Minneapolis: University of Minnesota Press.

de Chernatony, L., and R. F. Dall'Olmo. 1998. Defining a brand: Beyond the literature with experts' interpretations. *Journal of Marketing Management* 14:417–443.

Dees, J. G. 1998. The meaning of social entrepreneurship. Paper presented at the Frontiers of Entrepreneurship Research Conference, June, at Kauffman Center for Entrepreneurial Leadership, Babson College, Wellesley, Mass.

Dees, J. G., and B. B. Anderson. 2003. For-profit social ventures. *International Journal of Entrepreneurship Education* 2:1–26.

Deleuze, G. 2000. *Proust and signs*. Translated by R. Howard. London: Athlone Press.

———. 1994. *Difference and repetition*. London: Athlone Press.

———. 1988a. *Bergsonism*. New York: Zone Books.

———. 1988b. *Foucault*. Minneapolis: University of Minnesota Press.

———. 1995. *Negotiations: 1972-1990*. New York: Columbia University Press.

Deleuze, G., and F. Guattari. 1984. *Anti-Oedipus: capitalism and schizophrenia*. 1972. Reprint, London: Athlone Press.

———. 1994. *What is Philosophy?* London and New York: Verso.

———. 2000. *A thousand plateaus: Capitalism and schizophrenia*. Minneapolis: University of Minnesota Press.

Deleuze, G., and C. Parnet. 1987. *Dialogues*. 1977. Reprint, London: Athlone Press.

DeLillo, D. 1997. *Underworld*. New York: Scribner Paperback Fiction/Simon and Schuster.

de Monthoux, P. G. 1993. *Om det sublimas konstnärliga ledning*. Stockholm: Nerenius and Santerus.

———. 1998. *Konstföretaget: Mellan spektakelkultur och kulturspektakel*. Göteborg: Bokförlaget Korpen.

———. 2000. The art management of aesthetic organizing. In *The aesthetics of organization*, edited by S. Lindstead, and H. Höpfl. London: Sage Publications.

————. 2004. *The art firm: Aesthetic management and metaphysical marketing.* Palo Alto, Cal.: Stanford University Press.

de Monthoux, P. G., and S-E. Sjöstrand. 2003. Corporate art or artful corporation? The emerging philosophy firm. In *The northern lights: Organization theory in Scandinavia,* edited by B. Czarniawska, and G. Sevón. Malmö, Swed.: Liber.

Derrida, J. 1986. Das subjektil ent-sinnen. In *Antonin Artraud: Zeichnungen und portraits,* edited by P. Thévenin, and J. Derrida. München: Schirmer/Mosel.

Derrida, J. 1998. Ich mißtraue der utopie, ich will das un-mögliche. Ein gespräch mit dem philosophen Jacques Derrida über die Intellektuellen, den kapitalismus und die gesetze der gastfreundschaft. *DIE ZEIT,* 05 March, 1998, 47–49.

————. 2000. *Als ob ich tot wäre: Ein interview mit Jacques Derrida* (As if I were dead: An interview with Jacques Derrida). Wien: Turia + Kant.

Descartes, R. 1988. *Descartes: selected philosophical writings.* Cambridge: Cambridge University Press.

Dewey, J. [1934] 1980. *Art as experience.* New York: Perigree Books.

Dick, P. K. 1995.The Great C. In *Beyond Lies the Wub.* 1953. Reprint, London: Harper Collins.

Dick, P. K., and R. Zelazny. 1996. *Deus Irae.* Poznan: Zysk.

Dormer, P. 1990. *The meanings of modern design: Towards the twenty-first century.* London: Thames and Hudson.

Douglas, M. 1992. In defence of shopping. In *Produktkulturen: Dynamik und bedeutungswandel des konsums,* edited by E. Miklautz. Frankfurt am Main: Campus Verlag.

Downey, G. L. 1998. *The machine in me: An anthropologist sits among computer engineers.* New York: Routledge.

Dreyfuss, H. 2003. *Designing for people.* New York: Allworth.

Duchesnau, D. A., & Gartner, W. B. (1990). A Profile of New Venture Success and Failure in Emerging Industries. *Journal of Business Venturing* 297-321.

du Gay, P. 1996. *Consumption and identity at work.* London: Sage Publications.

————. 2000. *In praise of bureaucracy.* London: Sage Publications.

————. 2004. Against 'Enterprise' (but not against 'enterprise', for that would make no sense). *Organization* 11:37–57.

du Gay, P., and M. Pryke. 2002. Cultural economy. In *Cultural economy: Cultural analysis and commercial life,* edited by P. du Gay, and M. Pryke. London: Sage Publications.

Düllo, T., and F. Liebl, eds. 2005. *Cultural hacking: Kunst des strategishen handelns.* Wien: Springer.

Eco, U. 1972. The myth of superman. *Diacritics* 2(1)14–22.

Edström, A., Å. Beckerus, and B-E. Larsson. 2003. *Evenemangs företagande.* Lund, Swed.: Studentlitteratur.

Eisenhardt, K. M., and C. B. Schoonhoven. 1990. Organizational growth: Linking founding team, strategy, environment, and growth among U.S. semiconductor ventures, 1978-1988. *Administrative Science Quarterly* 35:504–529.

Eldridge, P., and J. Voss, eds. 2001. How to set up a film festival. The Buckminster Fuller Institute, www.bfi.org.

Eneroth, B. 1984. *Hur mäter man vackert.* Stockholm: Natur och kultur.

Engwall, M. 1999. *Jakten på det effektiva projektet.* Stockholm: Nerenus and Santerus.

Ericsson, L. O. 2005. *Mordet på Tensta konsthall: En anklagelseskrift.* Visby, Swed.: Books-on-demand.

Evans, G. 2003. Hard branding the culture city: From Prado to Prada. *International Journal of Urban and Regional Research* 27:417–440.

Eversmann, P. 2004. The experience of the theatrical event. In *Theatrical events: Borders, Dynamics, Frames,* edited by V.A. Cremona, P. Eversmann, H. van Maanen, W. Sauter and J. Tulloch. Amsterdam: Rodopi.

Fenwick, T. 2002. Transgressive desires: new enterprising selves in the new capitalism. *Work, Employment, and Society* 16:703–723.

Féral, J. 2002. Foreword. *SubStance 98/99* 31(2/3):3–13.

Fielding, L. W., and B. Pitts. 2003. Historical sketches: The development of the sport business industry. In *Contemporary Sport Management,* 2d ed., edited by J. B. Parks, and J. Quarterman, Jerome. Champaign, Illinois: Human Kinetics.

Findlen, P. 1998. Between carnival and Lent: The scientific revolution at the margins of culture. *Configurations* 6(2):243–267.

Finucan, K. 2002. What brand are you? In an age of hype, cities have scrambled to get name recognition. *Planning* (August): 10–13.

Fischer-Lichte, E. 1995. Theatricality: A key concept in theatre and culture studies. *Theatre Research International* 20(2):85–89.

Fleming, P., and A. Spicer. 2004. 'You can check out anytime, but you can never leave': Spatial boundaries in a high commitment organization. *Human Relations* 57:75–94.

Fletcher, D. 2003. Framing organizational emergence: Discourse, identity and relationship. In *New Movements in Entrepreneurship,* edited by D. Hjorth, and C. Steyaert. Cheltenham, U.K.: Edgar Elgar.

Florence, M. 1998. Foucault. In *Michel Foucault: Aesthetics, method and epistemology: Essential works of Foucault: 1954-1984,* vol. 2, edited by J. D. Faubion. New York: The New Press.

Florida, R. 2002. *The rise of the creative class: And how it's transforming work, leisure community, and everyday life.* New York: Basic Books.

———. 2005. *The flight of the creative class: The new global competition for talent.* New York: Harper Business.

Foley, A., and J. Fahy. 2004. Incongruity between expression and experience: The role of imagery in supporting the positioning of a tourism destination brand. *Journal of Brand Management,* 11:209–217.

Forrester, K. 1999. Work-related learning and the struggles for subjectivity. Proceedings of the first international conference, Researching Work and Learning, University of Leeds, United Kingdom.

Forty, A. 1986. *Objects of desire.* London: Thames and Hudson.

Foss, L. 'Going against the grain…' Construction of entrepreneurial identity through narratives. In *Narrative and discursive approaches in entrepreneurship*, edited by D. Hjorth, and C. Steyaert. Cheltenham, U.K.: Edward Elgar.

Foucault, M. 1977. *Discipline and punish: The birth of the prison.* London: Penguin Books.

———. 1980. *Power/knowledge: Selected interviews and other writings, 1972-1977.* Hemel Hempstead, U.K.: Harvester Wheatsheaf.

———. 1981. *The history of sexuality.* Vol. 1. London: Penguin Books.

———. 1982. On the genealogy of ethics: An overview of work in progress. In *Michel Foucault: Beyond structuralism and hermeneutics*, edited by H. Dreyfus, and P. Rabinow. Chicago: University of Chicago Press.

———. 1983. Afterword to *Michel Foucault: Beyond structuralism and hermeneutics*, edited by H. Dreyfus, and P. Rabinow. Chicago: University of Chicago Press.

———. 1988. Technologies of the self. In *Technologies of the self*, edited by L. Martin, H. Gutman, and P. Hutton. Amherst, Mass.: University of Massachusetts Press.

———. 1991a. Questions of method. In *The Foucault effect*, edited by G. Burchell, C. Gordon, and P. Miller. Hemel Hempstead, U.K.: Harvester Wheatsheaf.

———. 1991b. *Remarks on Marx: Conversations with Duccio Trombadori.* New York: Semiotext(e).

———. 1992. *The use of pleasure: The history of sexuality.* Vol. 2. London: Penguin Books.

———. 1993. About the beginning of the hermeneutics of the self. *Political Theory* 21:198–227.

Foucault, M. 1997a. Polemics, politics, and roblematizations. In *Michel Foucault: Ethics, subjectivity, and truth*, edited by P. Rabinow. New York: The New Press.

———. 1997b. What is critique? In *The politics of truth: Michel Foucault*, edited by S. Lotringer, and L. Hochroch. New York: Semiotext(e).

———. 1997c. The ethics of the concern for the self as a practice of freedom. In *Michel Foucault: Ethics, subjectivity, and truth*, edited by P. Rabinow. New York: New Press.

———. 1997d. What is enlightenment? In *Michel Foucault: Ethics, subjectivity, and truth*, edited by P. Rabinow. New York: New Press.

———. 1998. A preface to transgression. In *Michel Foucault: Aesthetics, method, and epistemology*, edited by J. Faubion. Harmondsworth: Allen Lane and Penguin Press.

———. 2004a. *Geschichte der gouvernementalität II: Die geburt der biopolitik.* Frankfurt am Main.: Suhrkamp.

———. 2004b. *Geschichte der gouvernementalität I: Sicherheit, territorium, bevölkerung.* Frankfurt am Main: Suhrkamp.

Frayling, C. 1998. Introduction to *Alessi: The Design Factory.* 2d ed. Chichester, U.K.: John Wiley and Sons.

Frederic, B. 2003. The last bricoleur. Paper presented at 17th Annual Conference on Research in Entrepreneurship, in Lodz, Poland.

Freud, S. 1972. *Das unbehagen in der kultur.* Frankfurt am Main: Fischer Taschenbuch.

Frisby, W. 2005. The good, the bad, and the ugly: Critical sport management research. *Journal of Sport Management* 19:1–12.

Fromm, E. 1961. *Marx's concept of man*. London: Continuum.

Gagliardi, P. 1996. Exploring the aesthetic side of organizational life. In *Handbook of organization studies*, edited by C. Clegg, C. Hardy, and W. Nord. London: Sage Publications.

Gardner, B., and S. Levy. 1955. The product and the brand. *Harvard Business Review* (March/April): 33–39.

Gartner, W. 1988. 'Who is an entrepreneur?' Is the wrong question. *American Journal of Small Business* 12:11–32.

———. 1989. Some suggestions for research on entrepreneurial traits and characteristics. *Entrepreneurship, Theory, and Practice* (Fall): 27–37.

———. 2004. The edge defines the (w)hole: Saying what entrepreneurship is (not). In *Narrative and discursive approaches in entrepreneurship*, edited by D. Hjorth, and C. Steyaert. Cheltenham, U.K.: Edward Elgar.

Gartner, W. B., N. M. Carter, and G. E. Hills. 2003. The language of opportunity. In *New movements in entrepreneurship*, edited by D. Hjorth, and C. Steyaert. Cheltenham, U.K.: Edward Elgar.

Genell, K. 1997. *Transforming management education: A Polish mixture*. Lund, Swed.: Lund University Press.

Gherardi, S. 1995. *Gender, symbolism, and organizational culture*. London: Sage Publications.

Goffman, E. 1959. *The presentation of self in everyday life*. New York: Doubleday.

Gold, J. R., and S. V. Ward. 1994. Place promotion. In *Place promotion: The use of publicity and marketing to sell towns and regions*, edited by J. R. Gold, and S. V. Ward. Chichester, U.K.: John Wiley and Sons.

Goldlust, J, 2004. Reprint. Sport as entertainment: The role of mass communications. In *Critical readings: Sport, culture, and the media*, edited by D. Rowe. Maidenhead/Berkshire, U.K.: Open University Press. Original edition, Melbourne: Longman, Cheshire, 1987.

Goldtwaite, R. 1993. *Wealth and the demand for art in Italy, 1300-1600*. Baltimore, Md.: Johns Hopkins University Press.

Gorb, P., and E. Schneider, eds. 1988. *Design talks! London Business School design management seminars*. London: Design Council.

Gordon, C. 1991. Governmental rationality: An introduction. In *The Foucault effect: Studies in governmentality*, edited by G. Burchell, C. Gordon, and P. Miller. Hemel Hempstead, U.K.: Harvester Wheatsheaf.

Gray, C. 1998. *Enterprise and culture*. London: Routledge.

Greenblatt, S. 1980. *Renaissance self-fashioning: From More to Shakespeare*. Chicago: University of Chicago Press.

Grossman, C. 1994. Carefully crafted identity can build brand equity. *Public Relations Journal* 50:18–21.

Gunnarsson, B. 2002. Interview held in ALMI Foretagspartner AB in Vaxjo, Sweden.

Gunér, G., and R. Hamberger, eds. 2002. Auteuren: Återkomst eller farväl? *Filmkonst* 77. Göteborg, Swed.: Göteborg Film Festival.

Gustafson, E., and L. Hadley. 1999. An overview. In *Sport economics: Current research*, edited by J. Fizel, E. Gustafson, and L. Hadley. Westport, Conn.: Praeger.

Gustafsson, C. 1992. Den dygdige företagsledaren. In *Företagsledning bortom etablerad teori*, edited by S. E. Sjöstrand, and I. L. Holmberg. Lund, Swed.: Studentlitteratur.

Gustafsson, C., and M. Lindahl. 2002. Improvisation and intuition: From a perspective of emergence theory. Paper read at 2nd European Academy of Management Annual Conference, Stockholm.

Hall, T., and P. Hubbard. 1996. The entrepreneurial city: New urban politics, new urban geographies. *Progress in Human Geography* 20:153–174.

Hadzima, J., and G. Pilla. 2006. Entrepreneurial success traits one: Seven characteristics of highly effective entrepreneurial employees, MIT Enterprise   Forum, http://enterpriseforum.mit.edu/mindshare/startingup/seven-characteristics.html. First published in the *Boston Business Journal*.

Handelman, D. 1990. *Models and mirrors: Towards an anthropology of public events*. Cambridge, U.K.: Cambridge University Press.

Hankinson, G. 2001. Location branding: A study of the branding practices of 12 English cities. *Journal of Brand Management* 9:127–142.

———. 2004. Relational network brands: Towards a conceptual model of place brands. *Journal of Vacation Marketing* 10:109–121.

Haunschild, A. 2003. Humanization through discipline: Foucault and the goodness of employee health programmes. *Tamara: Journal of Critical Postmodern Organization Science* 2:46–59.

Hedhammer, T. 2002. Interview held in the municipality of Växjö, Sweden.

Heidegger, M. 1971. The origin of the work of art. In *Poetry, language, thought*, translated by Albert Hofstadter. New York: Harper and Row.

Hirschman, A. O. 1997. *The passions and the interests: Political arguments for capitalism before its triumph*. Princeton, N.J.: Princeton University Press.

Hjorth, D. 2001. *Rewriting entrepreneurship: Enterprise discourse and entrepreneurship in the case of re-organising ES*. Växjö, SE: Växjö University Press.

———. 2003. *Rewriting entrepreneurship: For a new perspective on organisational creativity*. Copenhagen/Malmö/Oslo: Copenhagen Business School Press/Liber/Abstrakt

———. 2004a. Creating space for play/invention: Concepts of space and organisational entrepreneurship. *Entrepreneurship and Regional Development* 16(5):413–432.

Hjorth, D 2004b. Towards genealogic storytelling in entrepreneurship. In *Narrative and discursive approaches in entrepreneurship*, edited by D. Hjorth, and C. Steyaert. Cheltenham, U.K.: Edward Elgar.

———. 2004c. Design: In-between aesthetics and economy-bridging art and entrepreneurship. Paper presented at Diamond 2000, Art-Business Conference, Århus, Danmark.

————. 2005. Organizational entrepreneurship: With de Certeau on creating heterotopias (or spaces for play). *Journal of Management Inquiry* 14:386–398.

Hjorth D., and B. Johannisson. 2003. Conceptualising the opening phase of regional development as the enactment of a 'collective identity'. *Concepts and Transformation* 8(1):1–24.

Hjorth, D., and C. Steyaert. (2003). Entrepreneurship beyond (a new) economy: Creative swarms and pathological zones. In *New movements in entrepreneurship*, edited by C. Steyaert, and D. Hjorth. Cheltenham, U.K.: Edward Elgar.

————. 2004. Introduction. In *Narrative and discursive approaches in entrepreneurship*, edited by D. Hjorth, and C. Steyaert. Cheltenham, U.K.: Edward Elgar.

————. 2006. American psycho–European schizo: Stories of managerial elites in a 'hundred' images. In *Management education and humanities*, edited by P. Gagliardi, and B. Czarniawska. Cheltenham, U.K.: Edward Elgar.

Hjorth, D., and P. Pelzer. 2003. The fate of Phaeton: The glory of the sublime or the Hetzhteater of baroque art for management's sake. Paper read at 3rd European Academy of Management Annual Conference, Milan.

Hjorth, D., and P. Pelzer P. 2007. The fate of Phaeton: baroque art for management's sake?. *Organization* forthcoming.

Hjorth, D., B. Johannison, and C. Steyaert. 2003. Entrepreneurship as discourse and life style. In *The northern lights: Organization theory in Scandinavia*, edited by B. Czarniawska, and G. Sevón. Copenhagen/Malmö/Oslo: Copenhagen Business School Press/Liber/Abstrakt.

Hobsbawm, E. 2001. Reprint. *Om historia*. Translated by L. Lundgren. Stockholm: Bokförlaget Prisma. Originally edition, London: Weidenfeld and Nicolson, 1997.

Hollows, J. 1995. Mass culture theory and political economy. In *Approaches to popular film*, edited by J. Hollows, and M. Jancovich. Manchester: Manchester University Press.

Höpfl, H. 2002. Playing the part: Reflections on aspects of mere performance in the customer-client relationship. *Journal of Management Studies* 39(2):255–267.

Hosking, D. M. 2004. Conversation with author, in *Narrative and discursive approaches in entrepreneurship*, edited by D. Hjorth, and C. Steyaert. Cheltenham, U.K.: Edward Elgar.

Hoskins, W. G. 1985. Reprint. *The Making of the English Landscape*. London: Penguin Books. Original edition, London: Hodder and Stoughton,1955.

Hubbard, P., and T. Hall. 1998. The entrepreneurial city and the new urban politics. In *The entrepreneurial city: Geographies of politics, regime, and representations*, edited by T. Hall, and P. Hubbard. Chichester, U.K.: John Wiley & Sons.

Huizinga, J. 1950. *Homo ludens: A study of the play-element in culture*. 1944. Reprint, New York: Roy Publishers.

Hull, D., J. J. Bosley, and G. G. Udell. 1980. Renewing the hunt of means of identifying potential entrepreneurs by personality characteristics. *Journal of Small Business Management* 20:11–19.

Humphrey, C. 2000. Bakhtin and the study of popular culture: Re-thinking carnival as a historical and analytical concept. In *Materializing Bakhtin*, edited by C. Brandist. New York: Palgrave Macmillan.

Ilinitch, A. Y., R. D'Aveni, and A. Levin. 1996. New organizational forms and strategies for managing in hypercompetitive environments. *Organization Science* 7:211–220.

Jackson, N., and P. Carter. 2000. *Rethinking organisational behaviour*. London: Financial Times.

Jacobson, M. 1996. Art and business in a brave new world. *Organization* 3(2):243–248.

Jacques, R. 1996. *Manufacturing the employee: Management knowledge from the 19th to 21st centuries*. London: Sage Publications.

Jeffcutt, P. 1996. The organization of performance and the performance of organization. *Studies in Cultures, Organizations, and Societies* 2(1):95–110.

Jeffcutt, P., R. G. Small, and S. Stephen. 1996. Organization as a theatre of performance. *Studies in Cultures, Organizations, and Societies* 2(1):3–8.

Jensen, R.1999. *The dream society*. New York: McGraw-Hill.

Joerges, B. 1990. Images of technology in sociology: Computer as butterfly and bat. *Technology and Culture* 31(2):203–227.

———. 1994. Expertise lost: An early case of technology assessment. *Social Studies of Science* 24:96–104.

Johannisson, B. 1983. Swedish evidence of the potential of local entrepreneurship in regional development. *European Small Business Journal* 1:11–24.

———.1988. Business formation: A network approach. *Scandinavian Journal of Management* 4(3/4):83–99.

———. 2005. *Entreprenörskapets väsen*. Lund, Swed.: Studentlitteratur.

———. Forthcoming. Enacting entrepreneurship: Using auto-ethnography to study organization creation. In *Ethnographic organizational studies*, edited by T. S. Eberle, and C. Maeder.

Johannisson, B., M. Ramirez, and G. Karlsson. 2002a. The institutional embeddedness of inter-firm networks: A leverage for business creation. *Entrepreneurship and Regional Development* 14:297–316.

———. 2002b. Theoretical and methodological challenges: Bridging firm strategies and contextual networking. *International Journal of Entrepreneurship and Innovation* 3:165–174.

Johansson, U., L. Svengren, and K. Sköldberg. 2003. Industrial design as a balancing artistry: Some reflections upon industrial designer's competence. Paper presented at the 5th European Academy of Design Conference, 28–30 April, in Barcelona.

Johnson, B. R. 1990. Towards a multi-dimensional model of entrepreneurship: The case of achievement motivation and the entrepreneur. *Entrepreneurship Theory and Practice* 14:39–54.

Johnstone, H., and D. Lionais. 2004. Depleted communities and community business entrepreneurship: Revaluating space through place. *Entrepreneurship and Regional Development* 16:217–233.

Jones, C., and A. Spicer. 2005. The sublime object of entrepreneurship. *Organization* 12:223–246.

———. 2006. Entrepreneurial excess. In *The Passion of Organizing*, edited by D. Boje, J. Brewis, S. Linstead, and T. O'Shea. Copenhagen: Copenhagen Business School Press.

———. Forthcoming. Outline of a genealogy of the value of the entrepreneur. In *Discourse and economics*, edited by G. Erreygers, and G. Jacobs. Amsterdam: Benjamins.

Jorn, A. 1962. *Værdi og økonomi: Kritik af den økonomiske politik og udbytningen af det enestående*. Valby, Dk.: Borgens Forlag.

Julier, G. 2000. *The culture of design*. London: Sage Publications.

Jung, C. G. 1968. The archetypes and the collective unconscious. In *The collected works of C. G. Jung*, edited by H. Read. Vol. 9. London: Routledge and Kegan Paul.

Kallinikos, J. 1996. Predictable worlds. *Scandinavian Journal of Management* 12:7–24.

Kallinikos, J. 2003. Work, human agency, and organizational forms: An anatomy of fragmentation. *Organization Studies* 24:595–618.

Kamm, J. B., and A. J. Nurick. 1993. The stages of new team formation: A decision-making model. *Entrepreneurship Theory and Practice* 17:17–28.

Kanter, R. M. 1990. *When giants learn to dance*. London: Unwin Hyman.

Kavaratzis, M. 2004. From city marketing to city branding: Towards a theoretical framework for developing city brands. *Place branding* 1:58–73.

Keller, K. 1999. Designing and implementing brand strategies. *Journal of Brand Management* 6:315–332.

Kelly, G. 1955. *The psychology of personal constructs*. Vol. 1. New York: Norton.

Kempinski, A. M. 1993. *Slownik mitologii ludow Indoeuropejskich* (Dictionary of the mythology of Indo-European peoples). Poznan: SAWW.

Kets de Vries, M. F. R. 1977. The entrepreneurial personality: A person at the crossroads. *Journal of Management Studies* 14:34–57.

———. 1996. The anatomy of the entrepreneur: Clinical observations. *Human Relations* 49:853–883.

Kingdom of Crystal. 2000. Sweden's Kingdom of Crystal. Brochure edited by AB Glasriket, Nybro, Sweden.

Kirkeby, O. F. 2004. *Det nye lederskab*. Copenhagen: Børsens Forlag.

———. 2005. *Eventum tantum: Begivenhedens etos*. Copenhagne: Samfundslitteratur.

Kirzner, I. 1979. *Perceptions, opportunity and profit: Studies in the theory of entrepreneurship*. Chicago: University of Chicago Press.

KK-stiftelsen. 2001. *Aha Sweden: En industri utan skorstenar*. Stockholm: KK-stiftelsen.

KK-stiftelsen. 2003. *Upplevelseindustrin 2003: Statistik och jämförelser.* Stockholm: KK-stiftelsen.

Klamer, A. 2001. The mode of financing of cultural heritage matters. In *L'offerta culturale: Valorizzazione, gestione, finanziamento,* edted by G. Trupiano. Rome: Biblink.

Knights, D., and G. Morgan. 1993. Organization theory and consumption in a post-modern era. *Organization Studies* 14(2):211–234.

Knights, D., and H. Willmott. 2002. Autonomy as utopia and dystopia. In *Utopia and organization,* edited by M. Parker. London: Sage Publications.

Knights, D., and D. McCabe. 1999. 'Are there no limits to authority?' TQM and organizational power. *Organization Studies* 20(2):197–224.

Knox, S., and D. Bickerton. 2003. The six conventions of corporate branding. *European Journal of Marketing* 37:998–1016.

Kociatkieiwcz, J., and M. Kostera. 2001. Art and organizing: Lessons for organization theory from the humanities. *Master of Business Administration* 50(3):24–28.

Koivunen, N. 2003. *Leadership in symphony orchestras.* Tampere, FI: Tampere University Press.

Kommunstyrelsens Beslut. 2000. Träindutrin i Kronobergs län 1970-1990. Statistiks of
Länsstyrelsen in the County of Kronoberg, Smaland, Sweden.

Koskinen, M. 2002. Auteuren: Person eller konstruktion? *Filmkonst* 77. Göteborg, SE: Göteborg Film Festival.

Kostera, M. 1997. The kitsch-organization. *Studies in Cultures, Organizations, and Societies.*
3:163–177.

———. 2005. *The quest for the self-actualizing organization.* Malmö, Swed.: Liber.

Kotler, P., and D. Gertner. 2002. Country as a brand, product and beyond: A place marketing
and brand management perspective. *Journal of Brand Management* 9:249–261.

Kotler, P., D. H. Haider, and I. Rein. 1993. *Marketing places: Attracting investment,*
industry, and tourism to cities, states, and nations. New York: The Free Press.

Kotler, P., C. Asplund, I. Rein, and D. H. Haider. 1999. *Marketing places Europe: Attracting investment, industry, residents and visitors to European communities, regions and nations.* London: Pearson Education.

Krell, G., and R. Weiskopf. 2006. *Die anordnung der leidenschaften.* Vienna: Passagen.

Kvaratzis, M. 2004. From city marketing to city branding: Towards a theoretical framework for developing city brands. *Place Branding* 1:58–73.

Lantz, J. 2007. Gendered textbook filmmakers. In *Aesthetic Leadership*, edited by P. Guillet de Monthoux, C. Gustafsson, and S-E. Sjöstrand. Hampshire, U.K.: Palgrave Macmillan

Lapierre, L. 2001. Leadership and arts management. *International Journal of Arts Management* 3(3):4–12.

Lapsley, R. and M. Westlake. 1988. *Film theory: An introduction.* Manchester: Manchester University Press.

Latour, B. 1986. The powers of association. In *Power, action, and belief: A new sociology of knowledge?*, edited by J. Law. London: Routledge and Kegan Paul.

———. 1987. *Science in action.* Cambridge, Mass.: Harvard University Press.

———. 1993. On technical mediation. Working paper, Lund University.

———. 1996. *Aramis, or the love of technology.* Translated by C. Porter. Cambridge, Mass.: Harvard University Press.

Latour, B., and R. Powers. 1997. Two writers face one Turing Test: A dialogue in honor of HAL. *Common Knowledge* 7(1)177–191.

Law, J. 1991. Introduction: Monsters, machines, and sociotechnical relations. In: *A sociology of monsters: Essays on power, technology, and domination*, edited by J. Law. London: Routledge.

Lazzerato, M. 2004. From capital labour to capital-life. *ephemera: theory and politics in oganizations* 4:187–208.

Lee, D. Y., and E. E. K. Tsang. 2001. The effects of entrepreneurial personality, background, and network activity on venture growth. *Journal of Management Studies* 38:583–602.

Lee, J. H., and S. Venkataraman. 2006. Aspirations, market offerings, and the pursuit of entrepreneurial opportunities. *Journal of Business Venturing* 21:107–123.

Lefebvre, H. 1991. *The production of space.* Translated by D. Nicholson-Smith. Malden, Mass.: Blackwell Publishing.

Lindfelt, M. 1999. *Idrott och moral: Reflektioner över idrottens ideal.* Nora: Bokförlaget Nya Doxa.

———. 2005. Idrott, människosyn och religion: En tolkning av Pierre de Coubertins idrottsreligion med utblick på postmoderna höjder. *Idrottsforum*, (May 3, 2005), www.idrottsforum.org.

Lindfelt, M. 2006. *Meningsskapande idrott: Livsåskådningsrelevanta perspektiv och empiriska kontraster.* Nora: Bokförlaget Nya Doxa.

Lindqvist, K. 2004. *Att göra det främmande till sitt. Konstnärer och arbetsplatser i samarbetsprojekt. Erfarenheter från projektet Airis, fas I och II (2002-2004).* Research report, Swedish National Council for Cultural Affairs, Stockholm.

Linstead, S. 2002. Organizational kitsch. *Organization* 9(4):657–682. London: Sage Publications.

Lindstead, S., and H. Höpfl, eds. 2000. *The aesthetics of organization.* London: Sage Publications.

Link, J. 1998. Von der "Macht der Norm" zum "flexiblen Normalismus." In *Zeitgenössische französische Denker*, edited by J. Hurt. Freiburg im Breisgau: Rombach Verlag.

Linn, B. 2002. *Konsten 1915-1950.* Lund, Swed.: Bokförlaget Signum.

Linstead, S., and H. Höpfl, eds. 2000. *Aesthetics of organization*. London: Sage Publications.

Litgard, N. 2002. Interview held in Norrgavel in Lammhult, Sweden.

Löfgren, O. 2005. Cultural alchemy: Translating the experience economy into Scandinavian. In *Global ideas: How ideas, objects and practices travel in the global economy*, edted by B. Czarniawska, and G. Sevón. Malmö, Swed.: Liber.

Löfgren, O., and R. Willim. 2005. Introduction: The mandrake mode. In *Magic, culture and the new economy*, edited by O. Löfgren, and R. Willim. Oxford: Berg.

Lundequist, J. 1995. Design och produktutveckling: Metoder och begrepp. Lund, Swed.: Studentlitteratur.

Lundman, T. 2004. 1-0 till Operan. *Svenska Dagbladet* 13 December, 2004.

Louro, M., and P. Cuhna. 2001. Brand management paradigms. *Journal of Marketing Management* 17:849–876.

Low, G., and R. Fullerton. 1994. Brands, brand management, and the brand management
system: A critical historical evaluation. *Journal of Marketing Research* 31:173–190.

Lund, B. 2002. Interview held in Savsjo Naringslivs AB in Savsjo, Sweden.

Lyotard, J-F. 1993. *The postmodern condition: A report on knowledge*. Translated by G. Bennington, and B. Massumi. Minneapolis: University of Minnesota Press.

Matson, E. 1994. Can cities market themselves like Coke and Pepsi do? *International Journal of Public Sector Management* 7:35–41.

Mangham, I. L. 1990. Managing as a performing art. *British Journal of Management* 1:105–115.

Maraniello, G., S. Risaliti, and A. Somaini, eds. 2001. *Il dono: Offerta, ospitalità, insidia* (The gift: Generous offerings, threatening hospitality). Milan: Charta.

Margul, T. 1989. *Mity z pieciu czesci swiata* (Myths from five parts of the world). Warszawa: Wiedza Powszechna

Massumi, B. 2000. Too-blue: Colour patch for an expanded empiricism. *Cultural Studies* 14(2):177–226.

———. 2002. *Parables for the virtual (Movement, affect, sensation)*. Durham: Duke University Press.

McClealland, D. C. 1987. Characteristics of successful entrepreneurs. *Journal of Creative Behaviour* 21:219–233.

McClelland, D. 1961. *The achieving society*. Princeton, N.J.: Van Nostrand Publishing.

McCloskey, D. N. 1986. *The rhetoric of economics*. Brighton: Harvester.

McGehee, N. G., and K. Kyungmi. 2004. Motivation for agri-tourism entrepreneurship. *Journal of Travel Research* 43 (November): 161–170.

Michelson, E. 1999. Carnival, paranoia and experiential learning. *Studies in the Education of Adults* 31(2):140-154.

Miller, P., and T. O'Leary. 1987. Accounting and the construction of the governable person. *Accounting, Organization, and Society* 12:235–65.

Miller, P., and N. Rose. 1998. Governing economic life. In *Strategic human resource management:. A reader*, edited by C. Mabey, G. Salamon, and J. Storey. London: Sage Publications.

Mommaas, H. 2002. City branding: The necessity of socio-cultural goals. In *City branding: Image building and building images*, edited by T. Hauben, M. Vermeulen, and V. Patteeuw. Rotterdam: Nai Uitgevers.

Monö, R. 1997. *Design for product understanding*. Malmö, Swed.: Liber.

Montag, W., and T. Stolze, eds. 1997. *The new Spinoza*. Minneapolis: University of Minnesota Press.

Neill, J. V. W. 2001. Marketing the urban experience: Reflections on the place of fear in the promotional strategies of Belfast, Detroit, and Berlin. *Urban Studies* 38:815–828.

Neuberger, O. 2000. *Das 360 grad feedback: Alles fragen? Alles sehen? Alles sagen?* München/Mering: Hampp.

Newsweek, Aug. 29/Sept. 5, 2005.

Norman, D. 1988. *The design of everyday things*. 2d ed. New York: Currency and Doubleday.

O'Connor, J., and D. Wynne, eds. 1996. *From the margins to the centre: Cultural production and consumption in the post-industrial city*. Arena: Aldershot.

O'Leary, T. 2002. *Foucault and the art of ethics*. New York: Continuum.

Olins, W. 1989. *Corporate identity: Making business strategy visible through design*. London: Thames and Hudson.

O'Reilly, B. 1994. 360 degree feed back can change your life. *Fortune*, 17 October 1994, 93-97.

Orlean, S. 2001. Art for everybody: Thomas Kinkade, America's most profitable artist. *The New Yorker*, 15 October, 124–146.

Oslobodjenje. 1993. Program of the International Film Festival Sarajevo. Friday, October 22, 1993Papadopoulos, N. 2004. Place branding: Evolution, meaning, and implications. *Place Branding* 1:36–49.

Parker, M. 2002. *Against managament: Organization in the age of managerialism*. Cambridge, U.K.: Polity Press.

Parks, J. B., and J. Quarterman. 2003. Sport management: An overview. In *Contemporary sport management*. 2d ed. Edited by J. B. Parks, and J. Quarterman. Champaign, Ill.: Human Kinetics.

Patton, P. 1997. The world seen from within: Deleuze and the philosophy of events. *Theory and Event* 1(1):16–19.

Paulsson, G. [1919] 1995. *Vackrare vardagsvara*. Stockholm: Rekolid.

Peters, T., and R. Waterman. 1982. *In search of excellence: Lessons form America's best-run companies*. New York: Harper and Row.

Pfeffer, J. 1997. Pitfalls on the road to measurement: The dangerous liaison of human resources with the ideas of accounting and finance. *Human Resource Management* 36: 357–365.

Phillips, R. 2002. *Concept marketing for communities: Capitalizing on underutilized resources to generate growth and development*. Westport, Conn.: Greenwood.

Pine, B. J., and J. H. Gilmore. 1999. *The experience economy: Work is theatre and every business a stage.* Boston, Mass.: Harvard Business School Press.

Polanyi M. 1974. Reprint. *Personal knowledge: Towards a post-critical philosophy.* Chicago, University of Chicago Press. Original edition, New York: Harper and Row, 1958.

Postlewait, T., and T. C. Davis. 2003. Theatricality: An introduction. In *Theatricality*, edited by T.C. Davis, and T. Postlewait. Cambridge: Cambridge University Press.

Potter, N. 1989. *What is a designer: Things, places, messages.* 3d ed. London: Hyphen Press.

Powell, W. W. 1990. Neither market nor hierarchy: Network forms of organization. *Research in Organizational Behavior* 12:295–336.

Power, M. 2004. Counting, control and calculation: Reflections on measurement and control. *Human Relations* 57:765–783.

Prasad, P. 1995. Working with the 'smart' machine: Computerization and the discourse of anthropomorphism in organizations. *Studies in Cultures, Organizations, and Societies* 1(2)253–267.

Pratt, A. C. 2004. The cultural economy: A call for spatialized 'production of culture' perspectives. *International Journal of Cultural studies* 7(1):117–128.

Press, M., and R. Cooper. 2003. *The design experience: The role of design and designers in the twenty-first century.* Burlington, Vt.: Ashgate.

Rabinow, P. 1997. Introduction: The history of systems of thought. In *Michel Foucault: Ethics, subjectivity and Truth*, edited by P. Rabinow. New York: New Press.

Ramírez, R. 1987. Towards an aesthetic theory of social organization. Ph.D. dissertation, University of Pennsylvania.

Ramírez, R. 1996. Wrapping form and organizational beauty. *Organization* 3(2):233–242.

Ramírez-Pasillas, M. 2002. Realising regional brands through strategic networking: The cases of Como, Italy, and Lammhult, Sweden. Paper read at the 16th Annual Conference on Research in Entrepreneurship, in Barcelona, Spain.

Ramírez-Pasillas, M. 2004. *Embedded regional networking.* Master's thesis, Växjö Universitet.

Rhen, A., and S. Taalas. 2004. Crime and assumptions in entrepreneurship. In *Narrative approaches in entrepreneurship: A second movements in entrepreneurship book*, edted by D. Hjorth, and C. Steyaert. Cheltenham, U.K.: Edward Elgar.

Ristilammi, P-M. 2000. Cultural bridges, events, and the new region'. In *Invoking a transnational metropolis: The making of the Øresund region.* Edited by P. O. Berg, A. Linde-Laursen, and O. Löfgren. Lund, Swed.: Studentlitteratur.

Ritzer, G. 1999. *Enchanting a disenchanted world: Revolutionizing the means of consumption.* Thousand Oaks, Calif.: Pine Forge Press.

Rose, N. 1990. *Governing the soul: The shaping of the private self.* London: Routledge.

313

————. 1991. Governing by numbers: Figuring out democracy. *Accounting, Organizations, and Society* 16:673–692.

————. 1992. Governing the enterprising self. In *The values of the enterprise culture*, edited by P. Heelas, and P. Morris. London: Routledge.

Sandahl, B., and P. Sjöblom. 2004. Idrottsrörelse med identitetsproblem? *Svensk Idrottsforskning* 2:52–55.

Santagata, W. 1998. Beni d'arte, modelli di scambio, istituzioni per il mercato. In *Economia dell'arte: Istituzione e mercati dell'arte e della cultura*, edited by the author. Turin: UTET.

Saussure, F. [1916]1983. *Course in general linguistics*. London: Duckworth.

Sauter, W. 2004. Introducing the theatrical event. In *Theatrical events: Borders, dynamics, frames*, edited by V. A. Cremona, P. Eversmann, H. van Maanen, W. Sauter, and J. Tulloch. Amsterdam: Rodopi.

Scheibler, I. 2001. XXX. *International Journal of Philosophical Studies*, 9:151–176.

Schrag, C. O. 1997. *The self after postmodernity*. New Haven, Conn.: Yale University Press.

Schreyögg, G., and H. Höpfl. 2004. Theatre and organization: Editorial introduction. *Organization Studies* 25(5):691–704.

Schroeder, J. E. 2004. Aesthetics awry: The Painter of Light™ and the production of organizational values. Paper read at 2nd Art of Management Conference, Paris.

Schumpeter, J. A. 1934. *The theory of economic development: An equity into profits, capital, credit, interest, and the business cycle*. Cambridge, Mass.: Harvard University Press.

————. 1991. *Essays on entrepreneurs, innovations, business cycles, and the evolution of capitalism*. New Brunswick, N.J.: Transaction Publishers.

————. [1946]1991. Comments on a plan for the study of entrepreneurship. In *Joseph A Schumpeter: The economics and sociology of capitalism*, edited by R. Swedberg. Princeton, N.J.: Princeton University Press.

Sciascia, S., and R. De Vita. 2004. The development of entrepreneurship research. Research paper, LIUC papers no. 146, Università Carlo Cattaneo, Castellanza.

Scott, J. 1999. *Seeing like the state: How certain schemes to improve the human condition have failed*. New Haven, Conn.: Yale University Press.

Scruton, R. 2002. *Spinoza: A very short introduction*. Oxford: Oxford University Press.

Sevón, G. 2002. Att uppträda som publik. In *Öresundsbron på uppmärksamhetens marknad: Regionbyggare i evenemangsbranschen*, edited by P. O. Berg, A. Linde-Laursen, and O. Löfgren. Lund, Swed.: Studentlitteratur.

Shane, S., and S. Venkataraman. 2000. The Promise of entrepreneurship as a field of research. *Academy of Management Review* 25(1):217-226

Shelley, M. W. [1818]1989. *Frankenstein, or the modern Prometheus*. Poznan: Wydawnictwo Poznanskie

Shenhav, Y. 1999. *Manufacturing rationality: The engineering foundations of the managerial revolution*. Oxford: Oxford University Press.

Sievers, B. 1994. *Work, death, and life itself: Essays on management and organization.* Berlin: Walter de Gruyter.

Simon, H. A. 1996. *The sciences of the artificial.* 3d ed. Cambridge, Mass.: MIT Press.

Sjöberg, J. 2002. Interview held in Svenssons i Lammhult in Lammhult, Sweden.

Sjöstrand, S. E., and L. L. Holmberg, eds. 1994. *Företagsledning bortom etablerad teori.* Lund, Swed.: Studentlitteratur.

Sjöstrand, S-E., and M. Tyrstrup. 2001. Recognized and unrecognized managerial leadership. In *Invisible Management*, edited by S-E. Sjöstrand, J. Sandberg, and M. Tyrstrup. London: Thomson Learning.

Smart, B. 2005. *Sport star: Modern sport and the cultural economy of sporting celebrity.* London: Sage Publications.

Smith, A. [1776]2000. *The wealth of nations.* New York: Random House.

Soila-Wadman, M. 2003. *Kapitulationens estetik: Organisering och ledarskap i filmprojekt.* Stockholm: Arvinius.

Soila-Wadman, M., and A-S. Köping. 2004. Leadership in art and culture creating organizations. Paper read at the 2nd Conference on Art and Aesthetics, Paris.

Spinosa, C., F. Flores, and H. L. Dreyfus. 1997. *Disclosing new worlds: Entrepreneurship, democratic action, and the cultivation of solidarity.* Cambridge, Mass.: MIT Press.

Steiner, B., and D. Berger. 2001. On Superflex: Birgitte Feiring interviewed. In *Remarks on interventive tendencies.* The Danish Contemporary Art Foundation & Borgens Forlag, Copenhagen.

Stenström, E. 2000. *Konstiga företag.* Stockholm: EFI.

Stewart, M. Kronos. In *Greek mythology: From the Iliad to the fall of the last tyrant.* http://messagenet.com/myths/bios/kronos.html. (Accessed 19 September, 2005).

Steyaert, C. 2004. The prosaics of entrepreneurship. In *Narrative and discursive approaches in entrepreneurship*, edited by D. Hjorth, and C. Steyaert. Cheltenham, U.K.: Edward Elgar.

Steyaert, C., and D. Hjorth. 2003. Creative movements of entrepreneurship. In *New movements in entrepreneurship*, edited by C. Steyaert, and D. Hjorth. Cheltenham, U.K.: Edward Elgar.

Steyaert, C., and R. Bouwen. 1997. Telling stories of entrepreneurship. In *Entrepreneurship and SME research on its way to the next millennium*, edited by R. Dockels, and A. Miettinen. Aldershot, U.K.: Ashgate Publishing.

Stringer, J. 2003. Regarding film festivals (England). Ph.D. dissertation, Indiana University.

Stoddart, H. 1995. Auteurism and film authorship. In *Approaches to popular film*, edited by J. Hollows, and M. Jancovich. Manchester: Manchester University Press.

Storey, J., G. Salaman, and K. Platman. 2005. Living with enterprise in an enterprise economy: Freelance and contract workers in the media. *Human Relations* 58:1033–1054.

Strathern, M. 2000. Afterword to *Audit Cultures*, edited by M. Strathern. London: Routledge.

Strati, A. 1996. Organizations viewed through the lens of aesthetics. *Organization* 3(2):209–218.

———. 1999. *Organization and aesthetics*. London: Sage Publications.

Sundin E. 2004. Små företag: Lösning på vad och för vem? In *Det oavsedda entreprenörskapet*, edited by E. Daniel. Lund, Swed.: Academia Adacta.

Superflex. 1999. *Superflex: Biogas in Africa*. Woolloomooloo, Aust.: Artspace Visual Arts Centre,.

Superflex 2001. *Supermanual: The incomplete guide to the Superchannel*. Liverpool, U.K.: Foundation for Art and Creative Technology.

———. 2003. *Tools*. Cologne: Walther König.

Svendsen, G. L. H., and G. T. Svendsen. 2004. *The creation and destruction of social capital: Entrepreneurship, co-operative movements, and institutions*. Cheltenham, U.K.: Edward Elgar.

Svengren, L, and U. Johansson. Forthcoming. *Dynamiska relationer: Om motet mellan designer, marknadsförare och tekniker*. Lund, Swed.: Studentlitteratur.

Svenska Dagbladet, http://www.svd.se/dynamiskt/utrikes/did_8703270.asp, 14 February 2005. (*Protester mot pop-krubba i England*, publicerad 2004-12-08).

Sylvén, S. 2005. Idrotten är inte längre förebild. *Svenska Dagbladet*, 13 February, 2005.

Thornquist, C. 2005. The savage and the designed: Robert Wilson and Vivienne Westwood as artistic managers. Ph.D. dissertation, Stockholm University School of Business.

Thronley, A. 1998. Institutional change and London's urban policy agenda. *The Annals of Regional Science* 32:163–183.

Teitelbaum, S. H. 2005. *Sports heroes, fallen idols: How star athletes pursue self-destructive paths and jeopardize their careers*. Lincoln: University of Nebraska Press.

Text TV news, 07 March 2005, page 307, 10.50pm.

Tolkien, J. R. R. [1955]1990. *Wladca Pierscieni* (Lord of the Rings). Warszawa: CIA.

Townley, B. 1994. *Reframing human resource management: Power, ethics, and the subject at work*. London: Sage Publications.

———. 1995. 'Know thyself': Self-awareness, self-formation and managing. *Organization* 2:271–290.

———. 1998. Beyond good and evil: Depth and division in the management of human resources. In *Foucault, management, and organization theory*, edited by A. McKinlay, and K. Starkey. London: Sage Publications.

Tuan, Y-F. 1997. *Space and place: The perspective of experience*. 3d ed. Minneapolis: University of Minnesota Press.

Turan K. 2003. *From Sundance to Sarajevo: Film festivals and the world they made*. Berkeley: University of California Press.

Turkle, S. 1984. *The second self: Computers and the human spirit*. New York: Simon and Schuster.

————. 1991. If the computer is a tool, is it more like a hammer or more like a harpsichord? *National Forum* 71(3): 8–11.

Ulrich, K. T., and S. D. Eppinger. 1995. *Product design and development*. New York: McGraw-Hill.

Van den Berg, L., and E. Braun. 1999. Urban competitiveness, marketing, and the need for organising capacity. *Urban Studies* 36:987–999.

Van Ham, P. 2002. Branding territory: Inside the wonderful world of PR and IR theory. *Journal of International Studies* 31:249–269.

Van Maanen, J. 1988. *Tales from the field: On writing ethnography*. Chicago: University of Chicago Press.

Virilio, P. 2002. Reprint. *Ground zero*. Translated by C. Turner. Reprint, London: Verso. Original edition, Paris: Editions Galilée, 1998.

Vogl, J. 2002. *Kalkül und leidenschaft: Poetik des ökonomischen enschen*. München: Sequenzia Verlag.

Voß, G. G., and H. J. Pongratz. 2003. From 'employee' to 'entreployee': Towards a 'self-entrepreneurial' work force? *Concepts and Transformation* 8:239–254.

Ward, S. V. 1998. *Selling places: The marketing and promotion of towns and cities 1850-2000*. London: E and FN Spon.

Warhol, A. 1975. *The philosophy of Andy Warhol: (From A to B and back again)*. London: Cassell.

www.wapno.se. Site accessed, 18 September, 2004.

Weick, K. 1979. The social psychology of organizing. 2d ed. Reading, Mass.: Addison-Wesley.

Weick, K. 1995. *Sensemaking in organizations*. Thousand Oaks, Calif.: Sage Publications.

Weick, Karl E, et al. (2005), Sport and Organizational Studies: Exploring Synergy. In *Journal of Management Inquiry Volume 14(2): pp. 182-210.* London/Thousand Oaks/CA/New Dehli: SAGE.

Wikipedia, http://sv.wikipedia.org/wiki/Monopsoni, (4 February 2005).

Weiskopf, R. 2002. Deconstructing 'The Iron Cage': Towards and aesthetic of folding. *Consumption, Markets, and Culture* 5:79–97.

————. 2005. Gouvernementabilität: Die produktion des regierbaren menschen in post-disziplinären regimen. *Zeitschrift für Personalforschung* 19:289–311.

Welsch, W. 1998. *Undoing aesthetics*. London: Sage Publications.

Wennes, G. 2002. *Skjönnheten og udyret: Kunsten å lede kunstorganisasjonen*. Bergen: Norges Handelshöyskole.

Winnicott, D. W. 1971. *Playing and reality*. London: Tavistock.

Wise, J. M. 1997. *Exploring technology and social space*. Thousand Oaks, Calif.: Sage Publications.

Wynne, D., ed. 1992. *The culture industry: The arts in urban regeneration*. Avebury, U.K.: Aldershot.

Yukl, G. 2002. *Leadership in organizations*. New York: Prentice Hall.

Zizek, S. 2001. *Die tücke des subjekts*. Frankfurt am Main: Suhrkamp.

Zuboff, S. 1988. *In the age of the smart machine: The future of work and power*. Oxford: Heinemann.

Zukin, S. 1991. *Landscapes of power: From Detroit to Disney World.* Berkeley: University of California Press.